Gimme a THRILL

★

THE STORY OF

I'LL SAY SHE IS

THE LOST
MARX BROTHERS
MUSICAL
AND HOW IT WAS FOUND

★

NOAH DIAMOND

Bearmanor Media

BearManorMedia.com

GIMME A THRILL:
THE STORY OF *I'LL SAY SHE IS*,
THE LOST MARX BROTHERS MUSICAL,
AND HOW IT WAS FOUND

Published in the United States of America by:
BearManor Media
P.O. Box 1129
Duncan, OK 73534-1129
BearManorMedia.com

ISBN: 1-59393-934-5
ISBN-13: 978-1-59393-934-2

Printed in the United States.

Cover:
Photo of the Marx Brothers in *I'll Say She Is*, 1924, author's collection.
Photo of Noah Diamond as Groucho as Napoleon by Don Spiro.

Design and layout by the author.

illsaysheis.com

For Amanda,
Beautiful Beauty

Aristotle Stamat, Robert Pinnock, Noah Diamond, Melody Jane, and Seth Shelden in the 2014 New York International Fringe Festival production of I'll Say She Is. *Photo by Don Spiro.*

CONTENTS

ACKNOWLEDGMENTS

FROM THE BEGINNING, my work on *I'll Say She Is* has been elevated by the invaluable insight and assistance of old friends and new friends. From the earliest rumblings of the project, Mikael Uhlin, Kathy Biehl, and Margaret Farrell have kept it, and me, going with their support, enthusiasm, and feedback. The *I'll Say She Is* stage project (and, indirectly, this book) has been enabled by West Hyler, who guided the development of the script through its turbulent adolescence; and Trav S.D., who turned the script into a show. The work has been crucially enhanced by the ideas and encouragement of Martin Denton, Barbara Hogenson, Melody Jane, and Seth Shelden.

I'm deeply indebted to Robert S. Bader and Paul G. Wesolowski, for the trail they have blazed through the deep woods of Marx Brothers history, and for their great kindness and generosity in spending time with me, answering my questions, and sharing the fruits of their research. To Robert Moulton and Rodney Stewart Hillel Tryster, without whose research and insight this book would be (and was) much poorer; and Matthew Coniam, whose kindness, good humor, and fresh insight into the Marx Brothers' art are unparalleled. To Miles Kreuger and the Institute for the American Musical for expertise, generosity, and meaningful encouragement that came at just the right time. To Frank Ferrante, noble spreader of the Gospel of Groucho, whose thoughtful feedback and friendly support has meant a great deal; also for the use of some beautiful photographs, with the valuable assistance of Ralph Torres. To Miriam Marx Allen, for many things, including the use of a previously-unpublished portrait by Will B. Johnstone. To Bill Marx, Andy Marx, the Marx Brothers' estates, and Groucho Marx Productions, for kind words, encouragement, and general support of this work. To Pau

Medrano Bigas, Ira Dolnick, Bob Gassel, Michael J. Hayde, and Jay Hopkins for further insight, help, and kindness. To the entire Marx Brothers Council of Facebook—hi! To Wendy Shay, Maggie Drain, and Joe Hursey at the Smithsonian's National American History Museum Archives Center, which houses the astonishing Groucho Marx Collection; to Kenneth Johnson, Tomeka Jones, and Chamisa Redmond at the Library of Congress; and to Ben Ohmart and BearManor Media.

I am forever grateful to the 2014 cast, crew, and creative team of *I'll Say She Is*: Tom Bibla, Kathy Biehl, Amber Bloom, Helen Burkett, Sabrina Chap, Francine Daveta, Ivory Fox, Grace Gotham, David Green, Dan Hermann, Glen Heroy, Bob Homeyer, Melody Jane, Juliann Kroboth, Lefty Lucy, Emily Turner Marsland, Robert Pinnock, Frances Ines Rodriguez, Melissa Roth, Kita St. Cyr, Trav S.D., Seth Shelden, Aristotle Stamat, Alexis Thomason, Foxy Vermouth, C.L. Weatherstone, and Jamie C. Wells—the active ingredients in a dream come true. I am all gratitude to my colleagues on the Marxfest Committee: Kevin Fitzpatrick, Brett Leveridge, Jonny Porkpie, Kathy Biehl (again), and Trav S.D. (again); and adjunct committee members Don Spiro and Bill Zeffiro.

Love and gratitude to Cindy Lerner, Steve Diamond, Steven Nestler, Erica Backmann, Shayna Diamond, Joe Diamond, Margaret Aldredge, Liz Diamond, Stephanie Diamond, Ginny Sisk, Shea Sisk Wellford, and Alex Wellford.

And most of all, to Amanda Sisk, my wife, my best friend, my collaborator, my partner in life and art, my biggest fan and my biggest hero—more love, gratitude, and admiration than I can possibly express, though I would like to spend the rest of my life trying.

NOAH LERNER DIAMOND
NEW YORK
2016

GIMME A THRILL

OVERTURE

THIS IS A BOOK about a musical called *I'll Say She Is*.

The first half of the book is a history of the original production, which opened in New York at the Casino Theatre in 1924. Its stars were the Four Marx Brothers, Julius, Arthur, Leonard, and Herbert, making their Broadway debut after a twenty-year vaudevillian odyssey. *I'll Say She Is* was a phenomenal smash ("A masterpiece of knock 'em down and drag 'em out humor"—George Jean Nathan, *American Mercury*). The Marx Brothers drew raves from Algonquin Round Table tastemakers like Alexander Woollcott and Robert Benchley, and became the preeminent jesters of the Jazz Age and the darlings of the New York smart set.

I'll Say She Is was their first great work, the long-delayed bloom of the rose they'd been tending all those years in vaudeville. Joe Adamson, in his immortal book about them, calls *I'll Say She Is* "the beginning of the Marx Brothers Proper." It influenced all of the Marx Brothers comedies which followed, especially their next two Broadway musicals, *The Cocoanuts* and *Animal Crackers*. Those became the first two Marx Brothers movies, and are now beloved classics, often revived on stage. But *I'll Say She Is* slipped through history's fingers. For most of a century it was a legend, known only by anecdote, and only by the world's most passionate Marx Brothers fans.

The second half of this book is about one of those fans, touched by the Marxes in childhood, and never quite the same thereafter. You know the kind—in high school, he told you that your eyes shined like the pants of a blue serge suit. My fascination with the Marx Brothers (especially their Broadway period, and especially *I'll Say She Is*) eventually led me to spend years researching, reconstructing, and adapting the lost Marx Brothers musical. In the summer of 2014, it had its world re-premiere in the New

York International Fringe Festival, ninety years after its original Broadway opening.

So the first half of this book is about the first production of *I'll Say She Is*, and the second half of this book is about the second production of *I'll Say She Is*, and I figure now is a good time to tell the story, quickly, before there's another production of *I'll Say She Is*.

Act One

I.
BROTHERS

The Marx family, circa 1914:
Harpo, Chico, Frenchie, Zeppo, Minnie, Gummo, and Groucho

ONCE UPON A TIME, a hundred years ago, there were five brothers named Leonard, Arthur, Julius, Milton, and Herbert. They grew up in New York City, the sons of Jewish immigrants. Their father was Sam Marx, a dapper Alsatian, known to all who loved him as Frenchie. Their mother was Minnie Schoenberg, from the German village of Dornum. Minnie's parents, Lafe and Fanny Schoenberg, had been itinerant performers in the old country. Lafe lived long enough to become a towering figure in the boys' childhoods, but Fanny had left behind only a token of her existence. Her harp, played in German music halls in another age, sat in a state of unplayable disrepair in Lafe's bedroom. Although none of the Marx children ever played it, it was a powerful symbol.

Minnie's brother, Al Shean, had the showbiz bug, and he became a famous vaudeville comedian in America. Uncle Al's success was an inspiration in a way that Frenchie's humble career, as "the most incompetent tailor Yorkville ever produced," was not. One by one, in their teens, Minnie's boys entered vaudeville. Julius was the first to set foot on stage, after answering an ad in the *Morning World* seeking boy singers. In 1905 and 1906, he appeared in an assortment of trios, doubles, ensembles, and touring theatrical productions, which are remembered only through his own later reminiscences. In 1907, brother Milton joined Julius and a girl singer in an act known as Wayburn's Nightingales, managed by vaudeville teacher and impresario Ned Wayburn. That lasted about six months, until Minnie herself assumed control of the act. Initially billed as the Three Nightingales, they became Four when young Arthur (born Adolph) joined the act, at Minnie's insistence. For years they trudged through the trials and indignities of small-time vaudeville, getting tougher and tighter, and gradually evolving from a musical act with comedy to a comedy act with music. In 1912, Leonard joined them, and they became the Four Marx Brothers. Two years later, at a backstage poker game in Galesburg, Illinois, a comedian named Art Fisher gave them funny nicknames. These nicknames caught on instantly in private, but did not go fully public for another ten years. They were inspired by the comic strip characters of Gus Mager—a family of monkeys with names like Knocko, Yanko, Rhymo, and Groucho.

Leonard was the oldest surviving Marx brother. (Sam and Minnie's first child, Manfred, had died before his first birthday—of old age, Julius said later.) Leo was fast and fearless, Minnie's favorite, a joyously irresponsible gambler and reckless optimist. He entered showbiz by way of the piano keys, taking advantage of the lessons Minnie had dotingly purchased for him, and of his own prodigious mind for numbers and timing. Leonard joined the family act in a typically brash and impulsive manner. Arthur, Julius, and Milton were playing Waukegan. Leonard ambled into town, went to the theatre, and arranged to sit in for the piano player. In the middle of the act, he jumped up on stage, and he stayed there with his brothers for half a century. He had previously worked with their cousin, Lou Shean, doing a stock Italian dialect character. This was another choice he made and stuck to for half a century, along with voracious womanizing, which is why Art Fisher called him Chicko.[1]

Arthur idolized his big brother. He had Leo's cockeyed charm, but not his drive and sense of purpose. Leo had a sense of purpose even when he had no sense and no purpose. Arthur was up in the clouds. He was forced onto the stage by Minnie, and encouraged to sing as quietly as possible. His initial comedy role was another ethnic caricature, the Irish bumpkin—thus the red wig. By approximately 1914, he had abandoned onstage speech altogether. But the silent Marx Brother was never really silent; he was just non-speaking. He was perhaps the *noisiest* member of the team, his repertoire of sounds including whistles, stomps, honks, clangs, and the ethereal soundscapes woven at his harp. The harp was a gift from Minnie, no doubt thinking of her mother's instrument and of Arthur's fascination with it. He painstakingly taught himself to play, in his own idiosyncratic style, which earned him the nickname Harpo.

The third brother was often mistakenly thought to be the oldest, because he was the most serious, and the most articulate. Unlike his older brothers, he wasn't looking for a good time. Or his idea of a good time was a quiet room and a dense book, or civilized conversation with carefully-selected friends, rather than parties and games. He was sober and introverted, yet he was the first of the boys to enter show business, and in the early days, the one most determined to find success as a performer. Al Shean was his inspiration, and his first comedic specialty was a Dutch character in blatant imitation of Uncle Al. Julius was dour and cynical enough to be called Groucho.

Milton, nicknamed Gummo for the softness of his shoes, was in the act until 1918, when he joined the army. He survived the Great War, serving

---

[1] Although the *k* was later dropped, it's still pronounced *Chicko*.

Vaudevillians of 1916: Groucho, Chico, Harpo, and Gummo

bravely in Illinois, and when it was over he had no interest in returning to the stage. His role was filled by the baby of the family, Herbert, who had a burgeoning career as a juvenile delinquent until Minnie drafted him. Herbert was nicknamed Zeppo for several reasons, none of them true.

The early Nightingales act was mostly singing, with comedy provided mainly by Julius, playing a German butcher boy character named Hans Pumpernickel. By 1911, they had a full-fledged comedy act, *Fun in Hi Skule*. It was a school act, with Julius as the elderly Dutch teacher, and Arthur and Milton as unruly students. School acts were in vogue, due to the success of Gus Edwards' *School Boys and Girls*. The Edwards school act had premiered in 1908 and taken the country by storm, as had its hit song ("School days, school days / Dear old golden rule days"). The Marx Brothers' *Fun in Hi Skule* was liberally borrowed from the Edwards turn, and refreshingly advertised as "The Somewhat Original School Act." After Leonard joined the act, it evolved into *Mr. Green's Reception*, a more elaborate production built around the same schoolroom characters. This, in turn, was replaced by *Home Again*.

Home Again was their biggest hit in vaudeville, serving them for nearly a decade. It was written and staged by Al Shean, cementing his role as a primary shaper of early Marx Brothers comedy. Uncle Al didn't create the Marx Brothers, but they created themselves in his image, and without his example it's unlikely they would have happened as they did. However impressive Al had seemed to the boys in childhood, his greatest fame was still ahead of him, even when he worked on *Home Again* in 1914. At this point, he had worked with Ed Gallagher once, but it would be six years before their paths crossed again, with dazzling success, as Gallagher and Shean.

The Four Marx Brothers who gradually conquered vaudeville were not a simple comedy act "in one" (in front of the curtain). They were not embryonic standup comedians, like Fred Allen, Will Rogers, or Jack Benny. What the Marxes did was theatre. Their act was a production, a self-contained mini-musical known in vaudeville as a *tabloid* or tab. A typical tab was about forty minutes long, and encompassed comedy scenes, singing and dancing turns, and musical specialties, strung together by a thin storyline, with a carload of scenery and a cast of fifteen or twenty. Tabloids were the perfect format for the Brothers, comedians who did a little bit of everything: singing, instrumental solos, impressions, a little dancing. But they always had a context, a scene to play, and they got laughs by playing it in surprising ways, and eventually violating its whole intention.

By 1918, they were among the biggest comedy stars in vaudeville, and the act entered a period of restless introspection. The boys were now grown men, mostly on the road since childhood, and even Harpo was beginning to find it "grueling and tiresome." Everybody was exhausted and impatient with showbiz. The dream was Broadway, where if you were a hit, you could get rich without leaving New York. Chico, the ever-hopeful gambler, was sure that the Marx Brothers could be a hit on the Big Street, the Main Stem, the hardened artery. Groucho was sure they couldn't. Harpo agreed with both of them, and nobody asked Zeppo.

While the Brothers were trying to get out of one line and into another, the public and the press were having an increasingly hard time telling the difference. *Variety* concluded that "the 'revue' in vaudeville now amounts to what vaudeville does in musical comedy. If Broadway can sell vaudeville under the guise of musical comedy up to $3.50, there is no reason why vaudeville cannot sell musical comedy at one dollar, more or less." The Marx Brothers couldn't manage to cross the blurry line.

Theoretically, their tabloid style would transfer easily to the legitimate stage. As early as 1916, the *New York Clipper* was reporting that "an effort is being made to induce the Four Marx Brothers to desert vaudeville in favor of musical comedy. The idea is to build up their present act, which runs forty minutes, into a full time show." *Billboard* noted, three years later, that "in their frantic search for new material for musical comedy the producers seem to be overlooking the Four Marx Brothers…The comedy ideas and versatility of these boys could be well used in a revue." Yet whenever they tried to graduate from vaudeville, they flopped. In 1918, they attempted to "begin a career" and "forsake the varieties for a venture in musical comedy." The result, *The Street Cinderella* (sometimes called *The Cinderella Girl*), was significant for being the official stage debut of Zeppo Marx as part of the team. But they opened in Grand Rapids, Michigan in the midst of an influenza epidemic, and patrons were only permitted to occupy every other seat in every other row. The show limped onward to another booking or two, but to little effect, and the Brothers' hopes for legitimate theatrical success died of the flu.

At the end of 1919, they actually signed a contract with an esteemed New York producer, Charles Dillingham. He announced his intention to star them on the Main Stem in the 1920-1921 season, but nothing came of that. He made noises about getting Aaron Hoffman, an old Weber and Fields scribe, to write for them, but nothing came of that either. Dillingham finally offered the Marxes the third road company of an old Montgomery and Stone vehicle, which they turned down.

In 1919 and 1920, the Brothers worked a new tabloid entitled *N'Everything*, but it was really *Home Again* again. Still, their performances kept getting better, and their improvisations more daring. *N'Everything* was hailed as "a thousand per cent beyond what they ever did before" in a June 1920 Chicago item, which also noted that the team "panicked the house not once but forty times, and stole a clean, bombarding hit, and got very near and dear to the customers." In August, "more people were talking about Marx Brothers than about any other act on the bill...It is an entertainment that has pretty nearly everything, yet everything is worthwhile and some things are streaked with genius." In Newark on October 2, *Billboard* reported that the Marxes "were forced to respond to so many encores at last night's performance that the act, which ordinarily runs about forty-five minutes, ran over an hour."

Yet their consistent ability to score with audiences, and the resultant fawning of much of the vaudeville press, inevitably stirred the resentment of those few who *didn't* like the Marx Brothers. As would ever be the case, there were always some who looked down their noses at these brash boys and their unrefined "roughhouse" antics, and considered the whole enterprise tasteless and juvenile. The *New York Clipper's* vaudeville pages were especially harsh during the second half of 1920:

> The Four Marx Brothers, with an act that lacks class and has a lot of rough business such as slapping a girl in the back, washing the face and hands in a bowl of punch and tickling a girl under her arm-pit, dragged along without exciting any great amount of interest. (August 18)

> The harp is well played by one of the boys, but the act is just as sloppy and suggestive in places as it was when last reviewed at the Palace and makes one

wonder how they get away with it. (September 29)

The Four Marx Brothers slopped up the stage with water and wine and still have several pieces of business that are very coarse and vulgar. (October 20)

[The Marx Brothers] were a noisy stampede from the word "go." (November 3)

There is little class to the entire offering, practically everything being sacrificed for the sake of getting laughs, many of which could, with good taste, be eliminated. (December 8)

By most accounts, this was a frustrating period for the Marxes personally. The endless vaudeville grind would have been especially onerous for two of the Brothers, who were trying, in their ways, to be family men. Chico had married Betty Karp, a chorus girl from the act, in 1917, and quickly produced a daughter, Maxine. Meanwhile, Zeppo, the handsome teenager, fell for Ruth Johnson, another handsome teenager, who was his dance partner in the act. Then older brother Groucho swooped in, swept her off his feet, and married her. Their son, Arthur, was born in July of 1921. These joyous developments meant that the act *had* to keep going, and the team had to work harder than ever, because they had more mouths to feed.

T HE MARX BROTHERS began the 1920s with a crucial creative transformation. Up to this point, Uncle Al Shean had been their major influence, but his effect was waning. German dialect humor had lost its appeal during the war, causing Groucho to drop his Dutch affect in favor of an elderly Yiddish persona. Regardless, the character had become confining. Mr. Green, or Schneider, had served Julius Henry Marx nobly, but his day had passed, and from his ashes an immortal spirit would rise—a more brash and modern figure, for the more brash and modern world around him.

Harpo and Chico, meanwhile, had the fundamentals of their characters in place, but they'd been playing boys too long. It was time to grow up and play men who *behaved* like boys. It was a time of expansion and experimentation. To shepherd this process, the Marxes found an important new collaborator, whose contributions have largely been ignored.

Herman Timberg was a librettist, songwriter, producer, director, and star, prominent in vaudeville and on Broadway for decades. Today he would be remembered as one of the great old masters if only we had more of him on film. Born in New York in 1892, he was slightly younger than the three major Marx Brothers, but in the early days he always seemed to be one step ahead of them. While still a teenager, Timberg achieved celebrity as the star of Gus Edwards' *School Boys and Girls*. It was Timberg who introduced the song "School Days," in 1908. This was the act the Marxes shamelessly plundered in 1911, when they conceived *Fun in Hi Skule*. One review of the Marxes' version declared it "the best 'school act' seen since the Edwards turn had Herman Timberg in it."[2]

Timberg was successful enough to support his family before he was eighteen. His father, an immigrant violinist who'd been paying the rent as a barber, retired his shears and tended house, while Herman provided academic and musical education for two younger siblings, Sammy and Hattie. The Timbergs would work together, like the Marxes. Herman and Hattie had an act in which they played violins while dancing, and both Sammy and Hattie would appear in Herman Timberg tabs. Sammy began to contribute music to the act, and eventually wrote now-classic themes for Fleischer cartoons, including *Popeye*, *Betty Boop*, and *Superman*. Herman Timberg interrupted his career as a vaudevillian *auteur* to appear on Broadway in Shubert revues like *The Passing Show of 1916*, and eventually created his own revues. He was famous for "the Timberg crawl-off," in which he exited the stage on all fours.

---

[2] Some accounts of the Marx Brothers' early career have connected the wrong dots and assumed that Groucho appeared in the Gus Edwards school act. Not quite; in the spring of 1906, he appeared as one of Gus Edwards' Postal Telegraph Boys, a different act entirely. Sounds adorable, though.

Among his signature hits were a "big-little musical comedy...described as a Chinese-American fantasy" called *Chicken Chow Mein* (in mockery of the popular *Chu Chin Chow*), and a 1920 Broadway revue known as *Tick-Tack-Toe*. *Theatre Magazine* suggested that a more apt title would be *Herman Timberg in Three Acts*.

Despite this, Timberg was known for his generosity to other performers. Even when he was the centerpiece of the act, he made sure his fellow troupers had interesting and rewarding material to play. Over the years, he increasingly worked as a writer, producer, and director for other comedians, including Fanny Brice, George Jessel, Clark and McCullough, Benny Rubin, the *Our Gang* kids, and the Three Stooges. The Stooges' Larry Fine, according to his brother Morris Feinberg, "idolized Herman Timberg," and later hoped in vain that a Timberg-penned feature film would establish the Stooges as "successors to the Marx Brothers."

In 1921, Herman accepted the challenge of writing and producing a new act for Julius, Arthur, Leonard, and Herbert. The act he created was initially titled *On the Mezzanine Floor*, later shortened to *On the Mezzanine*, and eventually renamed *On the Balcony*. (Its elaborate second scene featured a mezzanine—or, if you prefer, balcony—built into the scenery.) Like many Timberg creations, it was a story about show business. He loved to write about managers, critics, actors, and showgirls. The first scene took place in a theatrical manager's office, and featured Zeppo as a playwright pitching a new play. The second scene was that play. This novel structure allowed for standalone revue material, including long-established specialties like Harpo's harp solo, Chico's piano solo, and Groucho's comic vocals. But all of this would take place in Timberg's Broadway milieu, and the Marx Brothers would "do away with their former characters," as *Variety* put it.

Most significantly, *On the Mezzanine* brought an important revision to Groucho's stage presence. For the first time, Julius would not be playing an immigrant; he would be what he was, a first-generation American Jewish New Yorker with a big mouth. The jokes Timberg wrote for him replaced

Uncle Al's singsong Dutch, or its variant, with modern New York jazz patter that fit Julius's distinctive speaking voice like a tailored velvet suit. This new character was called Mr. Hammer. (The name that had already been in use by Groucho in *N'Everything*, the hastily-conceived update of *Home Again* which the Brothers performed in 1919 and 1920.) We would recognize this Mr. Hammer as an old friend, if we saw him, and not only because the name would surface again in the film version of *The Cocoanuts*. The Mr. Hammer of *On the Mezzanine* is the first in a long series of illustrious aliases for the same character, a list which would grow over the years to include Captain Jeffrey T. Spalding, Rufus T. Firefly, and Dr. Hugo Z. Hackenbush.

This new character had a new look. Timberg wrote a line in *On the Mezzanine* in which Mr. Hammer says, when asked to describe himself: "Did you ever see Lincoln without a beard? Well, I look like Washington with a moustache." This is the dawn of the Groucho moustache! And the matching eyebrows, mentioned less often but no less vital to the impact of that face. Adam Gopnik observed that Groucho's makeup "allowed him to communicate ironically with a big theatre audience." The earliest known photographs of a mustachioed Groucho were taken late in 1921, in connection with *On the Mezzanine*; it appears as a smear of greasepaint not unlike the one that would become his signature for thirty years.[3] These photographs— two posed publicity shots taken on December 16, and one candid backstage photo from a couple of months earlier—show that Groucho retained the old schoolteacher's wire-rim glasses and frock coat, but abandoned the bald cap in favor of his own dark, frizzy hair. In one photo, he's wearing a bowler hat, also a Timberg trademark. In another, he's sprawled on the floor in a mock-provocative pose, eyeballs rolling, while his brothers cavort above him. In these pictures, Harpo's coat and hat look a little too crisp, and Chico doesn't

---

[3] Groucho often explained that he had begun with a stage moustache made of crepe or fur, but was late for an entrance one night—in some versions of the tale, due to the birth of his son, Arthur—and smeared on the greasepaint in haste. This seems entirely plausible, especially for a Groucho anecdote, but I've never seen a photograph to support the existence of the pre-greasepaint moustache.

have exactly the familiar clothes yet, but it's unmistakable: posterity's first glimpse of the Marx Brothers as we know them.

Icons emerging, December 1921: Zeppo, Groucho, Harpo, and Chico

There have been debates about who "created" the Groucho Marx character, most of which have rightfully concluded that Groucho Marx deserves most of the credit. *Groucho*, as he appears in the films of the Marx Brothers and in our wildest imaginations, is probably best explained as the personification of Julius Henry Marx's sense of humor. But there were important secondary father figures, starting with Al Shean, and later, Will B. Johnstone and George S. Kaufman. Herman Timberg belongs on this list, right after Uncle Al. He didn't wholly invent the modern Groucho character, and it's possible that the first-generation speech as well as the moustache originated during *N'Everything* or even *Home Again*, as part of a more gradual evolution. But what evidence we have suggests otherwise. Timberg probably found it easy to write for Groucho, because it was the kind of fast-talking wiseguy role he often wrote for himself. Surviving recordings of Timberg's voice reveal a throaty, velvety sound not unlike Groucho's (and even less unlike Eddie Cantor's), while surviving caricatures and publicity portraits of Timberg show him with glasses, leering eyebrows, cigar, tailcoat, and bent posture.

The best-known material Timberg wrote for the Marx Brothers was the opening scene of *On the Mezzanine*, generally known as "the Theatrical Agency sketch." It outlived *Mezzanine*, remaining a fixture of the Brothers' later vaudeville repertoire, then finding its way into *I'll Say She Is* in 1923, and even onto film in 1931. Marx fans know it well, and it must be considered canonical; it is classic Marx Brothers, but it is also *very* Herman Timberg.[4] A gruff theatrical manager presides over a Times Square booking office, into which the Marx Brothers barge, one at a time, each offering an imitation of the same popular star. The sketch is full of recognizable Marx Brothers comedy, but most of the dialogue is written in rhymed verse. The following review, which appeared in the *New York Clipper* in March of 1921, reveals a lot about Timberg's writing, as well as the Marxes' improvisational approach:

> Al Shean was supposed to have written the old vehicle of the Four Marx Brothers. Before they had used it one season, outside of the setting, and about three lines, the act was purely and simply the Four Marx Brothers, and their own ad lib material placed permanently into the act.
>
> Herman Timberg evidently wrote the new one, *On the Mezzanine Floor*. The program states "Herman Timberg Presents." However, there seems to be one infallible method of discovering a Timberg written act. That's by syncopated talk. Timberg had jazz patter in his own act some years ago. Then he wrote *Chicken Chow Mein*, and jazzed the talk. He did it in his production. He did it with

---

[4] A later Timberg extravaganza, *Laugh Factory*, played the Keith-Albee circuit in 1927. It included not only a "scene in a New York theatrical manager's office," but "Herman Timberg in a comedy skit entitled 'Monkey Business!'"

George Mayo's act. And he's done it with the Four Marx Brothers.

But what we're driving at is this. At present, *On the Mezzanine Floor* is mainly the act written by Timberg. What it'll be a few months from now is difficult to say. For even on the third day of this act's first appearance in the city, only a few weeks old, when the writer reviewed it, he recognized lines that never could be written by Timberg and must come from the Marx clan . . .

Most of the bits formerly done by the Marx Brothers are retained for the new act. The piano "Silver Threads" bit, done by "Wop" Marx for the past ten years, is still in, and seems to be as good for laughs as it was years ago. "Red" Arthur sprang a big surprise when reviewed, by actually playing his harp with hardly any clowning. Incidentally these two are now also playing the clarinet and harmonica. "Pop" Marx announces that he will imitate George M. Cohan and then sings "Roly Boly Eyes" with the "wha wha" business as done last season.

Despite the reviewer's certainty that Timberg's script would be abandoned—and despite the certainty that the Marxes *did* ad lib and rewrite—they were still performing the agency scene as a recognizable Herman Timberg creation in Hollywood in 1931. It was partly through Timberg's style, his milieu, and his "syncopated jazz talk" that the Marx Brothers assumed the breathtaking modernity that would make them the Broadway rage of the 1920s. (And perhaps it was through Art Fisher's nicknames, still yet to go fully public, that the boys avoided being permanently identified as Pop, Wop, and Red.) Chico would still be playing "Silver Threads Among the Gold" in the film version of *Animal Crackers* in 1930, and the earnestness of Harpo's solos would prove an even more lasting development.

On the Mezzanine was financed in part by prizefighter Benny Leonard, who joined the cast for a while, performing a comedy boxing scene with the Marxes and romancing the show's ingénue. The ingénue was Timberg's sister, now billed as Hattie Darling. She drew positive notices, singing, dancing, and performing the kind of violin specialty she'd been doing with her brother for years. She also served the act in a managerial capacity, as she would recall in conversation with Charlotte Chandler in the 1970s:

> Benny Leonard was in love with me, and he wanted me to marry him. My brother, Herman Timberg, was a great writer, and he wrote *On the Mezzanine*, and Benny Leonard put up the money for the show. I managed the act and collected the salary at the box office, which Chico couldn't stand. The four Marx Brothers were only getting a thousand dollars a week, and Chico was quite a gambler. He loved to gamble and was always losing, so he had to come to me for advances, and this would irk him so much. Groucho loved it because he didn't want Chico to gamble.

The act was a success. "It is the effrontery of these gifted boys that makes them so funny," said the *New York Dramatic Mirror*, "especially when they try their awkward manners on the society dames of the play." *Billboard*'s Chicago critic described the team as "an entire musical comedy show by themselves," and the *San Francisco Chronicle* found it "rough stuff, but hilariously funny," adding, "It's like a nightmare, so full of changes and surprises." There were still huffy objectors, now led by *Billboard*'s New York office, which had something snide and degrading to say almost every time the Brothers returned to the Palace. "Such stuff is hardly worthy of mention" was all *Billboard* could muster in March of 1921, saving the real knife-twisting for a return booking in the summer:

> The Four Marx Brothers top the bill at the Palace this week, which in itself is quite a compliment to the Marx Brothers, when one takes into consideration the quality of their entertainment. To find the Marx Quartet headlining leads one to believe that there must indeed be a tremendous shortage of really good acts. On the other hand, however, the showering of such honors upon the

four Marx Brothers may also be taken as evidence of a noteworthy inability on the part of the Palace management to judge an act of headline caliber.

Variety, in a kinder, more thoughtful, but similarly disapproving review of the same Palace engagement, detected the boys' restlessness:

> Since last seen here the act appears to have been roughened up considerably by the introduction of low comedy business, not in the original script as written by Herman Timberg. One bit had "Harpo" manipulating a rubber glove after the fashion of a person milking a cow. Pretty crude for any place. In another part Julius had a bit of dialog about something creeping over him—addressing his conversation to one of the women in the act—and following it up with another remark about "scratching it out." The Marx Brothers are an exceptional quartet, all talented, Harpo and Julius particularly, but they seem to need direction.

But on balance, the critical response suggests that Timberg had helped the Brothers get closer to their goal. The *New York Sun* noticed that *Mezzanine* was "more pretentiously in the nature of a revue than anything they have done heretofore." An earlier *Variety* account perceived "an outstanding smack of smartness…which, coupled with the Marx Brothers' low comedy clowning, constitutes a combination that's infallible." The notice closed with the promising observation that "the turn also has real values in a production way" and "it should lift the Marx family right onto Broadway."

But it didn't, and vaudeville felt like business as usual, with the Marxes still cranky and hungry for new vistas. They made a silent movie, the legendary, lost *Humor Risk*. It was shown once, never released, and apparently destroyed. (And yes, we sure would like to see it.) If film was not the answer, perhaps they could become International Artistes, like others who had conquered American vaudeville. They bought *On the Mezzanine* from Timberg and Leonard, for a price of $10,000, and headed across the pond to make their

European debut. The Four Marx Brothers, their two wives and two children, the cast of *On the Mezzanine*, and Minnie sailed from New York on the *Mauretania* on June 6, 1922. On June 10, they appeared on a special shipboard vaudeville bill, "in aid of seamen's charities," along with George Arliss, Clark and McCullough, Groucho's wife Ruth, and any other show people who happened to be aboard. This did not, however, include Hatty Darling. The ingénue role was filled by Helen Schroeder, soon to become famous as Helen Kane, one of the primary inspirations for Betty Boop.

The Anglicized tab, now called *On the Balcony*, opened on June 19 at the London Coliseum and scored at the matinee. The London *Daily Telegraph* celebrated "the maddest thing the variety stage has seen for a long time, conspicuous for its splendid inconsequence and clever back chat," while *The Stage* found the Brothers "immensely funny." On the strength of the audience's response, the act was moved from fifth on the bill to the star closing position, formerly occupied by a Russian dance troupe ("Lydia Lopokova, Leonide Massine, Lydia Sokolova, and Leon Wojcikowski in a 'Divertissement'"). But the evening show did not go well. Much of the audience was rude or indifferent to the Brothers' efforts, provoking Groucho's hostility and an unscripted aside: "They know *some* language, but what the hell is it?" Was his New York accent indecipherable to these British ears? He tried over-enunciating, in what might have sounded like mockery of the British, and this brought an aggressive hail of heavy British pennies upon the stage. Groucho marched to the footlights and pleaded, "Friends, it's been an expensive trip over. Would you mind throwing a little silver?" This earned the one genuine laugh of the evening, and was quoted everywhere the next day. "Following the conclusion," reported *Variety*'s British correspondent, "Julius Marx appeared before the curtain and apologized for what he termed 'the poor performance,' blaming it on 'the rowdyism of the gallery.' The apology was received with silence. Hearty applause greeted a frequently repeated line in the script by one of the characters: 'This is getting on my nerves.'"

The manager of the Coliseum later confronted the Marxes and was all apologies, explaining that the Russian dance troupe was furious at being asked to switch spots on the bill, and had arranged for a large contingent of angry fans to sit in the balcony and give the Marx Brothers a hard time. Groucho dispatched a terse letter to *Variety*, explaining that "ardent admirers of the Russian dancers, sometimes known as a claque, took exception to the switching of their favorites, and were responsible for the pennies that were thrown...Why your correspondent here gave such prominence to the penny throwing incident and none to the reasons thereof, I do not understand... The statements he sent in were injurious to our professional reputation."

But the tale of the vengeful Russian dancers, even if we assume it to be true, was likely a convenient cover for the fact that the Marx Brothers did not quite catch on with British audiences during this visit. The *London Times* approved only grudgingly, allowing that the boys seemed to enjoy their own performances so much that eventually the audience had to give in. On the fourth day of the booking, they abandoned *On the Balcony* and reverted to the old crowd pleaser, *Home Again*. Surely they would not have done this if they were really going over well. They moved to the London Alhambra, then Bristol, then Manchester. Although they completed their British experiment without further embarrassment, it didn't feel like much of a success. Perhaps they weren't International Artistes after all. Even when they did well, it was with their dusty old act from 1914. Every time they tried to do something new, they wound up having to do something old.

An even bigger disappointment awaited them upon their return to the States. E.F. Albee, president of the Keith circuit and fearsome kingpin of big-time vaudeville, was furious with the Marxes for accepting a foreign engagement without his permission. Apparently there was something written on a piece of paper somewhere. Albee was a seething, tyrannical authority figure who was just *born* to run afoul of the Marx Brothers; he was known for his iron grip on the major vaudeville circuits, and for his puritanical decrees. He banned Prohibition jokes, mother-in-law jokes, "jocular references to the picture players of Hollywood and Hollywood itself," and "all racial funny talk, grotesque make-up and offensive references." The Marxes' intention to tour Britain had been reported by the trades well in advance, and Albee surely could have warned them not to embark upon it, or risk their future in American vaudeville. But he waited for them to return, and then slapped them with his favorite punishment. And so, having resigned themselves to big-time vaudeville, the Brothers now suddenly found themselves blacklisted from big-time vaudeville.

TAKE IT FROM ME

Will B. Johnstone

MEANWHILE, ANOTHER IMPASSE was reached by another brother team.

William Breuninger Johnstone was born in 1881 in St. Louis, Missouri, and spent his childhood in Evanston, Illinois. Drawing was his great passion and his great gift, and although he would become many things, he was first and foremost a cartoonist. He studied at the Frank Holmes School of Illustration and the Art Institute of Chicago. In 1903, young Johnstone's

23

work was praised by the famous painter and art critic Henry Charles Payne, in the pages of the *Chicago Inter Ocean*: "Johnstone shows a fine quality of workmanship in his pen drawings… [Some] figures are drawn in such lines as the mind of the observer may easily fill in with what is only hinted at by the lines themselves." Johnstone took his work seriously, and had the driven artist's gifts of restless productivity and total concentration. One colleague observed that he "makes faces while drawing." Another was astonished to witness Johnstone completing three weeks' worth of comic strips, and several watercolor landscapes, over the course of a three-day train ride.

Will was an avid history buff who could take you to Revolutionary War battlefields and tell you exactly what had taken place during each battle. He was an enthusiastic athlete and sports fan. He was an avid chess player and an avid smoker, "fond of the drink, and fond of the joke," according to his great-granddaughter, Margaret Farrell. He was a man of serious social and political convictions, always on the side of the downtrodden and tempest-tost. In photographs, he tends to look scowling and disgruntled. But people who knew him described him as a figure of levity and playfulness, with "the most impish smile." He called himself Will B. Johnstone—whatever Will B. will be.

Today, Johnstone is remembered for his work with the Marx Brothers. That he wrote most of *I'll Say She Is*, and co-wrote *Monkey Business* and *Horse Feathers*, is already an extraordinary contribution to our culture. (He was also an uncredited writer on *A Day at the Races*.) In his time, he was known mainly as a popular political cartoonist, whose signature creation—the naked taxpayer dressed in a barrel—would become one of the iconic images of the twentieth century. B.J. Lewis, one of Johnstone's editors at the *New York Morning World*, credited him with "lampoon[ing] out of existence more American shams than you can remember." Lewis remembered Will walking into his office every day at 4:00 with a fresh cartoon, sharply satirizing some current hypocrisy or injustice, often with a surprising and thought-provoking take, and always with exquisite draftsmanship. "He was always good-humored, always ready with a smile," Lewis recalled, "but there wasn't any fooling Will. He could still be good natured as he busted the bubbles of conceit and deceit with his cartoons."

Will B. Johnstone was not the kind of man who did one thing. He was the kind of man who did ten things. He was restlessly creative. He was a fine painter, an author of humorous essays and parodies of the news, an illustrator of other people's writing. For the sports pages, he would draw diagrams of every single play in a football game. He wrote movies. He wrote musicals.

Just out of art school, he was drawing for the *Chicago Journal*, and then served as art editor of the *Inter Ocean*. He had a sweetheart named Helen Ross Beckman, whose disapproving father frowned upon their union. The Beckman family moved to East Orange, New Jersey in 1906, and Will followed them. He married Helen, had two children, and settled into a lovely routine of doting on his family and being frowned upon by his father-in-law. When the Beckmans wintered in California, Will, Helen, Jean, and Will Jr. would housesit for them in New Jersey. Will taught Mr. Beckman's pet parrot to greet his owner with, "Hello, you old son-of-a-bitch!"

Of course, living in New Jersey meant access to New York and its fathomless desirability. Johnstone worked as an illustrator for Hearst, then as an editorial cartoonist for the *World*. Mikael Uhlin, author of the website Marxology, describes the daily grind:

> Will commuted from his home in East Orange on the Lackawanna Railroad to Hoboken, then took the ferry to lower Manhattan, walking through the Fulton Fish Market and passing the Woolworth Building, to his office at the *World*, overlooking City Hall . . . Will went to the office in the morning, read all the papers, got an idea for that day's strip and then played chess in the office until it was time to actually draw up his cartoon, just in time for the deadline.

This was Manhattan's legendary Newspaper Row, once the nerve center of

American media. When Johnstone arrived, it was still thriving, but in the past decade it had suffered the departure of the *Herald* and the *Times*, to their eponymous Squares uptown.

Will drifted uptown too. He had a brother in New York, Alexander Johnstone. Alex was three years older than Will, and was a serious musician, concert violinist, and aspiring composer. It was perhaps through Alexander, in collusion with the city itself, that Will fell in love with the theatre. Then there was a third Johnstone brother, Tom, born in 1888 and also a composer (as well as a newspaperman, occasional playwright, and later, a pioneering ad man). The Johnstones are seldom remembered today for the authorship of musicals, but they were a presence on the Big Street for fifteen years, with twelve Broadway shows to their collective credit.

Will and Alexander first collaborated in 1911, on *Betsy*, adapted from *An American Widow*, a little-known Broadway farce by Kitty Chambers. Will wrote the lyrics, to Alex's music. The surviving songs from *Betsy* are charming but stiff, firmly rooted in operetta. In fact, *Betsy* was a prototypical musical comedy, at a time when the form was still too young to have a formula. The *New York Sun* began its opening-night review: "The experiment of putting music to an American farce was again tried at the Herald Square last night." Another critic noticed that Alexander's music was "of the popular Viennese type," and found Will's lyrics "strikingly original." *Betsy* starred Grace La Rue, who remained prominent on Broadway into the thirties. It was produced by Byron Chandler, her husband, who had produced her previous short-lived vehicle, *Molly May*. The second time around, both Ms. La Rue and the show drew respectful notices, but *Betsy* failed to excite the public and closed after thirty-two performances.

One year later, Will and Alex were back on Broadway, with a more traditional operetta, *Miss Princess*. This lasted a more traditional sixteen performances. It was a tale of romantic intrigue, set in Austria. It featured a popular star, the German soprano Lina Abarbanell, who got much better reviews than the show. "It is due to this energetic little singer that the show has any interest whatsoever," insisted *Variety*, even while admitting that the lyrics "are not half bad, and at times show positive genius for rhyme and reason," and the music is "buoyant and full of life." The *Dramatic Mirror* was impressed, but not moved. Alexander had "attempted to write Viennese music—he uses the whole bag of tricks," and "the orchestration is clever. And the music is, in spite of this, dull and flat, because of the lack of just one thing—real melody and inspiration."

Will and Alexander wrote again for Lina Abarbanell in *The Red Canary* in 1913 (this time with music by Harold Orlob, lyrics by Will, and Alexander co-writing the book with William Le Baron). It had a successful engagement in Chicago, but flopped on Broadway in April of 1914. In 1918, working not with Will but with librettist William Carey Duncan, Alexander scored a modest success. *Fiddlers Three* was an operetta set in "Cremona, the 'Violin City' in Lombardy." It lasted ten weeks on Broadway and then toured for many months. The complete score of *Fiddlers Three* survives, and it seems to have been Alexander's best work. The sound is still pre-jazz, but the structure is musical comedy, with memorable refrains and a new Broadway brashness.

According to Margaret Farrell, there was a falling-out between Will and Alex at this point, the details of which are unclear. They do not seem to have been professionally associated with each other ever again, and after 1918 Alex vanishes from Will's diaries. The collaboration between Alexander and William Carey Duncan continued with *Sunshine*, written and produced while *Fiddlers Three* was on the road. *Sunshine* was about "three Americans wandering through Spain, who in their wanderings, meet with Shimmying Spanish Señoritas, smugglers, gay and gallant matadors, and other humorous and picturesque personalities." The star was comedian Richard Carle. Alexander Johnstone, in addition to writing the music, was the show's producer. It never reached New York.

Alexander never got back to Broadway. Despite taking a loss on *Sunshine*, he continued as producer and composer on *The Sympathetic Twin*, again starring Richard Carle. He was also cultivating a producing partnership with the great comedian Bert Williams. But *The Sympathetic Twin* wasn't going well, and Alexander owed Carle money, and he owed Williams money, and everything was falling apart. His creditors attached the scenery and costumes, closing the show in Baltimore without notice, and he was unable to pay his actors. A week later, he was holed up in his apartment at the Hotel Sheridan Square in New York, when Equity officials came knocking. According to the *New York Clipper*, Alexander "pleaded for time to make up the deficiency. However, this was refused and some thirty summonses were dumped in his unsuspecting lap by the Equity representatives." The unpaid salaries were said to exceed $3,000 in aggregate, plus $500 still owed to Carle for *Sunshine*, and $7,000 to Bert Williams for underwriting *The Sympathetic Twin*.

Alexander Johnstone would live for another thirty-six years, to the age of 77, but *The Sympathetic Twin* was the end of his life in the theatre. There was another musical Johnstone brother waiting in the wings. But Alexander had been Will's way into showbiz, and if Will was to have his own life as a creator of theatre, he would need a new mentor, an advocate, a patron. What he got was a producer.

JOSEPH M. GAITES (the *M*, it was often said, stood for Minimum) was a producer with unlimited ambition but limited success, and he had been in the game for a long time. Born in Pittsburgh in 1874, he began his professional life as a railroad ticket broker, but his deepest interest was in the theatre. One day at the office, he told his partner, "I think I could write a play." His partner, a Mr. Blaney, said, "Well, you write the play and we will stage it." A few weeks later, Gaites strode into the railroad ticket office with a script entitled *A Railroad Ticket*. He and Blaney pooled their resources and consulted with some of the theatre people who bought train tickets. They managed to get *A Railroad Ticket* on its feet, but they wound up $8,000 in debt and had to go back to selling railroad tickets.

"It took several years to get out of the hole," Gaites recalled later, "and

Newspaper drawing of Joseph M. Gaites, 1910

we brought out no more plays, but I had been stung by the theatrical bee and I did everything in the business from painting scenery to a press agent." When even painting a press agent didn't work, Gaites began to worry. He kept writing plays, including *A Wild Duck* (1894), *The Air Ship* (1899), and *Shooting the Chutes* (1902), but each one failed. Gaites kept getting wiped out and starting all over again. His continual financial struggles fueled a chorus of irate creditors and legal adversaries. One cheeky reporter wrote, "It is hard to tell now just where the honor of being robbed by Gaites should go, as there are several claimants in the field."

Gaites eventually made money in show business, by abandoning his career as a playwright and becoming an impresario. He began to purchase secondhand attractions from other producers. He would cut costs by reducing the scale of the productions, and tour second- and third-string theatres all over the country. This proved highly profitable, with small-town audiences flocking to see popular hits like Weber and Fields' *Hoity Toity*, Ziegfeld's *The Red Feather*, and George M. Cohan's *Little Johnnie Jones*, on the strength of their titles. It was precisely the kind of operation Charles Dillingham had insultingly offered to the Marx Brothers. These endless copycat tours were something of a national epidemic, causing Groucho Marx to observe, in 1927, "Chicago has had . . . *Congo, One Man's Woman, Lucky Sambo* . . . a return engagement of *No, No, Nanette* . . . Cleveland has had a No. 8 company of *Blossom Time*, a No. 7 company of *Abie's Irish Rose*, a No. 6 company of *The Student Prince*, a No. 5 company of *Mutt and Jeff*, [and] *New York Exchange*, with the hot stuff eliminated."

Now Gaites had some money, but little prestige, as all of his successes were cheap versions of old properties associated with other producers. Perhaps fearing that he'd wind up back in the railroad ticket office, he cultivated other business interests on the side. He bought two grocery stores in Orange, New Jersey, and told *Variety* in 1912 that he planned to own a whole chain of them, so that eventually he "won't care what happens to the show business."

But he did care. In 1908, loaded with $50,000 worth of secondhand road show profits, he decided to sink it all into a new musical called *Three Twins* (book by Charles Dickson, music by Karl Hoschna, lyrics by Otto Harbach). Other producers had passed on *Three Twins*, and nobody believed in it, but Gaites declared, "I am always willing to bet when I think I am right. I believe this to be a good show and I am willing to take one chance and if I am wrong I will go back to work again." *Three Twins* was a hit on Broadway, running for ten months (very respectable in those days), and turning a large profit for Gaites and the authors. But this success was followed by a long series of dismal flops, including *Bright Eyes* (1910), *Dr. De Luxe* (1911), and *The Girl of My Dreams* (1911). George Jean Nathan observed that Gaites "gives the public exactly what it wants... [and] often achieves financial loss."

In a 1910 profile, Gaites is described as "a small man about five feet six inches, who looks more like a boy than the business man..."

> Mr. Gaites is good natured, mild mannered and exceptionally polite. No matter how small or important your business with him may be, he would receive you with a half smile and a hearty handshake, and the expression on his face would make it seem sincere.
>
> He has lots of nerve and nothing seems too big for him to undertake. He is unlike [rival producers] Frohman and Savage, for these gentlemen go to Europe. They look over a piece that has been tried out and if it is a success over there they will bring it to America and produce it. The risk isn't half as great as in the case of Mr. Gaites, everything he produces is by American authors. He reads it over and if it sounds good to him he is willing to gamble his opinion against the public's, for the show business is nothing more than a gamble...

Road receipts kept Gaites afloat during these tense periods. A show could be savaged by the New York critics and close in a week, then tour the country for years, "Direct from Broadway!" Even a turkey could turn a modest profit on the road, if it could be produced cheaply enough—thus, Joseph Minimum Gaites.

Joe M. and Will B. must have crossed paths at just the right moment. Both had reached crises of faith in show business, and the feeling that if the next one wasn't a hit, it might be time to hang it up. The next Gaites production was called *Take it From Me*, with music by Will R. Anderson. For Johnstone, it was a creative leap forward; now he was writing not just the lyrics, but the book, from his own original story—summarized for us in 1919:

It is an amusing yarn of a rich young spender's attempt to run a department store [the Eggett Company] which he has inherited and which is to go to the villain [named Cyrus Crabb] if it fail to show a profit under the young man's direction. The hero sees no chance of making a profit, so he determines to leave as little as possible for his enemies. His efforts to crush the business, however, prove its best advertisement, and it grows into a great success. After which he marries the prettiest of the stenographers.

Perhaps the spirit of a future Marx Brothers writer can be detected in this tale of Tom Eggett (and "two of his pals, as Efficiency Expert and General Superintendent") gleefully running roughshod over a staid department store: "The salesgirls are ordered to wear gay costumes to replace the severe black of the old regime, while the oldest employee in the store, for the sake of efficiency, is ordered to wear roller skates." The boys "put in one or two cabarets, make a bosom friend of a clever shoplifter, and hire scores of lingerie models, who delighted them and certainly delighted the audience." This part of the show included a song, "I Like to Linger in the Lingerie," featuring Johnstone the lyricist at his most playful:

I like to linger round the lacy,
pink and white and racy
little negligee scenes,
around the soft crepe dechines
For beautiful boudoir queens, ah me!
I like to peek-a-boo
around the chicky cheeky peek-a-boo fluffles
and silky ruffles.
There's no attraction stronger,
and so, the longer that I linger, goodness me,
it only makes me long to linger longer,
linger longer in the lingerie.

Their assault on the store complete, "the three pals stage a movie play on their very counters."

Take it From Me premiered on the last day of the Great War, November 11, 1918, in Providence, Rhode Island. Ultimately, the show lasted much longer than the war. Gaites, having learned his lesson about hasty New York openings, kept it on the road for twenty-one weeks before allowing it to meet

Advertisement for Take it From Me, *1919*

its fate at the Forty-fourth Street Theatre on March 30, 1919. The reviews were generally positive, though more than one critic felt that the first act was too slow. The stars of *Take it From Me* were the Gardiner Trio (Edgar, Arline, and Helen), dancing comedians, and their work was consistently praised. So was Johnstone's. "The author has done his work in clever style," said the *Brooklyn Eagle*. "There is considerable humor to the lines and his lyrics have a pleasing swing."

On Broadway, *Take it From Me* ran long enough to avoid embarrassment—twelve weeks—and was perceived as a modest, quirky success. Will enjoyed bringing his cartoonist colleagues to the theatre to witness his achievement in another medium. The April 15 performance was dubbed "Cartoonists' Night," with twenty newspaper artists attending as Will's guests. In May, the American Cartoonists Convention was held in New York, and its members eagerly lined up for tickets. "It is reported they will insist on a speech from Mr. Johnstone," said the *Evening World*. "At any rate, he's been busy for a week writing on something he won't let anybody get a peep at." The box office thrived for eight weeks, then hit a slump. During its last four weeks in New York, *Take it From Me* lost $12,000, but Gaites knew that they'd easily make it up on the road, especially with ads boasting of a twelve-week run on Broadway.

Almost the moment it closed, in June, the show was flourishing again out of town. It lasted ten weeks in Philadelphia, nineteen weeks in Chicago, and broke records in Kansas City. By the end of its first year, *Take it From Me* had raked in a net profit of more than $100,000. It had cost $28,000 to produce. The *New York Clipper* paid tribute to Gaites' gamble, describing his latest work as "one of the money-getting surprises of the last few seasons. It is considered by theatrical people a perfect example of the speculative element that attaches to the show business." *Take it From Me* lasted for years on the road. Gaites kept it going in increasingly pared-down iterations, until it finally became embarrassing. *Variety* caught up with the show in San Antonio in March of 1923 and reported, "The show was terrible and showed its six years' wear . . . Experienced producers like Gaites . . . ought to know better." In 1926, *Take it From Me* was the basis of a silent film starring Reginald Denny.

Now Will B. Johnstone was the author of a stage success, and a participant in its profits. In his diary he meticulously recorded the box office intake for each performance. His stock had risen in the theatre, and it was reported that he would write a new comedy for the Shuberts. This did not come to pass. Will's next theatrical work would be another Joseph M. Gaites production. In fact, *Take it From Me* was still in its first year when Gaites presented Johnstone with his next assignment.

The producer had managed to sign a big star, Kitty Gordon, for her return to the stage after years in pictures, and needed a vehicle. Johnstone's idea was not, in itself, much of an idea. But get used to it: *A bored heiress is looking for thrills, and each scene depicts an attempt to thrill her. In the end, she learns that the greatest thrill is the thrill of love.* It was a flexible revue plot, which could accommodate any kind of song, sketch, or specialty, and it was called *Love for Sale.* (It had no connection to the famous Cole Porter song of the same title, which it preceded by more than a decade.)

The comedian of *Love for Sale* was Jack Wilson, a blackface comic "who is reminiscent of Eddie Cantor." (Wilson provided some of his own material, and in trade notices he shared book credit with Johnstone.) Kitty Gordon starred as the thrill-seeking society woman. "Act 1 shows the chorus receiving marconigrams in Jazzmania from Kitty, who arrives from overseas in an aeroplane," one critic tells us. Another observed, "The authors have made use of many unique characters, among them the 'Rich Man,' 'Poor Man,' 'Beggar Man,' 'Thief,' 'Doctor,' 'Lawyer,' 'Merchant' and the 'Chief,' who vie with each other in an endeavor to please and entertain her." Those characters certainly do sound unique. Switching papers again: "Then ensuing scenes range from Wall Street to an opium den and the curtain falls on a resplendent Garden of Love, in which Kitty's costume reaches the height of stage magnificence." Ms. Gordon's attire was among the show's principal attractions. She had an uncanny ability to wear gowns, and in *Love for Sale* she could be seen in as many as nine of them, which collectively cost more than $20,000.

Toronto Evening Telegram, November 4, 1919:

> Last night's audience had a cruel shock when Jack Wilson appeared before the rise of the curtain to appeal for their indulgence because a railway had mislaid one whole baggage car! For a moment the audience wondered if it would have to prove its devotion to Kitty Gordon by sitting through her show minus her Queen of Sheba clothes it had come to see.
>
> Then came a snicker from the first row youths when Jack Wilson explained that it was the chorus girls who had lost their wardrobes, but would come on nevertheless.
>
> "I don't mean what you mean," said Mr. Wilson, who announced that the girls would wear their street clothes. That the show missed much of its sparkle without their glittering background seems almost superfluous to remark.

Kitty Gordon

Advertisement, Love for Sale, *1919*

Love for Sale was apparently not much of a thrill. It closed quickly, in Detroit, with the *Clipper* eulogizing "a rather disasterous [sic] tour" and noting Gaites' intention "to hold it until some time in the future."

On *Love for Sale*, Will B. Johnstone began a new songwriting partnership, or two. Musical duties were shared by Harry Auracher (later to achieve some fame as a bandleader, under the name Harry Archer) and little brother Tom Johnstone. This was Tom's first professional outing as a composer. He provided music that was less formal, and more fun, than Alexander's—perhaps for the simple reason that Tom was ten years younger, writing a little later. He didn't have Alexander's fealty to the Sigmund Romberg operetta tradition, which was growing stale. Tom's compositions are more recognizable to us as showtunes, in the modern idiom of Broadway; they are laced with ragtime. His contributions to *Love for Sale* included "Gimme a Thrill" (also known as "Give Me a Thrill") and "Wall Street Blues."

Tom worked with Auracher on *Frivolities of 1920*, then teamed up with Will again to write *Up in the Clouds*, the next Joseph M. Gaites spectacular. This was a frank (and successful) attempt to replicate the success of *Take it From Me*—though, thanks to the robust profits of *Take it From Me*, it was done on a larger scale. Once again, Will B. devised an offbeat plot which was inherently fanciful, and slightly arch. The *New York Dramatic Mirror* detected "more of a plot than most of the present-day musical comedies," but concluded that "whether or not the author is striving to inject a moral, not morals, into the musical comedy game had best be left to the audience."

Johnstone's story for *Up in the Clouds* concerned one Archie Dawson, who has served in the war and returned home with the ambition "to produce a picture which will unite all classes of men into a real democracy." Dawson's conservative father "threatens to disinherit him if he does not leave this 'movie bunk' alone." But Dawson perseveres, delivering "socialistic speeches" and making his movie against the wishes of his father, as well as the villain, "a philandering movie director." Establishing his own studio in "a musty old bank," Dawson recruits a cast of promising amateurs, including a beautiful

Tom Johnstone

young unknown named Jean Jones. Miss Jones has come to New York "to attend a school of motion picture acting in hopes of becoming a great star." The school turns out to be crooked, "run by schemers, whose methods are detrimental to the moving picture profession." But in the second act, Jean reveals herself to be "none other than Gladys Jewell, a great star of the silver screen, who has entered the school under an assumed name to expose its workings." She falls in love with Archie Dawson, stars in his "patriotic" film, and exposes the villains. The movie is a hit and the heroes get rich. Then "the heroine runs to the hero's arms and is caressed till the curtain shuts them from view."

The tale was decorated with a lively score by Will and Tom, including the beautiful title song ("We're dreaming daydreams / Up in the clouds…"), and a Cohan-like salute to Betsy Ross. The first act finale, "Jean," was musical comedy gold, in which Archie and his pals, Bud and Freddie, imagine Jean

Jones as the heroine of various films. All of the fun was delivered in a sparkling package, full of the spectacular effects which were part of the Joe Gaites formula whenever he could afford them. Audiences appreciated a "travestied medley of Months in girly satire," a "gaudily unusual male dancer in gilt from toe to head crown," "a beautifully effective statue pose . . . that broke into a human balancing act," and a "trio of elderly men" who turned out to be "a team of acrobats." According to *Variety*, "the real high point of the audience appeal was saved for a cloud effect a la 'movie' style on a plain screen drop."

Up in the Clouds, like its model *Take it From Me*, lasted a few months on Broadway (at the Lyric Theatre), and then cleaned up on the road,

Up in the Clouds *sheet music cover, 1922*

touring for more than two years and further enriching Gaites, Johnstone, and their partners (though it didn't make quite as much as *Take it From Me*, largely because it was more lavish and expensive). But Johnstone and Gaites couldn't let that other idea go—that thing about the society woman looking for thrills—and made periodic stabs at resuscitating it. In the summer of 1921, Gaites had announced "a condensed version" with female impersonator James Watts as the ingénue. Nothing came of that. But by the fall, Gaites found himself in need of a new musical property, and the Johnstones found themselves rewriting *Love for Sale*, and everybody, even the Marx Brothers, found themselves in Shubert Advanced Vaudeville.

THE SHUBERT BROTHERS, Sam, Lee, and Jacob (J.J.), had begun as theatre owners in upstate New York, nurturing a nascent empire in the dusk of the nineteenth century. They gathered successes like daisies, and by the new century were beginning a strategic conquest of New York City. Sam died in a railroad accident in 1905. Lee and J.J. kept buying theatres. By the twenties they owned hundreds of them, across the country, and they had become one of Broadway's most formidable producing organizations. The Shuberts were not exactly loved, but they were exactly feared. Lee was known for the staid, reserved personality which masked a ruthless and predatory approach to show business. J.J. was known as a vulgarian who physically attacked people.

Despite some earnest efforts, they never mastered vaudeville. Shubert Advanced Vaudeville was a doomed enterprise from the start, but it did momentarily create an entire new circuit just when our heroes needed one. Trav S.D., in his outstanding history *No Applause—Just Throw Money: The Book That Made Vaudeville Famous*, explains:

> In 1920, the Shuberts attempted once again to set up a rival circuit, called Shubert Advanced Vaudeville. Their plan was to outbid Albee for all his major acts until he went broke—at which point, presumably, they would buy out his theatres and then pay the acts whatever they wanted.

But Albee was not to be so easily cowed. He called the Shuberts' bluff by matching all their bids, no matter how high, and threatening to blacklist all those who went to their circuit. Strapped for acts, Advanced Vaudeville hung on for a few years by switching to touring revues and musicals as entire companies (as Weber and Fields and others had done in the 1880s and nineties), a move that was feasible since they owned all of their theatres. Weber and Fields themselves travelled with one of these Shubert units, as did the Marx Brothers, Ed Wynn, James Cagney, and Fred Allen. But this strenuous gambit defeated the whole purpose of switching to vaudeville, which was its increased cost-effectiveness. The Shuberts caved and went back to producing regular Broadway musicals, and Albee showed uncharacteristic grace toward the acts that had defected. He only blacklisted them for a year, after which they were allowed back on his circuit for a smaller salary if they would take out an advertisement in *Variety* apologizing for their foolish transgression.

The Marx Brothers, of course, had no such option. With their transatlantic transgression, they had offended Albee more deeply than an ad in *Variety* could fix, and at any rate, the Marx Brothers were no more inclined to public humility than Albee was. So they glumly plugged along, their fates tied to a sinking ship. In October of 1922, they signed a thirty-week Shubert contract and assumed control of a dying unit, the *Hollywood Follies*. Having collapsed in Chicago, deep in debt, the show was bailed out by a Milwaukee Chinese restaurateur named Charles Moy. (Or, in some sources, Chow Moy; in others, Sam Toy.) On Mr. Moy's dime, the unit again set sail, now entitled *The Twentieth Century Revue* and starring the Four Marx Brothers.

The first half of the show was a fixed vaudeville bill, with the Marxes as headliners, doing the Theatrical Agency sketch from *On the Mezzanine*. The second half was a full Marx Brothers tabloid, with more from *On the Mezzanine* and *Home Again*, a new routine revolving around a poker game, and a mysterious scene featuring Harpo and Chico as automobile mechanics.

Advertisement for The Twentieth Century Revue, *1922*

When the show played Chicago, the Brothers had an idea to make it rain on stage, an effect to be accomplished with falling rice. They wired their angel, Charles Moy or whoever, and he sent a hundred pounds of rice. The rice somehow got wet in the rigging above the stage, and when released, it fell in one goopy mass, landing on a member of the chorus, and inspiring some impromptu remarks from Groucho about paying off their creditors in rice pudding.

The vaudeville portion of the show was roundly panned ("*The Twentieth Century Revue* as a whole is not such a much"—*Billboard*), but our Brothers got their usual raves. In *Variety*, Sime Silverman mused, "The Marx boys may greatly profit in one way or another at the head of their own show in a Shubert theatre on Broadway." Wouldn't that be nice?

Even if *The Twentieth Century Revue* could get its management and finances in order, it was one car of a derailing train. *Variety* issued reports on the status of Shubert vaudeville in increasingly funereal tones, estimating a season's loss of $1,550,000, and announcing "SHUBERT UNIT LOSERS FOR THIS SEASON." On March 3, 1923, the Marxes were about to play the final show of a three-day run at the Murat Theatre in Indianapolis, but when they arrived they were greeted by a deputy sheriff, who strongly suggested that they were *not* about to play the final show of a three-day run at the Murat Theatre in Indianapolis. The partners were suing each other; the circuit was collapsing; the show was broke; the chorus was covered in wet rice; everything was a mess.

WHILE THE BROTHERS were beginning their Shubert Advanced debacle, Joseph M. Gaites was in Fall River, Massachusetts, rehearsing the Johnstones' "thrill show," now reduced to tabloid length and retitled *Gimme a Thrill*. This, too, was a Shubert unit. Soon before the show was to open at the Majestic Theatre in Boston, the Shuberts sent a representative to check on Gaites' progress. The Shubert representative went home and filed his report, and Gaites received orders from the New York office to cancel the opening immediately. Gaites refused. "I've got a reputation at stake, too," he said, "and I'm willing to play Boston billed as a Joseph M. Gaites show." As it happened, the show missed its opening matinee "due to delayed baggage." In lieu of the planned show, *Variety* reported, "the acts on the bill improvised a performance that was booed by the audience."

The Gaites unit show was the inverse of the Marxes', with the tabloid first, and the vaudeville acts second. The tabloid retained the plot and structure of *Love for Sale*, with "episodes showing the quest of Beauty in search of a thrill, the thrill coming at the finale, when she finds love," one reviewer helpfully explained. The "thrills" included the Wall Street number from *Love for Sale*, a Parisian Apache dance set in a Chinatown opium den, a scene in a sheik's tent, and a courtroom sketch. In the Chinatown sequence, there was an elaborate "love boat" or "dream ship"—a large art piece which moved across the stage. This was a favorite Gaites device, also used prominently in

Advertisement for Gimme a Thrill, *1922*

Up in the Clouds. The idea was popularized through its use in the operetta *San Toy* (not to be confused with any Milwaukee restaurateurs), which was lampooned in the Chinatown sequence in *Gimme a Thrill.* The Johnstone brothers added a charming new number called "I'm Saving You for a Rainy Day," which was staged without the use of rice.

At Shubert vaudeville prices, Gaites was unable to make *Gimme a Thrill* profitable if he produced it on the scale he envisioned—the scale of *Up in the Clouds* or at least *Take it From Me. Variety* reported that Gaites' expenditure on *Gimme a Thrill* was already enough to guarantee him no profit for the season, even if it turned out to be a big hit. It did not: "He apparently started off to do a real job…and when he found the proposition getting away from him as regards reasonable financial limitations along a dollar circuit, he just said, 'I'm going through regardless.'" It closed in February of 1923, leaving Gaites behind to the tune of $10,000.

The headliners of *Gimme a Thrill* were the Gardiner Trio, Edgar, Arline, and Helen, our old friends from *Take it From Me* (where in one critic's opinion, they "just simply walked away with the whole performance"). In

Gimme a Thrill, Arline Gardiner played the Kitty Gordon role, the unnamed Beauty. The roles of "rich man, poor man, beggar," and so on, remained. But the real crowd-pleasers in the *Gimme a Thrill* unit were Max and Moritz, a trained monkey act.

The Gardiner Trio in Gimme a Thrill

III.
YOU MUST COME OVER

The chorus of a revue on the Strand Theatre roof, 1919

THE MUSICAL REVUE is an art form which, depending on how you define it, either died in the middle of the twentieth century, or is still thriving today. It emerged at a time when "musical theatre," or what we now usually mean by that phrase, did not yet exist. There was opera, and its folksier and more dialogue-driven variant, ballad opera. Ballad opera was typified by a British work, John Gay's *The Beggar's Opera*, but the form had existed in America since the colonial period. Ballad opera scores usually consisted of existing folk songs. In the late nineteenth century, a lighter but more refined offshoot of opera, the operetta, emerged in Europe, exemplified by Jacques Offenbach and Gilbert and Sullivan. In New York, the hot operetta guys were Rudolf Friml and Sigmund Romberg, then Victor Herbert, and the Princess Theatre team of Jerome Kern, P.G. Wodehouse, and Guy Bolton.

Those Princess shows formed the bridge between operetta and a new form, musical comedy, which would dominate for the next fifty or sixty years. But while operetta was transforming into musical comedy, so was vaudeville, and that's why revues were born.

A common misconception of the revue is that it was, like vaudeville or the circus, a lineup of unrelated "acts," grouped for the sake of *variety*, but with no thematic principle or narrative. In fact, most revues had either plots or themes. The plots were simple and negligible, even less sophisticated than the plots of musical comedies, but they did serve to connect the material. Most revues strove to feel "of a piece," to add up to a thematic or stylistic whole, in a way that vaudeville did not. A revue is by definition more pretentious, more willfully artful, in its attempt at a cohesive and distinctive experience. It's also more self-conscious than the book musical, which can succeed by involving the audience in a story and its characters. One Chicago critic who saw *Up in the Clouds* said that he knew the difference between a plotted revue and a book musical when he saw one, but it was hard to say what it was: "*Up in the Clouds*…is heralded as a musical entertainment of hybrid tendencies, having an intelligible story to tell, but inclining in the telling of it to a scenic elaboration not usually manifested by plays with plots."

Other revues eschewed storylines and recurring characters, but were held together thematically. Two classic examples are *As Thousands Cheer* (1933), the topical Irving Berlin / Moss Hart revue in which each song or sketch was based upon a current story in the news; and Harold Rome's "labor revue" *Pins and Needles* (1936). The principal elements in a revue might be songs, dances, comedy sketches, stars, chorus girls and boys, elaborate visual spectacle, or all of the above. Story and character, even if they existed, were never the *principal* elements in an old Broadway revue, as they are in most book musicals, and in virtually all original musical theatre since World War II.

The paradigmatic old Broadway revue, of course, was Florenz Ziegfeld's *Follies* (1907-1931). Initially inspired by the *Folies Bergère* in Paris, these were dreams come to life. The *Follies* were synonymous with the glamour and decadence of Broadway. Their signature features were grandiose visual tableaus featuring the exalted, "glorified" Ziegfeld Girls, artfully arranged on sets by Joseph Urban and in costumes by Erté. The *Follies* is mostly remembered for the mystique of those Girls, and for showcasing the talents of legends like Josephine Baker, Ray Bolger, Fanny Brice, Eddie Cantor, Ruth Etting, W.C. Fields, Bob Hope, Marilyn Miller, Will Rogers, Sophie Tucker, Bert Williams, and Ed Wynn. But the real star of the *Follies* was the *Follies* itself, the gold standard of American entertainment.

Second to Ziegfeld's revues were George White's *Scandals* (1919-1939), a slightly more risqué series which featured, in early editions, the breakthrough compositions of George Gershwin; and the Shuberts' *Passing Show* (1912-1924, after a trendsetting *Passing Show* which opened at the Casino Theatre in 1894). Irving Berlin had the *Music Box Revue* (1921-1924), Earl Carroll had the *Vanities* (1923-1931), and Rodgers and Hart had the *Garrick Gaieties* (1925-1930). In addition to these major series, and a lot of minor ones (*Hitchy-Koo*, 1917-1920), every Broadway season had one-offs. Some of these were important and successful, like Eubie Blake and Noble Sissle's *Shuffle Along* (1921-1922) and the Four Marx Brothers' *I'll Say She Is*.

The line between a revue (or book revue) and a musical comedy (or book musical) was fluid and blurry. The Eddie Cantor show of 1923-1924, *Kid Boots*, was considered a book musical, but it contained plenty of interpolated, standalone material that had no real connection to the flimsy plot, involving Cantor as the caddy at a Palm Beach golf club. *I'll Say She Is* was described as a revue, but it wasn't plotless, and sometimes the songs nominally expressed the sentiments of the characters.

There were narrative musical comedies, too, straddling the line between operettas and modern musicals. But most of these were only vaguely more plot-driven than the average plotted revue. Despite some early leaps forward (*Show Boat*, *Porgy and Bess*, *The Cradle Will Rock*, *Lady in the Dark*), the form we now think of as "modern musical theatre"—the musical *play* as opposed to the musical comedy—was not popular until Rodgers and Hammerstein's

Oklahoma! (1945) and its successors. This was a sea-change, after which even the old masters began writing "modern musicals" of substance, whose songs expressed character or advanced the story (Irving Berlin's *Annie Get Your Gun* and Cole Porter's *Kiss Me Kate* being the best and most obvious examples). Richard Rodgers himself had gone from collaborating with Lorenz Hart, in the old approach, to Oscar Hammerstein, the foremost architect of the new.

This revolution in musical theatre edged out the revue, but there were exceptions. The comedy revue *New Faces* had a successful 1956 edition, and a less successful 1962 edition. Olsen and Johnson's very popular 1938 revue *Hellzapoppin* held Broadway's long-run record for a time. It was supposed to come roaring back in 1976, starring Jerry Lewis, but it died out of town. *Sugar Babies*, a cleaned-up homage to old burlesque, was a hit revue in 1979, largely due to the star power and nostalgic appeal of Ann Miller and Mickey Rooney (in his long-delayed Broadway debut). Eventually, the form found a new purpose, with the advent of the low-budget composer showcase. Despite the lavish physical productions associated with early revues, one could also be done on a bare stage with a small cast. In such a revue, it's the *material* that's emphasized, rather than the production or the performers. Throughout the later twentieth century, there were popular "songbook" revues on and off Broadway, including *Jacques Brel is Alive and Well and Living in Paris*, Ben Bagley's *The Decline and Fall of the Entire World as Seen Through the Eyes of Cole Porter*, *Eubie!* (Eubie Blake), *Ain't Misbehavin'* (Fats Waller), *Sophisticated Ladies* (Duke Ellington), *Side by Side by Sondheim* and *Putting it Together* (Stephen Sondheim), *Tomfoolery* (Tom Lehrer), *And the World Goes 'Round* (Kander and Ebb), and *Songs for a New World* (Jason Robert Brown).

Stephen Sondheim, the key figure of the postwar musical theatre, has often written character-driven scores which are hybrids of the narrative and revue forms (*Company, Follies, Pacific Overtures, Assassins*), and some of Sondheim's contemporaries made similar experiments (Kander and Ebb's *Cabaret* and *Chicago*, Stephen Schwartz's *Godspell*). Andrew Lloyd Webber's *Cats* is rarely described as a revue, but it is one. Today, the scourge of Broadway is the "jukebox musical," which shoehorns hit songs by popular bands or singers into a jerry-rigged plotline. Whereas *Jacques Brel* and *Side by Side* were designed to *familiarize* audiences with their composers' catalogues (and *Decline and Fall* featured *obscure* Cole Porter songs), the jukebox shows trade on the audience's lifelong familiarity with the songs—the musical revue as Greatest Hits album.

BY THE SPRING of 1923, *The Twentieth Century Revue* and *Gimme a Thrill* were both history, and so was most of Shubert Advanced Vaudeville, and the Marx Brothers and the Johnstone brothers all happened to be moping around New York trying to figure out what the hell to do. (The Shubert brothers weren't thrilled, either.) On March 15, Tom and Will B. Johnstone were summoned to the office of producer Ned Wayburn. There they were introduced to three of the Marx Brothers. "The boys were very nice," Will B. recalled in his diary. "They want a show written to fit them & Ned called us in. Fine of Ned, the great producer."

Wayburn was chiefly a choreographer, who'd made his name by running a dance school on Fourteenth Street. Through this laboratory, he would develop vaudeville acts, and then function as their manager. As noted earlier, he had managed the teenage Groucho and Gummo as Wayburn's Nightingales in 1907. Wayburn had then fallen on hard times, but by 1923 he had more than recovered. He was now a highly successful director of Broadway musicals, including two editions of the *Passing Show* and four of the *Ziegfeld Follies*, and perhaps the Brothers sought their old mentor's counsel in mounting a legit production.

All of the various brothers got along famously, and lingered for a while in Wayburn's office, kicking around ideas and making plans. Can you imagine what this conversation must have been like? At this point, Will B. Johnstone still had never seen the Marxes perform. Presumably, the whole thing had to be explained to him: "See, I play a wiseguy with a painted moustache, one of my brothers plays an Italian, another doesn't speak, and another doesn't do

Ned Wayburn's office

much of anything at all…"

Will and Groucho hit it off—Groucho, as ever, gravitating toward writers. Will called him Julie. On April 15, Will finally saw the Marx Brothers perform, at an independent vaudeville theatre in Brooklyn. The effects of that experience were recalled decades later by his son, Will B. Johnstone, Jr., in an interview with Mikael Uhlin: "That night he arrived at our home in East Orange, New Jersey, long after we had all retired. He woke everybody up shouting, 'I found them!'" Yet the impression Johnstone Sr. recorded in his diary was relatively reserved: "Very good indeed tho' not done expertly. Will fit into show O.K." Maybe he just felt like waking people up.

Johnstone was only the third or fourth man in history to sit down and try to write a script for the Marx Brothers. The old Kitty Gordon thing, about the heiress looking for a thrill, did not occur to him as an ideal vehicle. That's probably the *last* thing he wanted to work on, the idea having flopped twice in the last four years. Johnstone had something else in mind, called *Try and Get It*, which he pitched to the Marxes in Wayburn's office. "I spilled an idea that they seemed to like & we talked it over," he recorded in his diary.

Meanwhile, Joseph Minimum Gaites had picked himself up and dusted himself off again, and fallen in with wealthy industrialist James P. Beury (the *P* stands for *Pennsylvania coal magnate*). Beury had recently acquired the Walnut Street Theatre in Philadelphia, and was willing to finance Philadelphia's first summer revue. Joseph M. Gaites was a man of powerful convictions, and apparently he believed that *Love for Sale / Gimme a Thrill* had been the greatest idea ever, because by the end of April, Johnstone was writing it for the third time. Gaites wouldn't even let him choose the title. One of the earliest press mentions of the project, in *Variety* on May 3, 1923, held that "the attraction may be called *You Must Come Over*," a title Johnstone favored. He also suggested using the title of one of the new songs he and Tom had written, "The Thrill of Love." But Joe Gaites knew that the can't-miss title, the one that had everything, the one that was sure to create a stampede at the box office, was *I'll Say She Is*. These guys had a thing about four-word titles.

As for *why* the gimme-a-thrill plotline held such lasting appeal for its creators, we can only guess. In both *Take it From Me* and *Up in the Clouds*, Johnstone had shown a knack for fanciful conceits and complex plotting, much more sophisticated and more inherently satirical than the storyline of *Love for Sale* and *Gimme a Thrill* and *I'll Say She Is*. There is a temptation to attribute the premise to Gaites, the failed playwright with an eye for spectacle, but Johnstone's diaries suggest that it was his own concept, from the start— tailored first for Kitty Gordon and Jack Wilson, then for the Gardiner Trio, and now for the Marx Brothers. One critic would write, of the plot of *I'll Say She Is*: "It would seem that with such a vehicle as this, the writer of the book could keep the progress of the action clear and well defined. That he does not, of course, matters little…Like the beauty, the audience is looking for thrills and laughter, and it is satisfied when it gets either."

The thirty-three-page document that emerged from Will B. Johnstone's typewriter, which we shall call *the typescript*, dates from the spring of 1923. Some commentators have identified this document (which resides at the Library of Congress) as "the Broadway script of *I'll Say She Is*," which it is surely not. The typescript predates the Broadway opening by just over a year, and it's properly described as an outline with dialogue, clearly to be embellished in rehearsal and performance. (There is one additional known *I'll Say She Is* typescript, held in the collection of the Institute of the American Musical; it contains slight variations.) Two of the show's key comedy sketches survive in other, later versions, and an examination of these more detailed drafts clarifies that the typescript was a sketch, a guide. Much of the show, like the Marxes' vaudeville tabs, was written out loud, with the best improvisations made permanent. Moreover, there are references in the typescript which fix it in time. It contains Philadelphia jokes, obviously intended for the Philadelphia premiere, as well as a crack about President Harding. Harding was to die in office on August 2, 1923, two months into the Philadelphia run of *I'll Say She Is*; Groucho remembered having to announce the President's death from the stage. It was raining, too, and the sound of raindrops hitting the theatre's tin rooftop, mingled with the sounds of audience members weeping for the dead Commander-in-Chief, made for a surreal spectacle. "I got a lot of laughs, talking about Harding," Groucho sarcastically recalled. But the Harding joke in the typescript ("Why are you crying, little girl? Are you lonesome or have you been listening to some of Harding's speeches?") would certainly not have been spoken on Broadway in 1924.

What was retained from *Love for Sale* and/or *Gimme a Thrill* included the central narrative of Beauty looking for thrills, the "rich man, poor man" business, the Chinatown opium den sequence, the Wall Street number, "I'm Saving You for a Rainy Day," "Gimme a Thrill," and a pageant of cloth finery entitled "The Inception of Drapery." Added to the mix were some new songs, some new thrills, and the Marx Brothers.

The comedy material was distinctly Marxian, and if it now reads as a slightly more primitive Marxian dialect than what would later be put on paper by George S. Kaufman, Morrie Ryskind, Bert Kalmar, Harry Ruby, S.J. Perelman, and (by the way) Will B. Johnstone, let's remember that less than one year ago we were doing *Home Again* in London. *On the Mezzanine*, *The Twentieth Century Revue*, and *I'll Say She Is* (and possibly the Brothers' lost 1918 musical *The Street Cinderella*, too) represent a transitional period between the early vaudeville Marxes (Groucho's German schoolteacher, Harpo's Irish bumpkin, Chico's street Italian) and the later filmic ones (Groucho's New York wiseguy, Harpo's speechless demon, Chico's street Italian). *I'll Say She Is* contained three major elements clearly imported from the Brothers' existing vaudeville repertoire: The Theatrical Agency sketch from *On the Mezzanine*; Harpo's knife-dropping routine from *Home Again*, etc.; and the poker scene from *The Twentieth Century Revue* (a forerunner of the bridge scene in *Animal Crackers*, with many of the same gags). The typescript also contains Harpo's celebrated "cut the cards" hatchet gag, which surfaced nine years later in *Horse Feathers*. Typically, Johnstone does not illuminate Harpo's business with stage directions, but any Marxist who reads Chico's final lines in the bit ("Cut the cards. What's the matter you spoil cards like that?") knows exactly what happens in the space between those two sentences.

But, contrary to some accounts characterizing *I'll Say She Is* as wholly recycled, a lot of the Marx Brothers material was new. The courtroom scene, which incorporates both the poker game and the knife-dropping routine, is full of lines which are related to the plot and seem to have been written specifically for, or perhaps by, Groucho ("I would explain this case, but what's the use? He wouldn't understand it, you wouldn't understand it, and I wouldn't understand it"). Its similarity to the courtroom scene in *Gimme a Thrill* is difficult to assess, though apparently both were at least partially intended as parodies of a playlet called *Irish Justice*. There was another new scene called "Cinderella Backward," featuring Groucho in drag as Beauty's Fairy Godmother, or something. Some have proposed a connection between

"Cinderella Backward" and *The Street Cinderella*, which *seems* possible; almost nothing is known about *Street Cinderella*, though the title does suggest a similarly low-class take on the fairy tale. But Will B. Johnstone tells us, in his diary, that "Cinderella Backward" was a new idea he pitched to Groucho.

The best and longest scene in *I'll Say She Is*, assuredly new, was its great comedic triumph. It's the piece of material which most clearly anticipates future classics, and it disproves later claims that George S. Kaufman "invented" Groucho's familiar character or verbal style when he wrote *Cocoanuts*. The man who actually did invent those things, Groucho Marx, had a hand in writing this sketch. It's formally identified as "Napoleon's First Waterloo," but known simply as "the Napoleon scene." The concept—Groucho, as Napoleon, repeatedly returns to the palace to find Josephine entangled with her lovers, Harpo, Chico, and Zeppo—was Johnstone's.

On May 9, 1923, Will and Groucho discussed the scene while hanging out at the Century Roof. It's been said that their collaboration began "when they were attending a performance of *Chauve-Souris*," because *Chauve-Souris* was playing downstairs at the Century Grove Theatre. But up on the Century *Roof*, there was another show entirely. The Society of Illustrators, of which Johnstone was a proud member, staged a massive revue with a company of four hundred, for two nights, May 11 and 12. Johnstone was one of several authors and contributors; others included Will's brother Tom, their good friend James Montgomery Flagg, Rube Goldberg, Marie Dressler, and Sigmund Romberg! Surely *The Society of Illustrators Show* is what brought Johnstone to the Century that night, when he and Groucho "doped on ideas for [the] thrill show," as Will wrote in his diary—including an "idea I got of doing a Napoleonic comedy scene." This was probably the evening when, as Groucho specifically put it in a 1973 interview, "Johnstone and I sat down to write the Napoleon scene."

The Napoleon scene is one of two *I'll Say She Is* sketches which survive in later versions. (The other is Herman Timberg's Theatrical Agency sketch, which the Brothers actually filmed in 1931.) The later extant Napoleon script, which was likely used for personal appearances in the early thirties, is somewhat richer and fuller than the typescript version; it's probably the result of both Groucho and Johnstone making additions as the show went on. Later, when a reporter asked Groucho, "Do you write your own stuff?" he replied, "Only the good lines. We let the author write the rest." But the essence of the Napoleon scene is all there, including many of the good lines, typed up by Johnstone in the spring of 1923. He was probably working from loose pages, envelopes, and cocktail napkins scribbled upon with Groucho on the Century Roof. The Napoleon scene establishes that the first great Marx Brothers writing team, before Kaufman and Ryskind, before Kalmar and Ruby, was Johnstone and Marx.

The Napoleon scene on Broadway

IV.
I CAN'T GET STARTED

The Marx Brothers in Philadelphia, 1923

MARGARET FARRELL, IN her 2013 essay about the show, writes: "Here is where the origin legends of *I'll Say She Is* begin." Now that we're just one year from Broadway, and our heroes, after twenty years in showbiz, are finally about to have their glorious beginning, the tale muddies up with fanciful competing accounts, set down by such unreliable narrators as Groucho and Harpo Marx.

For example, it's not entirely clear how the Marxes got involved with James Beury and/or Joseph Gaites. Groucho, in his autobiography, writes that Chico met Beury at a card game, learned of Beury's desire to put his girlfriend on the stage, and promised that if Beury would finance a revue starring the Marx Brothers, they'd work for no salary, just a percentage. Groucho recast Beury as a New Jersey pretzel-salt manufacturer named Herman Broody, perhaps because he was writing about Beury's affair with the chorus girl. (In later interviews, Groucho correctly named Beury and identified him as being "in the coal business.") Groucho never mentions

Gaites at all. He does go on at some length about Beury/Broody's girlfriend, whom he calls Ginny. He says she was a terrible dancer; her dancing got bigger laughs than their comedy; someone slipped her a Mickey Finn to prevent her from appearing on opening night; she ran off with one of the musicians and then Beury/Broody said he would only back the show if she *wasn't* in it. Cut to a year later, and Ginny is waiting on Groucho in a Broadway diner. In later, less folksy tellings, "Ginny" is sexually involved not only with Beury but with Harpo as well.

In Harpo's version, Chico meets *Gaites* at a card game, and then Gaites has to consult with his backer—once again transformed into a New Jersey pretzel-salt manufacturer named Herman Broody—about whether to hire the Marx Brothers. Harpo writes that Gaites had been leaning toward "a blackface comedian named Wilson" (that would be Jack Wilson of *Love for Sale*), but that "Broody" convinced Gaites that four Marxes was a better deal. None of this would explain why Ned Wayburn was the link uniting the Marxes and the Johnstones. Yet another version of the tale, set forth in Kyle Crichton's authorized (but highly fictionalized) biography *The Marx Brothers* (1950), has Chico running into Tom Johnstone outside the Palace Theatre, and lamenting the Brothers' lack of prospects. Tom rushes Chico into Joseph Gaites' office on 42nd Street and suggests that *Gimme a Thrill* be rewritten for the Marx Brothers—with "the Philadelphia opening three weeks away!" Gaites has been paying Jack Wilson $600 per week. He offers the Four Marx Brothers $800 per week. Chico says, "Put us in for ten per cent of the gross… We don't want any salary."

The standard telling of the *I'll Say She Is* story, heavily influenced by the recollections of Groucho and Harpo, insists that James Beury was a fool, a businessman who knew nothing about the theatre, but was trying to impress a chorus girl, and thereby entangled the Marx Brothers in the total fluke of their ultimate triumph. The record suggests otherwise. Beury's background was indeed in the coal business he'd inherited, but show business had been his first passion as well as his second profession, long before he bought the

Walnut Street Theatre. In 1914, Beury became the major investor in the Conness-Till Film Company, a Toronto movie studio. The main creative force behind Conness-Till was Edward H. Robins, trumpeted in the press as "a Belasco leading man." (Robins had appeared in three Broadway shows to that time, and he would appear in over a dozen more. He would originate the role of Senator Carver Jones in *Of Thee I Sing* and its sequel *Let 'Em Eat Cake*, written by the Gershwins with Marx Brothers collaborators George S. Kaufman and Morrie Ryskind.) The idea was that Robins would star in a series of Canadian-made pictures for Conness-Till, underwritten by Beury.

Beury formed an amiable partnership with Robins, but neither of them cared much for Luke Edwin Conness and Louis A. Till, the guys whose names were on the company. In June of 1915, Beury bought them out, shared the controlling stock with Robins, and reorganized the studio as the Beury Feature Film Company. Numerous ambitious feature films were planned, but first the company undertook the filming of a hotly-anticipated Havana prizefight between Jack Johnson and Jess Willard. The resulting seven-reel film, which included close-ups and panoramic views of the ring, captured all twenty-six rounds of the match, with an abridged version prepared for commercial showings. The negatives were processed at Beury's Toronto studio, and prints were shipped to Europe, South America, Australia, and South Asia. But U.S. law had forbidden the importing of prizefight films, in the wake of riots following the Jack Johnson-Jim Jeffries match in 1910. Beury knew that "a fortune was waiting" if the Johnson-Willard film could be shown in the States. His company devised an inventive way of getting the film across the border. In his history of early Canadian cinema, Peter Morris explains that the law specifically forbade the *importing* of prizefight footage, so "Beury's technicians built a device which could project the negative across the border where it could be copied onto positive film in the United States." This process, performed in "a tent... straddling the border between New York State and Quebec" was successful. "But the resulting print was promptly seized by the American Customs officers who had been present throughout.

The American public never saw the film." (It is now, of course, on YouTube.)

The studio's next project was *Nicotine*, a seemingly ahead-of-its-time anti-smoking melodrama, funded by Beury and the Anti-Cigarette League of New York. It was to be a large and ambitious feature, and a make-or-break proposition for the Beury Feature Film Company. In Beury's willingness to stake everything on a project he believed in, we can see shades of Joe Gaites—a far cry from the hapless naïf depicted by some Marx Brothers and their biographers. But the *Nicotine* project, and Beury's film career, were doomed when on the night of May 31, 1915, a fire consumed the entire studio. Film reels exploded. The Johnson-Willard prizefight footage was saved, but little else survived. All of the studio's facilities and equipment were destroyed, along with the personal effects of the cast and crew of *Nicotine*. Beury sustained a loss of $100,000.

But the partnership between Beury and Edward H. Robins continued, now in the more familiar environs of the theatre. In June of 1917, Beury produced *Annabel Lee* on stage in Toronto, starring Robins. He managed a theatrical stock company, and produced the road tour of Victor Herbert's *The Girl in the Spotlight*. One newspaper item contends that at some point, Beury even "appeared behind the footlights himself."

In 1920, he purchased the Walnut Street Theatre from the heirs of the British actor John Sleeper Clarke, "for a consideration of $70,000, subject to an undisclosed mortgage." The Walnut was the oldest continuously-operating theatre in the United States, built in 1808 in the Colonial style. Beury preserved the 1808 exterior, but dramatically rebuilt the interior. The *Philadelphia Inquirer*'s theatre column gushed about the "up to the minute" renovations, including "a large comfortable lounging and retiring room for the women patrons, while the comfort of the males will be catered to with an elaborate smoking and retiring room." The women's lounge would include "writing desks and other conveniences," while the men's would be "almost club like in its comforts." Efforts were even taken to make the *actors* comfortable, with "the 'Green Room,' where the actors and their friends may assemble during a performance," as well as "a diet kitchen…where they can prepare light meals between shows on matinee days when they prefer to eat at the theatre instead of going to their hotels."

> [Beury] has been on the job daily with his architect and his contractors. Looking like one of the laborers but with a knowledge of architecture, iron construction, plastering, carpentering, and in fact, every angle of building …
>
> "And this cane, by the way," he added, shaking it in my face, "is one made from a piece of walnut taken from the rafters of the old theatre which was one of the original supports of the roof when the house was built in 1808."

Early reports were that Beury had signed an agreement to book attractions through the Shuberts, but this didn't happen. The initial offering, when the Walnut had its grand reopening on December 27, 1920, was George Arliss in *The Green Goddess*, a melodrama set in the Himalayas, and not a Shubert production. (It advanced to Broadway, and lasted there six months, the following year.) This, too, suggests a higher degree of independent ambition and theatrical savvy than is normally attributed to Beury. It's entirely possible that he *was* in love with a chorus girl in 1923, and insisted on her appearance in *I'll Say She Is* despite her incompetence. But if so, it was an incidental detail at most, and in no sense the impetus for the production. Beury was a man of the theatre, with or without Gaites, and with or without the Marx Brothers.

SOMEHOW, IT CAME to pass. By May 13, 1923, the new show was in rehearsal in New York, under the direction of Eugene Sanger and the choreography of Vaughn Godfrey. The cast of fifty-six (thirty in the chorus) included some veterans of earlier Gaites/Johnstone efforts, including

Cecile D'Andrea in 1922

the comedy dance team of Herbert and Baggott (from *Gimme a Thrill*) and a large portion of the 1922 cast of *Up in the Clouds*: Jack Sheehan, Gertrude O'Connor, Arnold Gluck, Florence Hedges, Ledru Stiffler, and the classical dance team of Cecile D'Andrea and Harry Walters. Choreographer Godfrey was an *Up in the Clouds* alum too.

Up in the Clouds had included a sequence called "The Pageant of Money," featuring Miss Hedges as financial fairy, with magic wand and dollar-sign tiara; and Mr. Stiffler, scantily clad and painted gold, as the embodiment of money. (He was the "gaudily unusual male dancer in gilt from toe to head crown" mentioned earlier.) It's not clear whether "The Pageant of Money" was a direct lift of the Wall Street number from *Love for Sale / Gimme a Thrill*, but Hedges and Stiffler did reprise their "Fairy" and "Gold" roles in the Wall Street sequence in *I'll Say She Is*. The first cast also featured Muriel Hudson, formerly of Ziegfeld's *Midnight Frolic* and *Flora Bella* on Broadway, in the central role of Beauty ("Musical comedy has so developed," Ms. Hudson told reporters, "that the best sort of acting is necessary to get it across"); and the Melvin Sisters, a novelty dance team from Edinburgh who had toured with Harry Lauder. In addition to the customary large pit orchestra, there was an onstage jazz band in Act Two (the Yerkes Happy Six, augmented), which was apparently judged the only form of entertainment energetic enough to follow the Napoleon scene.

As for Eugene Sanger and Vaughn Godfrey, the director and choreographer, their efforts were apparently unnoticed. Both had a smattering of Broadway credits. This was an age in which theatre directors functioned mostly as traffic cops. We've grown accustomed to thinking of the director as the primary creative force behind a project, partly because it tends to be

Muriel Hudson, the original Beauty in I'll Say She Is

so in film, and partly because post-World War II Broadway increasingly became "a director's theatre." You can probably name some famous playwrights, composers, producers, and performers of the twenties, and maybe some designers. But directors were more anonymous. The producer had the creative vision; the director told the cast where to stand.

While Sanger, Godfrey, the Johnstones, and the cast rehearsed in New York, Gaites and Beury labored in the Quaker City, tilling the soil to make sure it was fertile for the smash hit they needed. In the local papers, they planted items about the show which were flattering to Philadelphia ("Banking on their judgment of the city, [the producers] have assembled an exceptional aggregation of entertainers"). The *Philadelphia Inquirer* had a popular theatre column, "The Call Boy's Chat," which ostensibly consisted of quotations from a wizened character called the Old Stager. It was actually created and ghostwritten by the *Inquirer's* dramatic editor, Harry L. Knapp. On May 27, the Old Stager's readers encountered this:

> I ran into Joe Gaites on Chestnut Street, as he was dashing down to the Walnut to meet Jim Beury, his partner in the new Philadelphia summer revue, which, as you well know, is to be put on at that house...Joe is all het up about this show and believes that this town is at last due for a rousing musical show and that the people are just as keen on amusement in the summer months as they are in the colder ones, provided you give them what they want. He told me it was nothing short of a crime that the theatres here, with a population of two millions of people, should close just because a few hot weeks come along, and cited the fact that in New York, and other cities where the weather is just as warm, the show houses there keep going along just the same, and the musical shows turn some fancy profits. Regarding his first summer revue he is more enthusiastic than any show he has yet attempted. In elaborateness, youth, snap, comedy, melody, and dancing he declares he will give us

something that will open our eyes. He also hinted very broadly that he has a surprise up his sleeve that will set the town buzzing with gossip after it is seen.

Are you thrilled?

PRIOR TO THE PHILADELPHIA opening, the company travelled to Beury's hometown of Allentown, Pennsylvania, for a four-day trial run at the Lyric Theatre. On Monday, May 28, Will Johnstone caravanned by car with the Marxes—noting in his diary that Zeppo drove "a big Premier—foreign made," and travelled with his English sheepdog and his golf clubs. They arrived in Allentown eager to rehearse, but the Lyric was in use, so the company rehearsed on the top floor of the local newspaper's office building. *I'll Say She Is* was performed that night for an audience of newspapermen, who filled the stairs and doorways to watch an unexpected Marx Brothers extravaganza. The owner of the Lyric stopped by to watch, too, and pronounced the show "bigger and better than *Up in the Clouds*."

On Tuesday, the scenery was loaded into the Lyric. Rehearsal continued until after midnight. The next day, while the ensemble numbers were rehearsing onstage, Johnstone worked with Groucho, Harpo, Chico, and Zeppo in the lobby. "They are terrible on cues & lines," he wrote later. After dinner, the company rehearsed with the Walnut Street Theatre orchestra, up from Philadelphia: "We had frequent stops for lighting, etc. The usual tedious affair. Got through at 5 a.m. in the dawn's early light & to bed exhausted—by sunrise." On the evening of Thursday, May 31, the first proper performance of *I'll Say She Is* took place, and "went fine for the first performance," Johnstone noted. "Everything went big in Act I. Act II was all good except the Marathon dance which didn't come up to expectations. To my surprise the 'Cinderella backwards' was full of laughs & the 'Napoleon Scene' the high spot of comedy." The show ran three hours, and cuts were made right away. On June 3, the production moved to Philadelphia, and opened at the Walnut the following evening.

Newspaper advertisements for the Philadelphia run

Joseph Gaites' promotional zeal paid off. *Variety* critic "Waters," in his review of the opening, commented on "a great deal of mystery surrounding *I'll Say She Is*, and an unusual amount of interest and curiosity," but also noticed that the show "turned out to be…an expanded and very much elaborated version of the unit show, *Gimme a Thrill*, played over the Shubert circuit." (Another critic detected "some reminiscences of *Up in the Clouds*" as well). Waters was impressed with the production, noting its "speed and smoothness" and "perfect ensemble work," the "rather daring" Apache dance, and the "beautifully staged" dream ship specialty. "The Inception of Drapery" was "an elaborate, but rather out-dated number…in which various members of the ensemble brought silk, and lace, and feathers and jewels, and perfume to deck Miss Hudson, who at one time was clad in rather diaphanous garments." Well, the number *ought* to have been out-dated; Gaites and the Johnstones had been using it since *Love for Sale* in 1919.

Our Brothers were praised, though not without qualification. Some of the showbiz jokes in the Theatrical Agency sketch, "clever for those on the know, fell a bit flat here the opening night." Waters' observation that the poker routine "would have been funnier if trimmed" further confirms that the typescript was merely an outline; there, it occupies less than one page. Waters found the Napoleon scene "much too long, but…very funny in spots," and reported that Harpo "'ad-libbed' a great deal, even to the extent of getting the other performers laughing." It's hard to say whether Waters is referring to Harpo's physical improvisations as "ad libs," or confusing him with one of his brothers.

Of course, what Waters actually wrote was that *Arthur* ad-libbed a great deal. But, to this point, it's the cast listing that may be the notice's most interesting feature:

Zeppo—'Merchant'............Edward Marx

Chicko—'Poorman'.............Leonard Marx

Groucho—'Lawyer'..............Julius Marx

Harpo—'Beggarman'............Arthur Marx

What's noteworthy here is not the substitution of the mysterious Edward for Herbert, but the sudden public appearance of the Brothers' immortal nicknames. Privately, they'd been using "the O names" for almost a decade, and the nicknames had been occasionally referred to in press items since at least 1917. But as far as I know, this is the first example of the nicknames being used in official billing. Of course, here the nicknames are applied to the *characters*, rather than the performers (Julius Marx as Groucho-Lawyer, not Groucho Marx as Lawyer), but it's a prescient moment nonetheless. Also significant is the original, more phonetically accurate spelling of Leonard's nickname.

I'll Say She Is in Philadelphia was exactly what Gaites and the Marxes needed it to be—a smash hit, an event, a phenomenon. Conditions seem to have been exactly right. Even the infernal summer heat worked in the show's favor, because for the majority of its run, it was the only play in town. After June 16, when the Theatre Guild's production of *Scandal* closed at the Lyric, if you were going to the theatre in Philadelphia, you were going to *I'll Say She Is*. Furthermore, the Walnut advertised itself as "the coolest spot in town," thanks to "four enormous typhoon fans, two over the proscenium arch and two in the rear of the house, which drive the cool air from tons of ice directly into the theatre."

We might pause here and marvel at the powers of vocal projection once required of stage performers. Today, and for the last several decades, it would be unthinkable to present a large-scale musical, backed by a full orchestra, in a theatre with more than a thousand seats, without using microphones. The biggest stage stars of the pre-amplification era tended to be gigantic person-alities with voices of ear-splitting resonance—Al Jolson and Ethel Merman are prime examples. Even so, audiences not seated in the front of the orches-tra section were once accustomed to having to make an *effort* to hear what was being said, and sung, on stage. This led to a high degree of concentration. You had to actively *listen* in order to hear; you couldn't just relax and let the show wash over you. Now imagine having to project your voice not just over the sound of the orchestra, but over "four enormous typhoon fans" as well. It's a wonder anyone heard anything.

But they did hear it, and they liked it. "The show seems to be constantly gaining through 'word of mouth,'" *Variety* observed on June 27, when the engagement was in its fourth week. It was still selling out, with a two-week advance sale, and pulling in a very respectable $11,000 or $12,000 week-ly. Predictions of its longevity were constantly being expanded, from four weeks to eight weeks to ten weeks to the entire summer. Repeat business was common, because it was known that the Brothers ad-libbed every night, and Gaites kept telling the press about the constant updates and upgrades he was making. These included some additions and changes to the cast. On July 29, Muriel Hudson departed, and the "prima donna" role of Beauty was assumed by Peggy McClure, fresh from the Broadway production of George M. Cohan's *Little Nelly Kelly*. The Philadelphia press admiringly reported that Ms. McClure enjoyed horseback riding every morning, and made most of her own dresses and hats by hand.

Being the only show in town meant having almost total command of the local theatre pages. Through chatty profiles of the cast members,

Philadelphians learned that Florence Hedges, as a child, had longed to be "a second Lillian Russell"; that Cecile D'Andrea "has been dancing since a tiny tot"; and that Mildred Joy's father, a clergyman, had no objection to his daughter's work as a chorus girl. A great deal of ink was spilled in honor of the Marx Brothers. In one item, they offered an adoring tribute to their mother, which would be a frequent exercise for the rest of their lives. Minnie herself, explaining her former management of the team, told the press, "I just let the boys develop the way their inclinations led. I only made one rule—everything they do upon the stage must be clean. You will notice that the boys never do the same thing twice in the same manner. That is why, I believe, that they never grow stale."

One intriguing item in Knapp's "Call Boy's Chat" column has Groucho touting a book he claims to be writing, entitled *Compendium of Comedy*. "If the average theatregoer takes the trouble to dissect every joke hurled at him over the footlights," quoth the Grouch, "he will find its derivation in my book...It is impossible for a comedian to invent anything new. Since the days of the strolling players in England until the present time our funny men have been getting their laughs out of the same identical subjects." Sadly, Groucho's book on comedy does not seem to have been mentioned anywhere ever again.

In later recollections, Groucho often told a story about buying a new Studebaker during the Philadelphia run of *I'll Say She Is*, taking it out for a spin during intermission, getting stuck in traffic, and having to abandon the car and walk to the theatre in his Napoleon costume. It's a great anecdote, and the older Groucho reveled in such details as the car dealer's French accent, which rendered the car's brand name as "Stoo-duh-bay-*kaire*." But the tale's veracity is undermined by the fact that the Napoleon scene was not Groucho's first appearance in Act Two. Either Groucho had to walk through Philadelphia in his fairy costume for "Cinderella Backward"—even worse—or the story is apocryphal. If anything like this did take place, Groucho seems not to have mentioned it at the time. However, an August 26 item in the

Inquirer has him trying to buy a car from "the most rotund individual that I ever clapped my eyes upon." If you asked me to guess, I'd say the Studebaker anecdote is a fabrication inspired by this event. During a test drive, the vehicle stalled in traffic, and "my obese friend" could do nothing to revive it, causing Groucho to remark, "Of all sad words that from lips have parted, the saddest are these: I can't get started."

As for the surprise up Joe Gaites' sleeve—the one "that will set the town buzzing with gossip"—this turned out to be something called "the Who's Who curtain," which was displayed during intermission. It bore a large illustration depicting prominent citizens of Philadelphia. If we are to believe the press reports, audiences loved studying the faces and trying to identify

Two shots of Groucho outside the Walnut Street Theatre, 1923.
The image on this page is published here for the first time.
Courtesy of the Groucho Marx Collection / Frank Ferrante

their neighbors. "Philadelphia is still guessing as to the identity of many of the faces on the 'Who's Who' curtain," according to one item in late June, "and the manager is receiving scores of letters daily asking for the list of those celebrities."

This novelty was typical of the way the producers curried favor with their local audience. They did this relentlessly and quite successfully, extolling the greatness of Philadelphia just as passionately as they lavished praise on their hit show. They made sure that the town's favorite son, socialite and war hero Tony Biddle (Anthony Joseph Drexel Biddle, Jr.), was quoted declaring *I'll Say She Is* "the greatest show I've ever seen." Gaites and Beury planted one item declaring themselves "greatly pleased that by establishing in Philadelphia a summer girl and music show [we] have placed this city… on the same plane as New York, Chicago and Boston."

And here there was trouble. Although the Marx Brothers were surely grateful for their warm reception in Philadelphia, of course what they *really* wanted was to go home to New York, to make it on Broadway. That was the impetus for doing a legit revue in the first place. Their natural peers, in the opinion of the ambitious Chico, were not the workaday troupers of the circuits—what Trav S.D. calls "this army of scrambling hams"—but those who had transcended vaudeville and were enjoying the easy, glamorous, and lucrative lives of Broadway stars. In the early twenties, this crowd included Fanny Brice, Eddie Cantor, W.C. Fields, Al Jolson, Will Rogers, Ed Wynn, and even the Marxes' uncle and mentor, Al Shean, who was featured by Ziegfeld that very summer of 1923. All of these people were great entertainers, with their own claims to genius. But from today's perspective, the notion that the Marx Brothers were lesser artists than any of them seems absurd.

Nevertheless, Broadway plans for *I'll Say She Is* remained vague and contradictory. As far back as April, before the Napoleon scene had been written, the *New York Clipper* was reporting, "Gaites intends bringing the show to the Apollo Theatre, New York, early in October." (Not the famous Apollo Theatre on 125th Street in Harlem, but a Broadway house on 42nd

Street.) At the end of May, the *Clipper* had Gaites expecting to bring the show to New York in September. In mid-June, *Variety* reported that it "will probably be taken into New York later in the summer." Two weeks later: "It is understood that the producers are in a position to secure a New York house at any time now, but prefer to keep *I'll Say She Is* in Philadelphia as long as there is profit." Late August: "Gaites…will bring his musical revue…to a New York theatre at the termination of its [Philadelphia] run."

While the Brothers were fretting about these Broadway promises, Gaites was leveraging the notion of Broadway interest to sell more tickets in Philadelphia. On the theatre page of the *Inquirer*, on July 8, it was claimed that "practically every theatre owner or manager of a New York theatre has made a trip to Philadelphia and inspected [the show], and without an exception promptly an offer has been made to the Messrs. Gaites and Beury, the producers, to bring their offering to New York. But as each offer is made it is just as promptly rejected…with the terse retort: 'We created *I'll Say She Is* for Philadelphia consumption, and here it remains, and it now looks as though this excellent summer entertainment would at least be with us until Labor Day."

Gaites was almost exactly correct. *I'll Say She Is* played the final performance of its initial Philadelphia run on Saturday, September 1, capping off a locally-unprecedented thirteen-week summer fling. The "Old Stager," in a eulogy for the run, declared that the success of *I'll Say She Is* in Philadelphia "established the fact that our citizens are alive to the times." On Labor Day, September 3, the show opened in its next engagement, which turned out to be not Broadway at all, but Boston.

In the press, Gaites and Beury went out of their way to suggest that if it was up to them, *I'll Say She Is* would stay in Philadelphia even longer, perhaps forever. Alas, "due to previous bookings that cannot be cancelled," they were "obliged to regretfully announce" the September 1 closing, with assurances that "every effort has been made to secure an extension of time, but it has been impossible to do so." As it turns out, the booking which succeeded

I'll Say She Is at the Walnut was a melodrama called *Thumbs Down*, which had just received thumbs down from the Broadway critics and closed after twenty-four New York performances. Its producer was Charles Wanamaker, the manager of the Walnut Street Theatre, and of *I'll Say She Is*. Beury was the principal backer. If everyone *really* wanted to keep *I'll Say She Is* at the Walnut, it's puzzling that Beury and Wanamaker couldn't postpone their own lukewarm booking. But it reminds us again that Beury's interest in theatrical production was more than a supposed obsession with a talentless chorine.

Julius, Arthur, Leonard, and Herbert were professionals. They'd done it before and they'd do it again. The record shows their impatience for a New York run, but *I'll Say She Is* in Philadelphia at the Walnut Street Theatre had already been the greatest success they'd ever known. They were a phenomenon; they were on fire, and they knew it, and even Groucho must have been happy about it. And the Philadelphia flattery wasn't *all* hype. They were genuinely grateful to the city, and held it in high regard forevermore (in marked contrast with such peers as W.C. Fields, who made insulting Philadelphia a staple of his act). Groucho remained sentimental about the Walnut Street Theatre, and revisited the historic playhouse in 1974. Near the end of his life, Groucho said that the Walnut run of *I'll Say She Is* "was the most important thing that ever happened to me."

AND SO, TO THE Land of the Bean and the Cod. Disgruntled though the Brothers may have been, they undoubtedly rode into Boston with high expectations, having triumphed there in vaudeville, and having just had this smashing success in Philly. But *I'll Say She Is* flopped in Boston. It faced stiff competition, with five other popular musicals running at the same time, including a hugely successful road edition of the *Ziegfeld Follies* which was playing to capacity every night and causing a general riot. (Gallagher and Shean were among its top stars—the last time in history that

Uncle Al would ever be bigger than his nephews.) The Marx Brothers weren't clicking; spotty audiences sat in bemused silence. At one particularly lifeless performance, Groucho pierced the gloom by looking out into the audience and asking, "Will the chairman of the Bunker Hill delegation please stand up?" *Variety* concluded, "the nose dive that Joe Gaites' *I'll Say She Is* took in Boston after its Philadelphia success seems to be 'one of those things.'"

The notices were polite, but business was slow. The company stuck it out for four grim weeks. Toward the end of the run, making matters no better, Chico was arrested. It seems he owed $112 to Tom Patricola, then appearing in Boston with the *Scandals*. Chico was soon released and settled up with Patricola, but it was a harbinger of the eldest Brother's continual financial and legal trouble. It would resurface again and again to threaten his brothers' patience and their collective career.

Shortly after the Chico/Patricola trouble, the Eight Yankee Girls, a secondary chorus added to *I'll Say She Is* after the Walnut Street run, were at an all-night Boston diner frequented by showfolk. They overheard a couple of Englishmen at another table, loudly opining—specifically, I'd imagine, for the girls to hear—that British dancers were invariably better than American dancers. One of the *I'll Say She Is* girls, Joey Benton, rose from her table, approached the offending party, and said: "Say, Mr. Englishman, we are eight Yankee girls at the other table. We have seen your English girls dance, and if we eight cannot go on after a week's practice and do better than those beefy-looking girls that you bring over from the other side then we will all get out of the business. Won't we, girls?"

"Yes, we will," chirped Miss Benton's colleagues. At once they departed the diner and raced back to the hotel, where they urgently roused Mr. A.W. Bachelder, the company manager, from a deep sleep. I theorize that he didn't mind being awakened by eight chorus girls. He probably assumed he was dreaming. The girls convinced him to let them stage their own dance presentation, to show those Englishmen a thing or eight, and although the reaction is unknown, the piece wound up in *I'll Say She Is* for a portion of the

The Eight Yankee Girls

tour, billed as the "Legology Dance de Resistance."

Before we close the book on Boston for the time being, consider one more cast listing, as quoted by the *Globe*:

> Zeppo...............Herbert Marx
>
> Chicko............Leonard Marx
>
> Groucho.........Julius H. Marx
>
> Harop...............Arthur Marx

Here, the nursery-rhyme names are gone (though they remained in the show itself), Chico is still Chicko, and Harpo has become Harop. With the exception of that typo, however, this is perhaps the most accurate Marx Brothers cast list ever seen. The characters these men played were never really Merchant, Poorman, Beggarman, and Lawyer, nor were they, later on, Captain Spalding and Emmanuel Ravelli and the Professor and so on. Groucho, Harpo, and Chico didn't "play themselves," because they *weren't* themselves. They were Julius, Arthur, and Leonard, playing Groucho, Harpo, and Chico.

V.
ISN'T SHE A BEAUTY?

Florence Reutti in 1919

THERE WAS ANOTHER NEW NAME in the program when the show opened in Boston, a name that would remain associated with *I'll*

Say She Is through Broadway and beyond:

Beauty............................Lotta Miles

Ah, Miss Miles, that evasive enigma of Marxian lore! All that is widely known about her was summed up by Groucho Marx in 1973: "She was used in ads for the Springfield Tire Company, and her face was all over the place. Lotta Miles wasn't her real name, but they called her that because of the tires. She was beautiful, really beautiful."

Her real name was Florence Reutti. She was born on December 18, 1893

Florence Reutti as Lotta Miles

in New York, and grew up in Buffalo. Her mother, Anna Werner, was a German immigrant. Her father was Joseph Reutti, a onetime manager of the Hamilton, Ohio branch of the American Malting Company, who later moved to Buffalo to run a mercantile house. Florence's older sister, Henrietta, was a popular Buffalo singer and "pianologuist," who drafted Florence into show business. The Reutti sisters staged amateur vaudeville shows to benefit the local mission, and things like that. By 1914, Henrietta was embroiled in a very juicy scandal involving her wealthy lover and his mother, and Florence was seeking professional work as a performer and model.

Soon, she was posing for Kelly-Springfield Tire Company advertisements, which identified her as Lotta Miles. However, she was neither the first nor the last Kelly-Springfield girl, and they were *all* called Lotta Miles—though our Miss Reutti was alone in the temerity to continue using the name, outside her work for the tire company. The original Lotta Miles was Jean Newcombe, who went on to a long career in Broadway musicals. A later Lotta Miles, post-Reutti, was Norma Shearer. Fuzzy dates, rerun ads, artists' renderings, and a basic physical resemblance among all the Lotta Mileses, make identifying Florence Reutti in Kelly ads more difficult than it should be. At any rate, she had probably assumed the role by 1916, when an item in *Photoplay* included Lotta Miles, along with Cleopatra and Xantippe, on a list of "Notable Women of History." (The list also included our old friend Kitty Gordon, the Beauty of *Love for Sale*.)

So here she was, twenty-two years old and a Notable Woman of History. Naturally she sought film work. She was cast as the heroine of *Florence Rose Fashions*, a series of Pathé shorts conceived mainly to showcase fashionable clothing. By 1918, the press (or her publicist) was calling her "The Most Photographed Beauty in America," with the photographer Dr. Arnold Genthe declaring that he "has never before photographed so perfect a type of beauty." ("Incidentally, beauty in this case brings its own reward, as the advertisers willingly pay Miss Reutti a comfortably large income for merely looking like herself.") In January of 1919, theatrical manager B. S. Moss "discovered" her singing in a benefit for wounded soldiers, and signed her to a contract.

On October 26, 1918, she married Raymond Anthony Court, an interior decorator. The marriage was short and unhappy, and it further confounds us by adding to her long list of names: Florence Reutti, Lotta Miles, Carlotta Miles, Florence Court (sometimes Cort), Florence Reutti-Court (or Reutti-Cort)…it just goes on and on. Later, she was sometimes billed as Charlotte Miles, and everyone knew her as Nancy.

Her first legitimate role was in *Fifty-Fifty Ltd.*, a musical adaptation of William Gillette's *All the Comforts of Home*. (Jean Newcombe was also in *Fifty-Fifty Ltd.*, making it the only known instance of multiple Lotta Mileses sharing the stage.) Around the same time, she was billed as Florence Court in the musicals *Linger Longer Letty* and *Tangerine.* In 1922, she appeared in the road version of Ziegfeld's *Frolic*, with Will Rogers. This seems to have been the first time she used the stage name Lotta Miles outside the context of Kelly Springfield Tires.

The year of the *Frolic*, she sued Raymond for a separation, filing an affidavit "charging Court with 'gross intoxication,' riotous living and abusive language toward her, and making allegations of an affair with a manicurist in a fashionable hotel." In response, Mr. Court asserted that his wife "was not contented with being Mrs. Court" (imagine!) and "desired to go on the stage" despite his disapproval. Our heroine sought $150 per week in alimony and $1,000 in legal fees. The decorator countered that he was only making $100 per week, whereas "Mrs. Court received an income of over $10,000 in the past year." The verdict came down from New York Supreme Court: "Repeated intoxication is not alone a cause for separation in this state. It seems not always to have been considered a serious matter in this household. The plaintiff seems to have been the first to leave the home. Moreover, she seems adequately supporting herself in the profession of her choice."

I'll say she is! How she found her way to the Marx Brothers, though, is not clear. Perhaps B. S. Moss was still acting as her manager. (Moss, despite the B. S., was a significant figure in early twentieth-century Broadway. His family's organization, as well as his Broadway Theatre, survives today.) She was a good find for the show, not only because of her beauty and singing ability ("a rich clear soprano voice," according to the *Clipper*), but because she was already, in her way, a star. I'd like to think that her stage name, practically a Marx Brothers joke in itself, helped win her the role.

ALL WE HAVE OF HER, today, are these biographical fragments, and some photographs. Since so little of Miss Miles is available to us, I'll turn the microphone over to her at this point, with an extended quotation from the only substantial interview I've been able to discover, conducted by the Hamilton, Ohio *Evening Journal* during the *I'll Say She Is* tour.

Ladies and gentlemen, Miss Lotta Miles:

> I am the most photographed girl in America. You see, I started my career as a professional photographer's model. It is a regular business. I was posed in every possible way and my picture adorned tooth paste advertisements, automobile ads, ads for silk underwear and corset ads.
>
> That is how I happened to take the name of Lotta Miles. I am known all over the United States as the girl who is photographed in the ads about a certain well known automobile tire...When I went on the stage I took the name Lotta Miles—because the automobile tire is supposed to last a "lot of miles." Isn't that unique?
>
> ...I like musical comedies best. I never had the slightest desire to be a second Ethel Barrymore. I'm content to be myself as long as I can be a success. I worship success, and I don't care just how I make my success as long as it's genuine. If I have any ambition it is simply to be a success.
>
> I am not like many people you interview. Most musical comedy stars want to sing in opera, and most

operatic stars want to be acrobats or something similar. Well, I'm different. I want to be a musical comedy star. And that's that!…I'm not working towards anything, and I am content to let nature take its course. I have never played anything but leads in my life and I think that is a good reward.

I don't believe in starting in at the bottom and working up. I didn't enter the theatrical world by the cellar door—I'll say I didn't! No, I began on leads and I am continuing on them. My first show was *Fifty-Fifty, Ltd.* in which I played the ingénue lead. I started out big and I hope I'll keep on that way. No chorus for me. When I started playing pictures I never was an extra. They gave me featured parts from the beginning…

I had a two-ton asbestos curtain fall on my head, and I am the only person on the stage who ever had this happen and lived to tell the tale. I was in Brooklyn, New York, playing vaudeville. I was in the midst of one of my songs when the asbestos curtain, which had never been used, and was rotten for want of care, suddenly slipped down on my head. The crowd screamed and there was a tremendous panic as I was taken away to the hospital. It was believed that I was dead, but here I am, as good as ever. It takes more than a two-ton curtain to kill me.

She was consistently well-reviewed for her performance in *I'll Say She Is*. Most critics took a moment aside from praising the Marx Brothers and noted Miss Miles' beauty, charm, singing ability, and good-natured camaraderie with the unruly comedians. One critic held that "she has poise and acting ability that would be worth watching in something besides a revue" (although "whether Lotta obtained the desired thrill remains a mystery so far as this observer is concerned"). She stayed with *I'll Say She Is* through the rest of its tour, for the entire Broadway run, and for the post-Broadway tour, right up to its very last performance in Detroit in June of 1925.

And here the trail of Lotta Miles goes rather cold. At some point, she moved to Hollywood to pursue a film career, without much luck. (She may have moved west with her mother, sister, and brother-in-law, who relocated to Los Angeles around 1930.) In 1931, she was reunited with the Marx Brothers, appearing on stage with them in Buffalo. It's likely that they performed the Napoleon scene, which the Brothers are known to have revived during this tour, under the title "Schweinerei." In 1935, she supposedly had a bit part in the film *Waterfront Lady*, but I've watched the damn thing twice and I can't find her—nor can I find any film footage or voice recording of the woman whatsoever.

*A Kelly-Springfield ad from the Casino Theatre
program for* I'll Say She Is, *1924*

She died of a heart attack, in her Hollywood home, on July 25, 1937. She was forty-four years old. Her obituary in the *Hamilton Journal* said that "she was discovered by the Marx Brothers," and noted that "some time ago she suffered a nervous breakdown." At the time Beauty made her final exit, the Marxes were having their last big success as a team, *A Day at the Races*. There's no record of any association between Miss Miles and the Brothers after that 1931 tour. But she is remembered through them, and occupies a sliver of their immortality. Her name, whatever it was, will be known as long as the Marx Brothers are celebrated.

VI.
GUNNING FOR
HIGH NOTES

THE MARX BROTHERS, in their fervent desire not to be on the road, were on the road. Gaites didn't take *I'll Say She Is* to New York after its Boston run, either. He took it to Pittsburgh. Perhaps the tepid Boston experience dulled everyone's confidence about Broadway. After Pittsburgh, Detroit. Then Chicago. Then Kansas City. St. Louis. Cincinnati. And so on, and so on. And on and on and on. The show would even play the Shubert-Crescent Theatre in *Brooklyn!* Just across the river! Ten subway stops from 42nd Street! So tantalizingly close to home—but in effect, no closer to Broadway than Kansas City.

Chicago was rough, but not for the same reasons as Boston. The show itself was a smash in Chicago, where the boys were hailed as local heroes; they had lived in Chicago during the second half of their vaudeville career. ("Only those aware that *I'll Say She Is* contained 'Chicago stuff' weren't surprised at the quick hold the Studebaker [Theatre] piece grabbed shortly after the premiere," said *Variety*, in a rather awkward sentence.) Charles Collins, writing for the *Tribune*, found that "these Marxes bear the test of stellar quality in the theater; they are different. They are as strange as mooncalves, as incredible as unicorns. And their show has something of the same fabulous quality. The scientific playgoer, on seeing it, wipes his spectacles, knits his eyebrows, and then, in a puzzled way, declares that this must be an example of a new species." Another Chicago critic, O.L. Hall, mused: "If you take apart and examine what they do, you may wonder if a show can be made of that sort of stuff. Well, it can." So they were getting their full houses and their big laughs, and they were celebrated in the press. In Chicago the trouble was all offstage.

On November 14, at a "black and tan dive" called Edelweiss Gardens, a fight broke out between members of the *I'll Say She Is* company and one Tony Andole. What may have begun as a crude sexual overture resulted in chorus girl Jean Spencer punching Andole in the jaw, and other men in the bar choosing sides, and Andole choking one of Miss Spencer's defenders, and then stabbing another in the face.

One week later, *I'll Say She Is* was the subject of a lawsuit brought by costumer Brooks-Mahieu, expressing frustration at trying to collect on an outstanding invoice to Joe Gaites. In order to bring the curtain up, company manager Bachelder had to come up with $3,500 for the deputy sheriffs who arrived on the scene. And shortly after *that*, they had to go to court just to continue their run, when a dispute broke out involving the Stoo-duh-bay-*kaire*'s incoming tenant, *Abie's Irish Rose*. By court ruling, *I'll Say She Is* was permitted to complete its intended run, but the company's trunks had been repeatedly packed and unpacked, its nerves rattled, its patience spent. Groucho continued his lifelong career as an insomniac. "I have tried this sheep-counting business for wooing sleep innumerable times," he wrote, "but the only effect it has had on me is to give me a terrible distaste for mutton chops. A far better way to fall asleep is to count not sheep but money." So much for the oft-told tale that Groucho's sleepless nights began with the 1929 stock market crash.

There were bright spots in the Chicago experience, too. It was during this run that the Brothers met and befriended Ben Hecht and Charlie MacArthur. Groucho and Harpo were admirers of Hecht's *1001 Nights in Chicago*, and one evening the four Brothers figured out where he lived and dropped by unannounced. They spent the entire night clowning around with Hecht, "improvising dirty parodies of popular songs," as Harpo remembered. Also during the Chicago run, Charlie Chaplin breezed through town, hung out with Groucho, and went on record calling *I'll Say She Is* "the best musical comedy revue I've ever seen."

At the end of 1923, the plan was to stay on the road for a while longer and reach Broadway around the first of March. The Marxes' sagging spirits were perhaps buoyed by the addition of Ed Metcalfe to the cast. Metcalfe was one of their favorite foils, and he's among the longest-serving supporting players in their career. His association with the team had started with *Home Again*, run through *The Street Cinderella*, and lasted all the way through the film version of *Animal Crackers*. There, he's the cop who shakes Harpo's hand during the silverware routine. In *I'll Say She Is*, he played the Agent in the Theatrical Agency scene, then morphed into the Johnstone character of "Richman" (rich man), one of the eight suitors seeking to give Beauty a thrill. It was probably backstage at *I'll Say She Is* that Metcalfe introduced Groucho to the Savoy Operas, which would become one of the comedian's great passions. Metcalfe was absently singing some Gilbert and Sullivan patter, and Groucho's ears perked up. "That's a goddamn good lyric," he said.

I'll Say She Is was a big show, and it was getting bigger. It turned out to be too big for the Shubert Missouri Theatre in Kansas City, where it opened on December 23. Groucho and Lotta Miles were in front of the curtain, doing the Cinderella Backward bit, and getting near their exits, when frantic whispers could be heard from the wings: "*Stall! Stall!*" Backstage, according to an eyewitness account, stage hands "struggled and toiled with heavy properties that needed almost twice the room for storage and display than was given them...[they] worked like demons, perspiration pouring off of them, and were so beset and upset by it all that they even forgot to swear."

During this Kansas City engagement, the boys were interviewed backstage by a youngster named Goodman Ace, of the *Kansas City Star*. They subjected Ace to their usual battery of uncooperative interview techniques. One of their favorites was to confuse an interviewer by asking *him* questions: "So, how do you like the newspaper game?" After the show, Ace accompanied the Brothers to a nightclub, where "chorus girls dressed as bell hops have a specialty paging number where they page people in the audience," as Ace described it. One of the girls sang, "Call for Mr. Davidson," whereupon Groucho rose from their table and shouted, "Did you say Mr. Davidson?" Goodman Ace, who was only twenty-four and wasn't used to this kind of thing, said, "Sit down! You'll be thrown out." Groucho was unfazed: "I don't mind being thrown out under somebody else's name." Groucho and "Goody" became dear friends, for the three-week engagement of *I'll Say She Is* in Kansas City, and for the rest of their lives. Before leaving Kansas City, Groucho presented his friend with a copy of James Thurber and E.B. White's *Is Sex Necessary?*

On January 27, 1924, the show played a one-nighter in Hamilton, Ohio, the original hometown of the Reutti clan, where Lotta Miles naturally walked away with the notices. "In a word," swooned the *Hamilton Journal*, "Miss Miles was 'the' attraction…[she] was the embodiment of personality, good will and stage ability and her comedy while playing with the Marx comedians was exceptional to behold. Especially in the Napoleon scene did the comedy of Miss Miles delight." (It's true—the Napoleon scene really was one of the great Lotta Miles comedy scenes of all time.) "To Miss Miles," concluded the *Journal*, all but proposing marriage, "goes the largest part of the credit for the success of the show." The *Hamilton Daily News* noted that "Miss Miles has a special song, 'The Thrill of Love,' which we are told makes every young lady touch the arm of her escort with a knowing grip." Hotcha!

Days later, the show played a week in Buffalo, where the Reutti sisters had grown up, and the same thing happened again. It was at this juncture that Lotta/Florence gave the interview quoted earlier. Her mother, Anna, and sister, Henrietta, attended the February 4 performance. The *Buffalo News* critic, apparently too familiar with the actress to use her stage name with a straight face, wrote, "Florence Reutti did as well as could be expected with an inane role." The same critic wrote that in Beauty's search for thrills, "she experiences everything but a meeting of the local city council and the glory of boarding a car at Shelton Square during the rush hour," but "the costumes of the chorus were such as would delight the eye of a pneumonia germ."

The reviews, in every town, were *almost* uniformly positive, with the usual smattering of scolds who didn't cotton to the comedy, but enjoyed the piano and harp specialties. In Syracuse, one critic reported, "Leonard Marx stopped the show with nothing more than his first finger with which he went gunning for high notes on the piano." As for Groucho: "Julius with his cadaverous humor just misses ranking with the big stars of the day. Just when you think, 'this guy is sure knocking them out of their seats,' he steps over the line with a cheap crack and you have to lower his rank a little." Still, "you'll remember the Napoleon and Josephine scene long after you forget the name of the play."

THE FIRST OF MARCH came and went, and the show was nowhere near Broadway. It was back in Ohio, playing one-nighters wherever there was an empty theatre. Most Marxian literature suggests that Gaites believed the show would be dismissed by the New York critics, and that before he appeased his stars by allowing them to flop on Broadway, he wanted to squeeze as much money as possible on the road. Gaites, The Marxes might have appealed to James Beury instead, but in March of 1924 Beury was far away, on a cruise to sunny Panama.

According to Harpo, the Marx Brothers *demanded* that the show be taken to New York. "Ever since we first opened in Philadelphia, we had been promised that the show would go to Broadway," he remembered. "The management kept stalling, saying the show still needed more testing out of town. Now we held them to their promise...Either *I'll Say She Is* went to New York or the Marx Brothers took a walk." But they were convinced, at least, to play a return engagement at the Walnut in Philadelphia, with the understanding that *this* Philadelphia run, nearly a year after the original opening there, would be expressly devoted to grooming and polishing the property for the Main Stem. One Gaites priority was to replace the jazz band whose set followed the Napoleon scene. He hired The Southerners for Philadelphia, but also negotiated with Vincent Lopez and the Bohemians, with an eye toward New York.

By this time, *I'll Say She Is* was a point of pride in the City of Brotherly Love, like the Liberty Bell. Philadelphia supported the show just as eagerly as it had in 1923. "With the prestige for 'summer' shows in this city and the distinction of having broken a lot of records for musical productions in various parts of the country, *I'll Say She Is* returned to the scene of its original triumph—the Walnut—last night, and it was received with all the warmth and sincerity of an old friend who had returned from a long trip," sighed the *Inquirer*. It was reported that the return engagement in Philly would last two or three weeks, and that the length of the run was to be set by the still-to-be-determined, but now absolutely imminent, Broadway opening.

Joseph Minimum Gaites now made an abrupt departure, turning producing authority over to Beury and the Walnut's manager, Charles Wanamaker. It's not clear why Gaites dropped out of *I'll Say She Is*, or whether he knew he was going to do so all the while he was negotiating with jazz bands and debating the move to Broadway. Perhaps he was inflamed by the Brothers' threat to walk. Maybe Gaites honestly felt that the show was embarrassingly below Broadway standards, and he didn't want to face the New York press again. (In fact, it would be more than a decade before he was associated with another Broadway production.) Or maybe Beury wanted control, and bought Gaites out for some irresistible sum.

Three days into the second Walnut engagement, *Variety* reported that Gaites was preparing a new summer musical for Detroit: "Gaites is something of a summer show pioneer outside of New York. He opened up Philadelphia last summer with *I'll Say She Is*... Gaites is entirely out of that attraction. Beury and Wanamaker intend strengthening the show and bringing it to Broadway soon." One year later, Gaites was out of the producing game altogether, acting as a salaried agent and business manager on other people's shows. "And Gaites isn't hiding a thing," noted the press. "He says he's happier than he has been in many years." When the producer of *The Sapphire Ring* booked a ritzy hotel suite for Gaites during that production's tryout in Washington, Gaites refused to accept, instead paying for his own modest room in a cheap hotel. "I'm only an agent, and I'll live according to my position," he insisted. He had had, *Variety* recalled, "some of the most famous triumphs and failures in the show business."

As for *I'll Say She Is*, some efforts were made to improve its chances in New York. Costumes were replaced and refreshed. It was reported that Herbert Ward, art director of five consecutive editions of *George White's Scandals*, was engaged to redo the scenery. The Southerners were dismissed, and Nat Martin and his Orchestra hired. On May 11, the *Inquirer* gently broke the news to its readers that *I'll Say She Is* "will positively leave Philadelphia at the close of this week. On Monday evening, May 19, the show opens at the Imperial Theatre, New York." Well, the Casino Theatre, actually, but they got everything else right.

APPARENTLY," WROTE HARPO MARX, "the plot was this: Open at the Casino, get crucified...run a couple of weeks to appease the Marx Brothers, then head back out on the road. We were warned not to put our trunks in storage." The fingerprints of Joseph M. Gaites are all over that plot. But I'd like to think that Beury knew what he had, and was giving it an honest shot. He didn't *have* to go to the trouble and expense of refitting the production, and presumably wouldn't have, if he saw no chance of Broadway success. The physical production had mostly been well-received on the road. And maybe, just maybe, Broadway audiences would be more interested in the greatest comedians who ever lived than a bunch of overproduced pageantry, anyhow.

Gaites had been hardened by decades of getting kicked around in cold, cynical showbiz. Beury was still enterprising, and increasingly a man of the theatre. He would produce two more Broadway musicals, in quick succession, after *I'll Say She Is*. Perhaps Beury bought Gaites out because he felt Gaites didn't believe sufficiently in the show, and that the Marxes deserved more than Gaites was willing to give.

On the other hand, even if Beury thought he had a hit on his hands,

Groucho and Harpo have both told us that they did not. "Look, Chico, we're not good enough," they say to their big brother, in the pages of Groucho's memoir. "We wouldn't be a hit on Broadway. We're vaudeville actors." In his own recollections in *Harpo Speaks*, Harpo claims that the afternoon before the Broadway opening, he was sitting in Lindy's, preemptively despondent at what he was sure would be the resounding flop of *I'll Say She Is* on Broadway. Lindy's felt like home to Harpo, as it did to an entire generation of Broadway characters:

> I was back with my own people, who spoke my language, with my accent—cardplayers, horseplayers, bookies, song-pluggers, agents, actors out of work and actors playing the Palace, Al Jolson with his mob of fans, and Arnold Rothstein with his mob of runners and flunkies. The cheesecake was ambrosia. The talk was old, familiar music. A lot of yucks. A lot of action. Home Sweet Home.
>
> I got up to go to work, with absolutely no enthusiasm, and told the boys to save my seat. I took a cab down to the Casino. The marquee lights had just been turned on. THE FOUR MARX BROTHERS IN "I'LL SAY SHE IS." I was not impressed. I was a realist. I kept hearing the words: *Sorry, boys—you're shut.* But what the hell, I thought, remembering the empty seat in Lindy's, it was going to be fun while it lasted.

The story of the brilliant success of *I'll Say She Is* is *always* told this way—darkest before the dawn—but the Marx Brothers had already been a big hit for a long time. Their act had been plagued by administrative issues following the English tour, but their problem had never been a failure to connect with audiences or critics. It's difficult, today, to comprehend why it was such a mighty leap to be a Broadway hit at the Casino Theatre, on Broadway and 39th Street, when they had already been a vaudeville hit at the Palace Theatre, on Broadway and 47th. But we can understand that these four boys, no longer boys, wanted to go home.

And if nobody had any confidence in *I'll Say She Is*, why let the first-string critics take a crack at it at all? The old legend, in which success can only be a fluke, says that the important New York critics would never have even *seen* the show if another, more important opening hadn't been postponed. The serious critics had gotten all dressed up to attend some lofty, high-minded drama, and then accidentally wandered into *I'll Say She Is* with no clue what it was. Groucho biographer Hector Arce debunked this myth, identifying the "more important" show as *Innocent Eyes*—not a high-minded drama at all, but another musical comedy revue. *Innocent Eyes* was at the Winter Garden, and it featured the Parisian cabaret star Mistinguett. Arce notes that the Winter Garden and the Casino were both Shubert theatres, and asserts that the two openings had been *inadvertently* scheduled for the same night, and then changed. The Shuberts were also the producers of *Innocent Eyes*, a show that was by no means a sure thing. There was general interest in Mistinguett, but the show got middling notices on the road, and it was assumed to be a limited Broadway engagement. So the Shuberts didn't reschedule *Innocent Eyes* to give *I'll Say She Is* a chance; if anything, they did it to protect their investment in *Innocent Eyes* from the popularity of the Marx Brothers. The postponement, if it occurred, was hardly last-minute; the correct opening dates of both *I'll Say She Is* and *Innocent Eyes* are listed in the papers as early as May 14.

The success of *I'll Say She Is* can be seen as a final rebuke to Shubert Advanced Vaudeville, and the Shuberts can be seen as the losers of this saga. (But don't worry, the Shuberts did okay in the long run.) *I'll Say She Is* was a product of Shubert vaudeville, having been assembled largely from the broken pieces of two Shubert units, *Gimme a Thrill* and the *Twentieth Century Revue*. The Shuberts had gone from having a big stake in these properties to merely being their landlords. In the summer of 1924, the Casino was the only Shubert house in New York not on cut rates, and also the only one housing a non-Shubert production.

Innocent eyes: Mistinguett

I'*LL SAY SHE IS* took its place in a Broadway season that was fairly typical of its time, but is awe-inspiring today for its breadth and depth. Two hundred and forty productions opened on Broadway in 1924, and a surprising number of them are works that are still known today, or which featured the talents of writers or performers whose names we remember.

The Marxes opened in the later, lighter part of the season, but the Big Street was still bursting with activity. Besides *I'll Say She Is* and *Innocent*

Eyes, theatergoers looking for thrills during the week of May 19, 1924 could choose among *Beggar on Horseback*, a satire by George S. Kaufman and Marc Connelly, starring Roland Young; *Show-Off*, a comedy by George Kelly; *Abie's Irish Rose*, no worse than a bad cold; *Moonlight*, a musical comedy with Julia Sanderson; *Cyrano*, directed by and starring Walter Hampden; *Cheaper to Marry*, a comedy by Samuel Shipman; the Theatre Guild's production of Shaw's *Saint Joan*; *Meet the Wife* with Mary Boland, Humphrey Bogart, and Clifton Webb; *Stepping Stones* with Fred and Dorothy Stone; *The Nervous Wreck*, a comedy by Owen Doyle, starring Otto Kruger (later to form the basis of Eddie Cantor's *Whoopee!*); Jeanne Eagels in *Rain*; Norma Talmadge in *Secrets*; Ada May in *Lollipop*; Emily Stevens in *Fata Morgana*; Lionel Atwill in *The Outsider*; Peggy Wood in *The Bride*; Bertha Kalich in *The Kreutzer Sonata*; Eddie Cantor in *Kid Boots*; W.C. Fields in *Poppy*; Fred Allen in *Vogues*; Lew Fields in *The Melody Man*; Beatrice Lillie and Gertrude Lawrence in *Charlot's Revue*; *Sitting Pretty*, the final musical comedy by Bolton, Wodehouse, and Kern; and *Plain Jane*, with music by our own Tom Johnstone.

Or if you'd already seen all of those, you might try *7th Heaven, Blossom Time, Cobra, Expressing Willie, Little Jessie James, The Miracle, Mr. Battling Buttler, Paradise Alley, Peg O' My Dreams, The Potters, The Shame Woman, Spring Cleaning, The Swan, Two Strangers from Nowhere, White Cargo*, or *The Wonderful Visit*. If you were willing to wait, you could add to the mix *Antony and Cleopatra, Artists and Models, The Brothers Karamazov, The Cherry Orchard, Desire Under the Elms, Earl Carroll's Vanities, The Greenwich Village Follies, Hedda Gabler, Ivanov, Keep Kool*, George and Ira Gershwin's *Lady Be Good, Macbeth, The Merchant of Venice*, Irving Berlin's *Music Box Revue, The Passing Show, Peter Pan, Rose-Marie, She Stoops to Conquer, Six Characters in Search of an Author, The Student Prince, The Taming of the Shrew, Uncle Vanya, What Price Glory*, and *The Ziegfeld Follies*; as well as Alfred Lunt and Lynn Fontanne in *The Guardsman*; and Paul Robeson in Eugene O'Neill's *All God's Chillun Got Wings*; and if you were willing to venture beyond the midtown theatre district, you could find the roots of New York's downtown theatre scene at such venues as the Greenwich Village Theatre, the Provincetown Playhouse, the Neighborhood Playhouse, and the Cherry Lane Theatre.

New York theatre in the 1920s was *the* popular culture of its time and place. It was a gleaming supermarket, with aisle after electric aisle, shelves bursting with everything from Aeschylus to Ziegfeld. To compare Broadway then to Broadway now is to miss the point entirely. If you're trying to fathom the range and the primacy of Jazz Age Broadway, think of it as the equivalent of not only our contemporary Broadway and Off Broadway scene, and the independent theatre scene which surrounds and sometimes tops it, but also of films, television, radio, concerts, and the internet, all together. And the musical revue, a form represented by more than a dozen 1924 productions besides *I'll Say She Is*, was a supermarket in itself. Watching a revue was like flipping channels. An audience might enjoy, over the course of a few hours, comedy, drama, a concert, a dance recital, a circus, and a fashion show. It was vaudeville for sophisticates.

THE CASINO THEATRE (1404 Broadway) had stood on the southeast corner of Broadway and 39th Street since the dawn of the theatrical era in midtown. It was built in 1882, in extravagant Moorish style, by Francis Hatch Kimball and Thomas Wisedell. By the time the Marx Brothers got to it, the Casino was already 42 years old and richer in history than any other Broadway house. It had been the first theatre lit by electricity, and it had the city's first public roof garden. The Casino was known primarily for comic operettas, like *Erminie*, which opened in 1886 and had a stellar two-and-a-half-year run. In 1894, the Casino became the birthplace of the Broadway revue, with the opening of *The Passing Show*—a production which set the tone not only for the later *Passing Shows* of 1912-1924, but for virtually all American revues, including the *Follies*. Four years later, with *Clorindy*, the Casino became the first Broadway theatre to present a musical

The Casino Theatre in 1900

written and performed by African-Americans (though, alas, not in the main auditorium, but upon a smaller stage, on the roof). In 1900, when *Floradora* opened at the Casino, New Yorkers saw their first line of modern chorusgirls, and the city was abundantly chorus-girled forevermore.[1]

---

[1] It's obligatory to mention here that among the *Floradora* girls, for a time, was Evelyn Nesbit. This is where Stanford White discovered her. Jealousy! Murder! Statutory rape! Read all about it, but not here.

The interior of the Casino Theatre, 1900

The more recent history of the Casino was almost all operetta. A lot of Gilbert and Sullivan. Whenever the Kern-Wodehouse-Bolton juggernaut was ready to open a new show at the Princess, their current production (*Very Good Eddie*; *Oh Boy*; *Oh, Lady! Lady!*) generally transferred to the Casino to make room for it. Casino highlights of the twenties had been *Sally, Irene, and Mary*, a shameless but successful attempt to capitalize on the popularity of three other shows entitled *Sally*, *Irene*, and *Mary*; and *Wildflower*, the third collaboration between Otto Harbach and Oscar Hammerstein II.

Despite the theatre's dazzling past, and its opulent design, by 1924 the old Casino was in a somewhat ramshackle state. (Later, when the boys were starring in *The Cocoanuts* at the newly-renovated Lyric, John Anderson of the *Post* wrote that because the Brothers were "accustomed to the magnificent decrepitudes of the Casino," they "probably will have to nick the furniture before they feel at home.") But this mixture of splendor and ruin was the perfect environment for *I'll Say She Is.* The shabbiness of the production has probably been overstated; Groucho called it "a poverty-stricken revue." But it is noteworthy that on the road the physical production was well-received, while in New York, it was mostly snickered about, despite whatever Beury may have done to spruce it up. Groucho was fond of explaining that all of the scenery in *I'll Say She Is* was left over from other shows, and rescued from Kane's Warehouse, a New Jersey repository for the wreckage of theatrical failures. He once claimed that among the scenic elements of *I'll Say She Is* he had identified pieces from *The Girl of the Golden West, The Squaw Man, Way Down East, Turn to the Right,* and *Uncle Tom's Cabin.* Will Johnstone, in his diary, gives another accounting:

> We sure have a "Turkey Show" as far as scenery goes . . . [with] odds & ends from other productions. *Up in the Clouds* industrial scene, *Girl in the Spotlight* first drop, *George White's Scandals* old art curtain, *Give Me a Thrill* drops, Nile scene from *As You Were,* costumes from *49ers,* rented office furniture. The joke is that the stuff looks O.K. from the front.

For the audience gathered on opening night at the Casino, there was a feeling of *quaintness* in the air—the old, ornate playhouse; the refined prettiness of the Shuberts' Casino program cover; the familiar art curtains on stage; the calm before the storm.

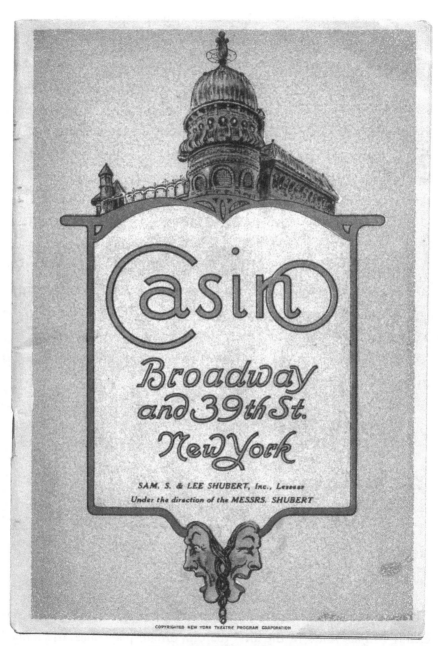

Casino Theatre program

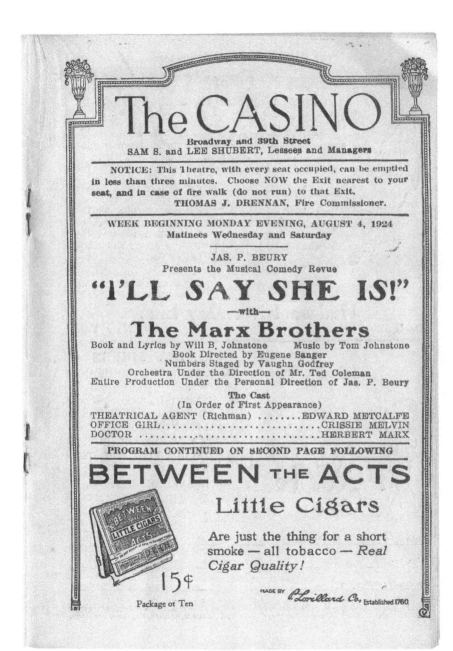

The CASINO

Broadway and 39th Street
SAM S. and LEE SHUBERT, Lessees and Managers

NOTICE: This Theatre, with every seat occupied, can be emptied in less than three minutes. Choose NOW the Exit nearest to your seat, and in case of fire walk (do not run) to that Exit.
THOMAS J. DRENNAN, Fire Commissioner.

WEEK BEGINNING MONDAY EVENING, AUGUST 4, 1924
Matinees Wednesday and Saturday

JAS. P. BEURY
Presents the Musical Comedy Revue

"I'LL SAY SHE IS!"

—with—

The Marx Brothers

Book and Lyrics by Will B. Johnstone   Music by Tom Johnstone
Book Directed by Eugene Sanger
Numbers Staged by Vaughn Godfrey
Orchestra Under the Direction of Mr. Ted Coleman
Entire Production Under the Personal Direction of Jas. P. Beury

The Cast
(In Order of First Appearance)
THEATRICAL AGENT (Richman) ....EDWARD METCALFE
OFFICE GIRL...............................CRISSIE MELVIN
DOCTOR ....HERBERT MARX

PROGRAM CONTINUED ON SECOND PAGE FOLLOWING

Week of August 4, 1924

VII.
MAY 19, 1924

ON THE DAY of the night that *I'll Say She Is* opened on Broadway, Heywood Broun's newspaper column ("It Seems to Me") featured a letter from Julius H. Marx. The comedian had written in to chide Broun for appearing on stage in the revue *Round the Town*:

> Mr. Benchley really started all the trouble. After he saw *Abie's Irish Rose*, he reasoned, "Well, if that show can make a million dollars, I certainly ought to be able to make a little money as an actor." Then I suppose you saw Mr. Benchley, and you figured, "Well, if he can do a monologue, I might as well take a crack at it." And so it goes in an endless and vicious chain.
>
> The next step will be the Messrs. Hammond and Woollcott doing the Rath Brothers' stuff, and Alan Dale batting for Marilyn Miller.
>
> Unless we get relief from Congress or the Equity, all the actors will wind up doing free performances for the radio, and all the critics will be getting fat salaries from Broadway revue managers. So please go back to your farm and column and don't take the bread out of our mouths.

The day of the opening, here is Groucho, bantering in print with the same crowd that suddenly "discovered" the Marx Brothers later that evening! They weren't *really* such an unknown quantity uptown. They had already romped through Chicago with Ben Hecht and Charles MacArthur. It was MacArthur who supposedly dragged Alexander Woollcott to the Casino Theatre on May 19. The legend has it that Woollcott protested, saying he had no interest in watching "some damn acrobats." This is especially remarkable in light of

Groucho's reference to the Rath Brothers in that morning's paper. The Rath Brothers actually *were* acrobats. Groucho's casting of Woollcott and Percy Hammond in their roles is an exact reversal of the legend! Perhaps Woollcott, miffed after reading Broun's column, deliberately turned it around on the Marxes: *I'm* an acrobat? *You're* an acrobat!

A N INTENSE FOUR DAYS stood between the Philadelphia closing and the New York opening. Will B. Johnstone had stayed in the city during this period, as the show's scenery was loaded into the Casino, and the company engaged in its very last rehearsals. On May 19, Helen Beckman Johnstone joined her husband in the city, bringing his dress clothes from their home in East Orange, and checked into the Waldorf. "When I got there she'd gone to hair dressers," Will recorded tersely in his diary later that night. "My flask had leaked out all over our clothes. Ruined my shirt, etc."

After attending a rehearsal for a new Society of Illustrators show at the Central Theatre, the Johnstones dined with friends at the Cornell Club. "Then we all went to the Casino for that 'Thrill of a Lifetime,'" Will wrote. "Big N.Y. opening night at the show…wondered what the verdict would be…The first nighters were all in—curious about this show that had come in after a year on the road…"

So now we must face a question that's of great interest to us, as followers of the Marx Brothers. It's a question of limitless importance to an understanding of their art, and their history. It should be of at least *some* interest to any student of comedy, musicals, revues, or Broadway. But it's a difficult question to answer. The answer to this question exists only in fragments, and although these fragments tell us a lot, they form an incomplete picture. There will always be a sense of loss. The question is: What happened onstage at the Casino Theatre on May 19, 1924?

The show began at 8:42 pm. Act One, Scene One, Theatrical Agency! "As Curtain Rises," wrote Johnstone, "Richman is discovered." This is Ed Metcalfe. In the program he's "THEATRICAL AGENT (Richman)."

Anyway, he is *discovered*—now bring on the girls. The girls and Metcalfe perform a song called "Do It," of which I have found no trace. *Variety* called it "a hum-dinger of a chorus number" that "gets the show under way with a bang." Yet the same notice describes "Do It" as "unpretentious," noting that "it [seems] to be the fashion lately to do away with the usual colorful and elaborate opening number." So it was a nifty song and dance, but not a spectacular Opening Number in the structural sense.

After the song, the girls vamoose, and Metcalfe sits down at his desk. He opens a newspaper and gives us the headline: "Oh boy! Society Woman Craves Excitement." An "office girl," played by Crissie Melvin of the Melvin Sisters, enters and announces: "Good morning, Boss. Here is an actor out of work." Zeppo Marx walks in, pausing to chuck Crissie Melvin on the chin. "How dare you!" she exclaims, and she's off.

From here, the Theatrical Agency scene from *On the Mezzanine* proceeded as usual. Each Marx Brother tries to impress the Agent/Richman with impressions of the same popular star. As for which star, it varied. In *On the Mezzanine*, they'd impersonated buck-and-wing dancer Joe Frisco. In England, they had done Chaplin impressions. In the Johnstone typescript for *I'll Say She Is*, and on opening night in Philadelphia, they'd impersonated Gallagher and Shean, with parody lyrics for their famous theme song:

> Our song's a lot of junk,
> and as actors we are punk.
> Positively, Mr. Gallagher.
> Absolutely, Mr. Shean.

Take that, Uncle Al!

When they changed the celebrity they were impersonating, they also had to change Chico's character name, even though it was only used in this one instance. This, you will recall, was a Herman Timberg jazz-patter sketch, and Chico's name had to approximately rhyme with the name of the star they imitated. *On the Mezzanine*: "What's your name?" "Zbysko / But the best thing I do is give the imitation of Frisco." *I'll Say She Is* typescript: "My name is Sabisco Chicaline / And the best thing I do is give the imitation of Gallagher and Shean." (I don't know what Chico's name was when they impersonated Chaplin in *On the Balcony* in Britain, but Mikael Uhlin suggests Napolin, which strikes me as a very good guess.) The version filmed in 1931 had the boys doing their Maurice Chevalier impressions from *Monkey Business*: "What's your name?" "Tomalia / But the best thing I do is give the imitation of Chevalier."

It's through that 1931 short that the Theatrical Agency scene has endured as the best-known extended sequence from *I'll Say She Is*. The Marxes filmed it for inclusion in a Paramount promotional feature, *The House That Shadows Built*. It's the only existing Marx Brothers short, and today it's in the public domain and readily available. Except for some incidental gags and Harpo's knife-dropping routine, it's the only part of *I'll Say She Is* for which we have an original cast performance on record. Of course, they're on a Paramount soundstage in 1931, not the Casino in '24; and that isn't Ed Metcalfe, it's Ben Taggart. But it's as close as the Marx Brothers ever got to making a movie of *I'll Say She Is*.

The sketch contains much Timbergian verse, which deteriorates toward the end, along with the scene itself. There's some signature physical business from Harpo and Chico, a few great Groucho lines, and an unusually prominent role for Zeppo. Each Marx Brother comes in and auditions, impersonating the same star and singing the same song; Harpo, fourth, whistles it. The scene eventually degenerates into a cacophony of shouting, arguing, and random gags exploding everywhere. Harpo milks a rubber glove into his hat and drinks it, as he later will in *A Night at the Opera*. (As we have seen, the gag went back at least as far as *On the Mezzanine*.) Groucho and Chico rearrange the furniture.

The film fades to black at this point, so we turn to Johnstone's typescript: *Another* showbiz hopeful wanders into the Theatrical Agency, asking about "an opening for a juvenile." This is Chief (tenor Lloyd Garrett), but he doesn't even get to do his imitation of Frisco, Gallagher and Shean, or whoever. Agent Richman tells the strivers he has no work for them, but he does have "an idea whereby we can all make some money." He shows them the newspaper.

> RICHMAN: Here's a wealthy young lady who claims
> she will give her heart, her hand, and her fortune
> to the man who gives her the greatest thrill. She is
> a victim of suppressed desires.
>
> GROUCHO: She's a nut.
>
> RICHMAN: She has complexes because she has never
> been in love . . . We will give her the whole range

If the Nightingales could sing like you:
The Brothers on the set of the Theatrical Agency short at Paramount, 1931

of masculine thrillers. Boys, do you remember the
old fable of Richman, Poorman, Beggarman, Thief,
Doctor, Lawyer, Merchant, Chief.

EVERYBODY: I'll be the Richman.

RICHMAN: Let's pretend. I'll be the Richman,
Poorman, Beggarman, Thief, Doctor, Lawyer,
Merchant, Chief. Are we all agreed?

EVERYBODY: Agreed!

RICHMAN: Isn't she a beauty?

EVERYBODY: I'LL SAY SHE IS![1]

Two more men have been introduced; inevitably, they are Merchant and
Thief. The former was played by Phillip Darby, and the latter by Edgar Gardiner, of the Gardiner Trio (and *Gimme a Thrill*). All eight of these men now
perform a song called "Pretty Girl," and the curtain falls. Not just any curtain, mind you—Art Curtains.

Scene Two, which takes place in front of said Art Curtain, begins with
the household staff. The typescript gives us a butler named Simpson, a social
secretary named Ruby, and some maids. But no butler appears in any program or cast listing I've seen. Ruby, the social secretary, was played by Ruth
Urban at the time of the Broadway opening. Johnstone wrote some fantastic
lines for Simpson which I hope were spoken by somebody: "Some gentlemen are calling who wish to give the Mistress a thrill. Some very peculiar
gentlemen...Ah, they are devastating the dining room. I fear for the silver."

At this point, the eight men enter, four of whom are Marx Brothers. They
immediately mistake Ruby for the Society Woman who Craves Excitement.
She tells them that she is "only the social secretary," but then "Goes L. [stage
left]" to add: "But I too, have complexes like my mistress." Groucho asks if
she has any liquor. "No, but I have suppressed desires." "Oh," says Groucho,

---

[1] In these pages, quotations from the Johnstone typescript replicate its spelling
and punctuation, with occasional exceptions for the sake of clarity.

"we don't mind what we drink." Ruby asks Harpo, "Could *you* give me a thrill?" This inspires "Business of Breaking Arm," which we can picture Harpo doing, and it's much better than it sounds. Everyone sings "Gimme a Thrill."

Art Curtains open, and Scene Three! Beauty's Reception Room. Here she is, folks, at the top of a modest hand-painted staircase—the enchanting Lotta Miles as Beauty. Her first words are "Gentlemen . . . it is indeed my good fortune to be flattered like this." She descends the stair, toying with her prey. "But how am I to choose from among you," she asks, "with a whole range of masculine society so perfectly represented?" She favors them with a song, which had been "The Thrill of Love" for much of the tour, but was now "Only You."[2] The song is a pleasant fox-trot, with a banal lyric ("I love, I love you, dear / I only want you near") elevated by a sweet ragtime undertow.

Ms. Miles suggests that the men draw lots to determine who gets the first chance to thrill her. The Thief, piping up for the first time, says ominously, "But remember this is going to be decided upon by a battle or a bullet." (Really?) This Thief certainly seems like a scoundrel, but it's Chief who takes matters, and Beauty, into his own hands. "Do you really want a thrill?" he asks. "Well, here's a real thrill!" He "gives her a long kiss," prompting the classic response, "Go! I never want to see you again!"

> CHIEF: I'll go, but before I go there is one last
>   request that I wish to make.
> BEAUTY: What is it?
> CHIEF: Will you please let go my hand?
> BEAUTY: Oh Chief, what must you think of me?
> CHIEF: I think you're a treasure, but all you need is—

That was originally the cue back into the refrain of "The Thrill of Love,"

---

[2] Not to be confused with the well-known 1955 song of the same title, recorded by the Platters, Louis Armstrong, and others.

whose lyric began, "Just a little bit of fondness…" By May 19, there was apparently no reprise here. The men, having drawn lots, now have various complaints about the results. Groucho snarls, "This is a frame up! Only eight voting and I got number 35." Chico, to Harpo: "What did you get?" Harpo shows him some stolen silverware. Old Richman has drawn number one, and implores Beauty to accompany him to Wall Street. But now the Thief asserts himself ("I'm the thief," he explains) and backs the other men offstage. "I'm going to take you to Chinatown and give you the thrill of the underworld," he tells our heroine. "Savvy? The thrill of the underworld."

The Chinatown sequence begins on the street, with Phillip Darby, the Merchant, singing "When Shadows Fall." The song has one of Tom Johnstone's loveliest melodies. The lyric, also by Tom, is about coming home at the end of the day "when lovers seal each love vow with a kiss." It's plausible that the Merchant was actually supposed to be a *merchant* in this street scene, and was singing about closing the store for the night and going home. Maybe *too* plausible. Next we have the Thief saying scary things to Beauty, such as "I'll show you the life of a thief, the thrill of getting away with murder, the thrill of being chased by the bulls[3] . . . The thrill of a gat spitting crimson in the dark . . . Say kid how about a little opium?" Beauty is apprehensive, but game, until footsteps are heard. "Somebody's coming," says the Thief. "Get in that doorway and I'll join you later." Some date! Here there was a "burglar number" entitled "Break Into Your Heart," performed by the Thief along with Marcella Hardie and chorus (impersonating "Burglar Girls and Street Gamins").

And now we move into the Opium Den, where the typescript must be seen to be believed.

> (*Chinaman discovered asleep on bench. Enter Policeman who looks at Chinaman, smiles and puts toy balloon in Chinaman's mouth and exits L. Business with balloon.*)

---

[3] Twenties slang for police officers.

CHINAMAN: Ang Quang Pong Hil.

*(Noise and whistle heard off R. Door slams. Enter Thief
and Beauty.)*

THIEF: Huan, Quiet, Safe.

BEAUTY: What a funny place.

THIEF: . . . Why you're in the lowest dive in the City,
where wrecks of humanity drug their brains with
poisonous poppy.

BEAUTY: The despicable vice.

THIEF: It's a tough break, ain't it? *(Chinese talk…)*
Say kid, the machinery of the brain wasn't planted
in the bean for nuttin, and if you'll stick by me kid,
you'll dress better than any of these dames. Experience the thrill of a balmy imagination.

BEAUTY: What?

THIEF: Take a few puffs—dream.

BEAUTY: I'll try anything once.

(Chinese talk to Thief)

(Sits on couch) Does this guarantee me a round trip to
China?

*(Smokes pipe, drops pipe and falls asleep. Chinese talk
and Exit. Enter another Chinaman and girl)*

2ND CHINAMAN: Young Ton Fir How. *(Rubbing
finger along knife)*

1ST CHINAMAN: *(Bowing out)* Alla Hic, Alla Hic.
(Exit)

APACHE DANCE

*(End of dance, Chinaman enters, sees a dead body,
throws him over his shoulder and exits singing)*

This does not guarantee us a round trip to China, and if it makes us
cringe, it's slight comfort that *I'll Say She Is* was hardly alone in perpetuating
this kind of thing, and lots of people were doing it long after the twenties.[4]

---

[4] See *Breakfast at Tiffany's* (1961).

But the dance was something else. Described confusingly as a "Chinese Apache Dance" in the program, this Parisian street dance actually had nothing to do with either China or Native Americans. (It's pronounced *ah-PAHSH*.) It's a rough, daring, acrobatic style of dancing, which involves a man and a woman violently throwing each other around the room. Apache dances were in vogue in the twenties, invariably performed to the strains of Offenbach's "L'Amour de L'Apache." (Mistinguett's *Innocent Eyes*, the revue which opened the night after *I'll Say She Is*, also included one.) The piece was performed throughout the run by the show's featured dance team, Harry Walters and Cecile D'Andrea, as "Hop Merchant" and "White Girl." Near the conclusion of the piece, as one Chicago critic noticed, "Mr. Walters rips off the front elevation of Miss d'Andrea's bodice, making disclosures which are common enough in life classes at the Art Institute . . . But to show that this is a revue as well as a life class, Mr. Walters roughly removes the facade of Miss d'Andrea's skirt, disclosing what slight lingerie she steps in." The Apache number caused some out-of-town reviewers to wonder if *I'll Say She Is* might be busted by the police for obscenity—and it caused the Philadelphia police to do just that, following the show's closing performance at the Walnut Street Theatre. Beury and Wanamaker "laughingly" spent an hour or so in jail, before they managed to get some fellow Philadelphia millionaires to come and bail them out.

At some point in this sequence, under the influence of opium, Beauty falls asleep and imagines the Dream Ship, which moves across the stage, in all its splendor. After the singing Chinaman exits with a dead body over his shoulder, there's a musical number entitled "San Toy." It's not clear whether this was an actual selection from the mock-Chinese operetta *San Toy* (which had four Broadway engagements between 1900 and 1905), or a pastiche devised by the Johnstones. This song accompanied the Dream Ship (a device which was itself borrowed from *San Toy*, as noted earlier). This was followed by the entrance of the Policeman, a Chinaman, the Thief, and Groucho, who for some reason suddenly becomes the embodiment of law and order and says, "Officer, arrest that woman." *Variety*'s New York critic recorded an ad lib in this scene, when "an underworld character with a gun appeared and Julius Marx said, 'Go ahead, shoot; you're on Broadway.'"

The most vivid surviving description of the Chinatown sequence, complete with ethnic slurs, comes to us by way of a review from the show's stay in Boston in the fall of 1923:

> Undoubtedly the sensation provided by the thief is the most "thrilly." Set in a dimly lighted opium den, "de woist in de city," as its sponsor proudly proclaims, it reeks with the flavor of crime, with pistol shots, with the weird whistles of police, with the unutterable depravity of Chinese jargon, muttered by sleepy-eyed Orientals. There is a wild Apache dance in which the bodice of the girl is half torn from her shoulders and her skirt is similarly damaged. But there is no cause for alarm by the censor, for the young lady has evidently foreseen such an emergency and is sartorially prepared. In conclusion the episode rises to a spectacle of real beauty, an opium dream, presumably, in which a Chinese junk set with a sail of gleaming burned bronze, appears in a background of blue, while a Chinese maiden sings the charming melody of "San Toy," one of the best of the numbers of the piece.

Beauty is arrested for the opium den murder, and Art Curtains open on the Courtroom Scene. The set for this piece was black-and-white, designed in the cubist style, very fashionable at the time.

In the courtroom, we are given only a moment to process the idea that Harpo is now playing a judge, when we are asked to accept Chico as the district attorney. This highly suspect D.A. tells the attending officer, "Don't let anyone in. The judge has something important he wants to talk to me about," and Harpo and Chico go into their poker routine. All the typescript offers here is two-thirds of a page of Chico patter, leaving us to imagine Harpo's gags and reactions. ("All the time you want to play with your cards. Play with my cards, I like to win sometimes too, you know . . . Why don't you play like I play. I don't cheat much.") It ends with the cut-the-cards gag later reprised

The Marx Brothers on the set of I'll Say She Is *at the Casino, in tuxedos made for them by their father, Frenchie.*

in *Horse Feathers*, and then the entrance of Groucho, who is *also* introduced as the district attorney.

> GROUCHO: How do you do your honor. I am here to convict a beautiful woman of murder in the first degree, homicide in the second degree, and suicide in the third degree. Let me know when I get to seventy degrees. Are you with me? Here's a dollar on account. I would explain this case but what's the use. He wouldn't understand it, you wouldn't understand it, and I wouldn't understand it. I am certainly glad to be before a judge whose hand has never been tainted by the lure of gold. A man who is not only unbiased and unemotional but is practically unconscious. Judge, you have no idea how you look.

In Johnstone's typescript, what follows is a sort of skeletal Marx Brothers scene, but it is still unmistakably a Marx Brothers scene. Groucho, as was ever to be, has good lines and bad lines. A repetition of the word *business* impels Chico to ask, apropos of nothing, "How is business?" The typescript specifies some Harpo business with a gun, anticipating later gags in the film version of *Animal Crackers*. When Harpo shoots the hat off a member of the "dummy jury," Groucho rewards him with, "The boy wins a gold cigar," which will later turn up in *The Cocoanuts* (and again, slightly varied, in *Duck Soup*). A Detective (apparently played by Ed Metcalfe, but as another character distinct from Agent/Richman) enters, opens his coat, and displays his badge; Harpo opens *his* coat to reveal a flask—yet another gag which will be back next year in *The Cocoanuts*. So will Chico's answer when the Detective notes suspiciously that Chico's suit doesn't fit: "I know. I had it made to order." It's not clear whether George Kaufman was leaning on Johnstone for some of these gags, or whether both were leaning on the Marx Brothers.

With the appearance of the Detective, all notions of Beauty being on trial for murder are abandoned; now it's man against boys.

> DETECTIVE: *(To Harpo)* Come down out of there you. Come on, make it snappy. *(To Chico)* Well, who is this guy?
>
> CHICO: That's my brother.
>
> DETECTIVE: *(To Harpo)* Is that your brother?
>
> *(Business of shaking head—yes—no.)*
>
> GROUCHO: Figure that out.
>
> DETECTIVE: *(To Groucho)* Are these your sons?
>
> GROUCHO: Yes.
>
> DETECTIVE: Are you their father?
>
> GROUCHO: No.
>
> DETECTIVE: *(To Harpo)* Is that your father? *(To Chico)* Is that your father?
>
> CHICO: I'm not sure. It was during the epidemic.
>
> DETECTIVE: Who are you?
>
> GROUCHO: The Shepherd of the Hills. I lost my sheep.

Even in embryo, in Johnstone's pre-rehearsal pages, what we have here is clearly Marx Brothers material, written specifically for them by a writer who understands them. Embellished by the performers as well as the librettist, there's every reason to assume that the courtroom scene was a comedy highlight of the evening. In fact, we *know* it was, because it contained Harpo's knife-dropping routine, already a favorite, and from *I'll Say She Is* onward, a classic.

It also contained two of the aforementioned "local" jokes, which verify that the typescript was prepared for the Philadelphia engagement. First, "a dummy jury is pushed on" from offstage, and Groucho says, "I thought the Phillies were on the road." Then he has an exchange with Beauty, the defendant: "I am going to send you to Harrisburg for twenty years." "Why?" "Capital punishment." It's easy to imagine either gag revised according to whatever town they were playing.

After Harpo's knife-dropping routine reduces the entire affair to a delirious shambles, Art Curtains quickly intervene. We can assume that during the ensuing scene "in one," the dialogue and music were punctuated by the sounds of stagehands gathering up silverware. The scene, as it happens, is the next chapter in the would-be romance of Beauty and Chief. See, this is the kind of guy Chief is—he's not interested in contests. Beauty asks if he intends to give her a thrill ("Engagements eight weeks in advance"), but he says, "I am not a fortune teller. You alone are the treasure I want," and then he starts singing "I'm Saving You for a Rainy Day."

> When I was much younger than this,
> somebody would always say,
> You must put some treasure aside.
> Save up for a rainy day.
> I have saved a treasure, priceless too.
> I'll be better off than any fellow, I don't care who.
>
> I'm saving you, dear, for rainy weather.
> So what if all the skies are gray . . .

Art Curtains open and—Wall Street! The Wall Street sequence, which was the first piece in the show to make use of the entire stage, had a black-and-white "futuristic" set resembling a spider's web, "flanked on one side by the bull and on the other by the bear of the stock market," one observer noted. Enter our old friend Richman, escorting our wayward Beauty toward her next thrill. Johnstone gave us some delightful hardboiled dialogue in the opium den scene, and there's more here. ("And am I to be crushed like a fly in this monstrous web?"... "The stake I'm playing for is you, you beautiful doll.") Johnstone excelled at this kind of thing. I bet he had something to do with the gangster dialogue in *Monkey Business* (though Perelman was also quite capable of hardboiled parody). It's a tone we might now describe as Runyonesque, conceived a decade before Damon Runyon's Broadway stories

Marcella Hardie in I'll Say She Is

entered the popular consciousness.

Runyon's stories were mostly written during the Great Depression, in *recollection* (despite their perpetual present tense) of the *I'll Say She Is* era. The Depression seems to loom over this Wall Street sequence, too, even though the Crash is more than five years away. In the shadow of that calamitous event, we tend to forget that there was also a severe depression in 1920-1921. This was typical of the transition from a wartime economy, and it fed investors' worries well into the Roaring Twenties, which is why Wall Street humor of the period often seems oddly prescient.

The scene began with "Wall Street Blues," sung principally by Marcella Hardie, along with Crissie Melvin (of the Melvin Sisters), Hazel Gaudreau, Edgar Gardiner (the THIEF!), and Ensemble. This was perhaps the only part of the Wall Street sequence that dealt with Wall Street directly. There was a large tickertape machine on stage, which issued streamers, and the aforementioned Bull and Bear. The largest part of the sequence was about gambling, as a metaphor for high finance. The program identifies it as "The Tragedy of Gambling," and it encompasses everything in the typescript for Wall Street (two pages). It was a pageant, with members of the ensemble emerging from the center of the spider's web, dressed as various gambling icons like dice, a roulette wheel, and playing cards. ("The costumes in this sketch," according to one critic, "are virtual objects of art.") Richman grandly announces each dancer's solo: "First the thrill of cards...Next the rattle of the bones." They are summoned with waves of the wand of the Fairy of Wall Street, embodied on Broadway by Mary Melvin (the other Melvin Sister). Then there was Ledru Stiffler's "Greed of Gold" dance specialty, in shimmering body paint. "His almost unclothed body burnished with shining gold," runs one description of the piece, "he whirls like a dervish among the gaily-clad figures which have preceded him, weaving them into one coordinated whole, while showers of ticker-tape fall in shifting lines of white from above and a rising curtain discloses the panorama of New York, the 'plaything of Wall Street.'" There was a dance duet by D'Andrea and Walters here, entitled "The Lure of Gambling," and something identified as "Scene 13—Industry—The Plaything of Wall Street." (*Variety* was impressed to find that the Wall Street sequence was "considerably built up"—having seen it in various forms since 1919, and probably earlier.) These final moments of Act One may have involved Beauty, perhaps establishing that although all of this has been very interesting, she is not exactly thrilled.

It's a difficult thing, to write a play in which spectacular things keep happening and your lead character is always saying, "Nope, that wasn't thrilling either." A bit too easy for the critics, if they hadn't liked the show. Anyway, it's time for intermission, and the opening night program contains a very convincing advertisement for Lorillard's "Between the Acts" Little Cigars. ("Just the thing for a short smoke—all tobacco—*Real Cigar Quality!* 15¢,

Package of Ten.") Let's go up to the Casino roof, gaze down at glittering Broadway, and have one.

THE MELVIN SISTERS open Act Two, dressed as pages. They sing and dance, then open the Art Curtains and walk upstage, where Lotta Miles is discovered lying on a couch, with Zeppo Marx seated at her feet. Girls enter with draperies and flowers. Zeppo attempts to thrill Beauty by offering her material things, in the memorably-entitled pageant "The Inception of Drapery." Here is where *I'll Say She Is* shows its roots as a Kitty Gordon vehicle. Zeppo announces all the exotic gifts he's purchased for her (though how he's managed to do this is a question, as just a little while ago he was an unemployed actor) and each gift is carried in by a chorus girl attired in the manner of the gift's country of origin. "Silks from Japan," intones Zeppo. "Perfume from Hindustan." I would have loved to hear him do this. (Marx Brothers completists may note that "The Inception of Drapery," or the cliché in which it participates, is referenced in the Brothers' 1949 film *Love Happy*.) Threaded through this scene there was a song, "Beauty's Dress," performed first by Beauty and the Merchant, and then, in front of the curtain, by everyone on stage.

"The Inception of Drapery" was singled out for particular derision by the New York press. Franklin P. Adams, the Algonquin Round Tabler forever known as F.P.A., reported in his column ("The Conning Tower") that *I'll Say She Is* contained "one of those songs wherein the young women caparisoned as this or that enter to announcements like 'Furs from Russia' and 'Fans from Timbuctoo.' After the fifth of these, the cynical pressman in C 110 turned to his neighbor and said 'Love from Elsie.'" John Anderson of the *Post* wrote in his opening-night review that "The Inception of Drapery" "ought to get the 1924 prize for wanton stupidity," and speculated that the Marx Brothers "probably got their laughs by sitting back stage and watching the show when they weren't on." Four days later, Anderson was at it again, reiterating his high opinion of the Brothers, but hastening to add:

The Melvin Sisters in *I'll Say She Is*

There is one spectacle, however, which represents a new high water mark for something or other. It is entitled "The Inception of Drapery," a ceremonial so unintentionally funny that the Marx brothers themselves might have appeared in it, but they didn't. Since this has occurred it might be well to look to the future. There is no valid reason why other sartorial developments should not be celebrated with similar pontification. Consider, for instance, what a gracious interlude might be arranged with the theme "The Instigation of Socks," "The Invention and Preparation of Suspenders," or perchance "The Use and Development of Detachable Cuffs." It ought to prove a thrilling panorama for those persons who designed and executed the Odyssey of draperies now on display at the Casino.

After presenting this Odyssey to Beauty, Zeppo turns out to be something of a quitter.

> ZEPPO: Now dear, admit you are thrilled by this exquisite finery.
>
> BEAUTY: Yes, it thrills the flesh but the thrill is only skin deep. My heart still remains unmoved.
>
> ZEPPO: I give up!
>
> BEAUTY: Oh, don't go. I want to be thrilled.
>
> ZEPPO: I'm through. It's the Beggarman's [5] chance now. He will give you the thrill of Cinderella backwards. He will take you from riches to poverty. Good-Night! *(Exit L.)*

Zeppo Marx, ladies and gentlemen.

After he leaves, Beauty suddenly longs for a life of poverty, as though she'd just thought of it herself.

> BEAUTY: Must I always be left here surrounded by company, forced to listen to wonderful opera singers, doomed to carry our anchovies and sparkling burgundy. What wouldn't I give for a single cinnamon bun and a piece of scrapple. Oh, Cinderella, you had a fairy godmother,

---

[5] This may be an error in the typescript, for it's Groucho (Lawyer, in the program) who manages the next thrill, and it's Harpo whose nominal character, according to the program, is Beggarman. Or maybe Groucho was originally Beggarman. It hardly matters—Zeppo was the Merchant in Philadelphia, and on Broadway, we find that he's been promoted to Doctor.

where, where can I today find a real fairy?

"Yoo hoo! Here I am," exclaims a familiar voice. It's Groucho. He enters, hilariously attired in fairy godmother drag, with wings, a tiara, and black garters. He is smoking a pipe. He explains that he's "a regular union fairy," and offers to wave his magic wand to transform her into Ella Cinder, the backwards Cinderella, who is "wretchedly poor like everybody else." Beauty asks if there will be a ball, and demonstrates her dance skills, which inspires the Fairy Grouchmother to exclaim, "Hot cole slaw! Why, with those dogs I will make you the Queen of the marathon dancers."

> BEAUTY: And will I meet Prince Charming, my
>   beloved vagabond?
> GROUCHO: I don't know but you will meet a
>   tramp who has danced himself ragged.

"Cinderella Backward"

> BEAUTY: Is he poor?
>
> GROUCHO: He is so poor, he even owes me money.
>
> BEAUTY: Is he actually starving?
>
> GROUCHO: He is practically in Armenia.
>
> BEAUTY: But will he dance with rich little Ella Cinder?
>
> GROUCHO: He doesn't discriminate. He's a Horn and Hardartite. He'll dance with anybody—even you.
>
> BEAUTY: He doesn't look down on riches?
>
> GROUCHO: He can't, he lives in the basement.
>
> BEAUTY: *(Taking Groucho's hand)* Then come, take me to Prince Charming.

Groucho refuses ("Who, me, the head fairy? Ridiculous"). Saying he has "other Cinderellas to call on," he names the female title characters of other Broadway shows. He promises that "one of my assistant fairies" will escort her.

This led, logically enough, to a marathon dance sequence. The Broadway program tells us that this was also a "Hawaiian Scene." Sure, why not? It began with a quartet of women from the ensemble, who were then joined by "The 16 Yankee Girls," though these Yankee Girls were apparently the regular ensemble (oddly, seventeen of them), not the aforementioned Yankee Girls who'd appeared in the show on tour. The Yankee Girls perform some kind of Hawaiian marathon dance, after which Beauty finds herself alone onstage with Chief again. He tells her that "adventure is no substitute for love," then says, "You are cold, cold as a marble statue. Pygmalion carved a statue of Galatea and so great was his love for this marble image that he brought it to life." Beauty asks if Chief expects to bring *her* to life. So Chief sings "Only You" again. That's his solution for *everything*.

At some point in the show—it's not clear where—Harpo performed his much-admired rope gag, in which he appeared at one end of the stage, tugging a big rope. His effort and struggle suggest that affixed to the other end of the rope, offstage, is an elephant. He tugs and tugs, until he's disappeared offstage, when in an instant, at the other end of the rope, appears—Harpo himself!

The next scene, a classical interlude entitled "The Marble Fountain," picks up the Pygmalion cue. Supported by twelve ladies of the chorus, Harry Walters and Cecile D'Andrea appear in ancient Greek costumes, and perform their Pygmalion and Galatea ballet, "The Awakening of Love." Then a group of men led by Groucho, Harpo, and Zeppo perform a "Tramp Ballet" called "The Death of

Harry Walters and Cecile D'Andrea in the Pygmalion and Galatea ballet

Love," burlesquing the serious ballet we have just seen. The Tramp Ballet, and possibly the entire Pygmalion dance sequence, were accompanied by the strains of Mendelssohn's "Spring Song." This concept was nothing novel. In fact, it had been in *Gimme a Thrill*, and *Variety* traced it to *Pinwheel*, "a highbrow revue" that ran for twenty-eight performances in 1922. Yet most of the notices out-of-town, and quite a few in New York, praised the Tramp Ballet as a highlight of the show; only the Napoleon scene got more attention.

It's strange that the second most successful Marx Brothers comedy piece of the evening was not Marx Brothers material at all—though undoubtedly they made it their own, and made it funnier than anyone else possibly could. This places the Tramp Ballet from *I'll Say She Is* on an oddball list of classic Marx Brothers scenes that are inherently uncharacteristic of them. The stateroom scene in *A Night at the Opera*, the "Tootsie-Frootsie" scene in *A Day at the Races*, the train sequence in *Go West*, and much of the physical comedy in *Duck Soup*, including the justly celebrated mirror scene, are not what we expect from the Marx Brothers. Yet these seem to be their best-remembered scenes among general audiences. These scenes comprise, along with a few others, the standard Marx Brothers Greatest Hits playlist. The Tramp Ballet is as elusive to us as the mirror scene would be, if we had never seen *Duck Soup*. It's hard to imagine the Marxes doing it because we've never seen them do anything like it.

After the Tramp Ballet, Chico "enters through curtains" and announces that he is a hypnotist, which I have to say is news to all of us. (When a reporter asked the Marxes what inspired the "funny hypnotic scene," they said, "Trying to induce the Broadway producers to give us an engagement." Nevertheless, they had used hypnotism as a comedic premise back in *On the Mezzanine*, too.) There follows a scene between Chico and Ed Metcalfe (Richman) in which Chico declares his intention to thrill Beauty through hypnosis: "I take her back centuries and centuries. I make her think she is Josephine, wife of Napoleon Bonaparte, Empress of the World." Richman declares Chico a fake, and by way of argument, Chico hypnotizes him and gets him to make dog and cat noises. But Richman doesn't know how to be a snake. "Just like a worm," Chico helpfully explains, "only more." Richman is onto him. "Yes," he says, exasperated, "but I don't *think* I am a snake." Chico accepts this: "But I will give $1,000 to anyone who can prove that *I* don't think you are a snake."

Or that's how the scene goes in Johnstone's typescript. Other sources indicate that it was *Metcalfe* who played the hypnotist on Broadway—opposite Chico. Perhaps the bit was rewritten. I assume Chico's participation in it is the only reason why he wasn't in the Tramp Ballet, so he must have done *something* funny in the hypnotist scene. Maybe he preferred to be instructed to bark like a dog, rather than do the instructing, because it was easier to remember his lines that way.

The hypnotist scene was followed, for reasons absent or unknown, by two chorus girls, Jane Hurd and Helene Bradley, doing a Pierrot Dance. I picture two young women in black-and-white costumes and pointy hats, with black-and-white painted sad clown faces. Perhaps the idea was to set a French mood for what was to follow.

THE NAPOLEON SCENE stands like Olympus at the end of the second act, beckoning to us from behind layers of history. This is the key evolutionary moment from the roughhouse vaudevillians of *Home Again* and *On the Mezzanine* to the archer satirists of *Cocoanuts* and *Animal Crackers*. It is dominated, as those two shows generally are, by relentless,

Groucho, Lotta Miles, and Harpo

sparkling verbal humor from Groucho. But his brothers are afforded plenty of opportunities, both for the precision physical farce that they'd honed for years onstage together, and for the customary harp and piano specialties. The Chico and Harpo solos were *both* embedded in the Napoleon scene. There was also a musical number, a lovely moon-in-June waltz entitled "Glimpses of the Moon," performed by Ruth Urban (as the Court Singer at Versailles) and the Melvin Sisters (as pages). In format, we're really not far from *The Twentieth Century Revue*, with the Napoleon scene serving as the Marx tabloid at the end of the bill.

Placing the Marx Brothers in this historical setting is the master stroke. It gives them a higher level of refinement and formality to play against, and it seems to parallel the Brothers' ascent from vaudeville to Broadway. No more schoolroom shenanigans or roughhouse antics on the Cunard docks—now we're going to be *Napoleon*, and watch what a mess we make of *that*.

The scene turns Groucho, for the first time, into an icon. Groucho as Napoleon was *not* Julius H. Marx playing a comedic version of the actual Napoleon. There was no attempt at a French characterization, or *any* characterization other than *Groucho*, the man we've been watching all night. This is the way he'd play *any* role—Caesar, Romeo, Oedipus. Napoleon isn't a character he's playing, just a situation in which his usual character finds himself, for no reason at all. So although this Napoleon may babble urgently about defeating his historical enemies ("I'm off to make Russia safe for French pastry"), he also cautions Josephine (Beauty) not to open sardines with his sword, because "my infantry is beginning to smell like the Lenox Avenue local." This coupling of old European gentility with twentieth-century New York ethnic color would become a paradigm in American comedy. It was Groucho's particular gift to the constellation of comic geniuses around Sid Caesar, thirty years later.

Each Marx Brother is announced at court and gets his own entrance, much as he will in *Animal Crackers* a few years from now. Zeppo, Harpo, and Chico are Alphonse, Gaston, and François—*Alphonse and Gaston* being a then-popular comic strip about two Frenchmen (catchphrase: "After you, my dear Alphonse"), and *François* being French for Frenchman. Each enters on the pretext of being one of Napoleon's "trusted advisers," but each offers only the slightest glance toward the emperor before pouncing upon Josephine, who, it is painfully clear, is involved in romantic entanglements with all of them. So Groucho keeps making long speeches about the war and the Lenox Avenue local, exchanges romantic goodbyes with Josephine, and charges off to battle, setting off choruses of "Vive La France!" As soon as he's gone, one, two, or three of his brothers materialize from under the couch or behind the curtain, and woo Josephine in various ridiculous ways, until Groucho comes stomping back in with the announcement that he's forgotten his sword. The exits and entrances come faster and faster, and the verbal humor builds and builds until the very notion of meaningful speech is left gasping for air. Groucho goes from almost catching Josephine to deliberately *refusing* to catch her, despite the fact that she is plainly sitting on Harpo's lap.

When the jig is up, Groucho sprinkles snuff everywhere, which draws his brothers, in sneezing fits, from the recesses of the room, Harpo perfectly happy in a gas mask. A later version of the scene, probably dating from the 1931 "Schweinerei" tour, provides an ending in which Alphonse, Gaston, and François are sent to be executed, but Gaston outsmarts the royal guard. The typescript has another ending, which was used throughout the *I'll Say She Is* tour, and on Broadway. Groucho, having exposed Josephine's infidelities, snarls, "You minx-eyed wastrel! You titian-haired traitor! Do you know what I'm going to do to you now?" Josephine is terrified: "You're not going to kill me!" Groucho, calmly: "Kill you? I should say not. I'm going to sell the couch." Whereupon the others start yelling, "Oh, no! Please don't sell the couch!" as the curtain falls.

THE NAPOLEON SCENE was such a success that Napoleon was assimilated into Groucho's public persona. He's one of twenty popular comedians and humorists caricatured on Ralph Barton's "Meet the Editors"

The Marx Brothers and Lotta Miles perform the Napoleon scene on Broadway

cover for *Judge* magazine, February 21, 1925—and he's pictured in his Napoleon costume. (Harpo is there, too, in a modern shirt and tie.) Assigning the Groucho visage to historical figures or archetypes would remain an occasional Marx Brothers device, the most obvious example being the succession of iconic military uniforms he wears in *Duck Soup*. But this aspect of the Marx Brothers' image is dominant only in their Broadway period. The Napoleon scene was the clear template for the "Spanish Knights" scene in *The Cocoanuts* and the DuBarry scene in *Animal Crackers* (sadly not included in the film version). Neither quite matched the relentlessness or joke-density of the Napoleon scene. But there was a time when a big farcical set piece, with elaborate period costumes, was as expected of the Marx Brothers as the harp and piano solos. Early in 1928, it was reported that the Brothers had been offered a silent film parody of Napoleon's life story (though with *Harpo* in the central role). That film, of course, was never made. In the films they *did* make, opportunities were found to wear all kinds of costumes, but only one Marx Brothers movie is a true period piece: *Go West*, generally regarded as one of their weakest efforts.

The more lasting legacy of the Napoleon scene is the Brothers' gift for old-fashioned, precision-timed, exit-and-entrance farce. They worked together like clockwork, and any scene in which they dart in and out of rooms, avoiding each other, or hiding from someone, or trying to get something, or preventing someone from finding something, is always a highlight. The split-scene in two hotel rooms in *The Cocoanuts*, Groucho's stuff with Thelma Todd and Alky Briggs in *Monkey Business* (co-written by Johnstone), the scene in Thelma Todd's apartment in *Horse Feathers* (Johnstone again), all that scurrying around the mansion in *Duck Soup*, the scene with Henderson and the beds in *A Night at the Opera*, the Esther Muir seduction scene in *A Day at the Races*, the Lisette Verea seduction scene in *A Night in Casablanca*—these are all descendants of Napoleon.

But what the Napoleon scene most clearly prefigures is Groucho as Captain Spalding in *Animal Crackers*. Spalding plainly cannot be an African explorer (Simon Louvish writes that he "does not seem to have come from anywhere further than the Carnegie Deli"), just as the man who lopes in and out of Versailles here is plainly not Napoleon. This is the grandiose, literary Groucho, of long, wonderful speeches, rambling avalanches of jokes that keep coming until he leaves the room, only to reappear moments later, spouting another torrent of language.

> I lost my sword. I had a swell chance to shoot one of those Russians, too. It was right near the gates of Moscow. If I find my sword, I Moscow and get him. He promised to wait, but I'm getting disgusted with the whole war. If it rains tomorrow, I think I'll stay in bed. What are

your plans, babe? The only thing that keeps me going is your devotion. It keeps me going and it keeps me coming back. It's women like you that make men like me like women like you. I guess I said something that time. Jo, you're as true as a three-dollar cornet. And believe me, that's nothing to blow about, and if you don't like it, you can trumpet. Ah! There it is. I wish you wouldn't open sardines with my sword. Oh, no, we had that, didn't we? Well, looks like I'm off again. The Russians are in full retreat, and I'm right in front of them.

Groucho's facility with this kind of material is undoubtedly why the Kaufmans and Perelmans of the world rose so brilliantly to the challenge of writing scripts for the Marx Brothers. Joe Adamson notes that "even among Marx Brothers, and even as late as the Fifties, the sentiment was expressed that nothing they ever did could beat the fast and furious *I'll Say She Is* and that wonderful Napoleon scene." It's among the most important and influential comedy sketches in the history of showbiz.

AFTER THAT, THERE WAS really not much to do but let the band take over. Here's Nat Martin's Orchestra, playing a jazz set right there on stage in the middle of the show. The engagement worked out well for Martin's band, and led to regular radio and nightclub work in which they were billed as "Nat Martin and His *I'll Say She Is* Orchestra." During the run of the show, the band became a feature every Saturday night on WGBS radio.

The jazz set was followed by one more sequence, of which very little description survives. The playbill calls it "Beauty's Russian Garden," and I suppose it must have had some nominal connection to the gimme-a-thrill plotline, but who knows. Ruth Urban performed a song called

Nat Martin and his orchestra on the set of I'll Say She Is *at the Casino Theatre*

"The Wonderful River"; Hazel Gaudreau performed an unspecified specialty; Ledru Stiffler performed "The Blue Tartar" (in which he was painted blue, instead of gold—versatile fellow); and Marcella Hardie performed the "Marcella Dance." And that was "Beauty's Russian Garden." It was common for shows of the era to conclude with an extra, unimportant sequence, which the critics could safely miss while running out to file their reviews. The typescript gives us a final exchange among Beauty and her suitors, in which she declares that "the greatest thrill in life is the thrill of love!" Everyone shouts, "That's me!" Beauty says, "No, that's the chief!" and everyone sings. The end!

VIII.
"A MASTERPIECE OF KNOCK 'EM DOWN AND DRAG 'EM OUT HUMOR"

Five of the "dangerously beautiful girls" in I'll Say She Is

IN PRESS NOTICES FOR *I'll Say She Is*, 1923-1925, there are occasional references to the show being "burlesque," or "a burlesque show," which are potentially confusing.

The Marx Brothers' revue contained no overt sexual content, nor nudity,

139

nor anything that could be called striptease. (Its only remotely strip-like number was the Apache, with Harry Walters relieving Cecile D'Andrea of much of her clothing.) Nevertheless, *Variety* called *I'll Say She Is* on tour "frank burlesque, but good burlesque," and on Broadway, "the best burlesque show (extravaganza, if you wish) of the season." One critic chortled, "Regular burlesque stuff! The difference is that the scenery and costumes cost a great deal of money and the girls are beautiful." Another considered *I'll Say She Is* "as good a burlesque as ever turned a wheel"; yet another called it "a girlesque tutti frutti" but hastened to note that "there is nothing risqué in the piece...If there is comedy evident, it never degenerates; if burlesque, it never slapsticks."

As with the *Follies*, and all musical theatre of the time, *I'll Say She Is* featured its chorus girls prominently, and female pulchritude was among its selling points. Advertisements for the show touted its "dangerously beautiful girls," with one ad even asserting that these girls were "vibrating with the pure joy of life." Arthur Pollock, the theatre critic for the *Brooklyn Eagle*, acknowledged that "perhaps it isn't fair to brand *I'll Say She Is* a burlesque show...but the moment the curtain rises and a group of chorus ladies dash on and let loose their voices and their legs *I'll Say She Is* defines itself."

But in fact, the work done by burlesque dancers and Broadway chorus girls was not all that similar. Perhaps some critics, after noticing the abbreviated costumes of both types of performers, were unable to think clearly. Generally, the burlesque performance is a display of individual virtuosity, with the emphasis on the style and personality of the performer. The chorus girl is just the opposite. Her role is to blend in with the rest of the chorus, operating as a seamless, synchronized unit.

Chorus girls were essentially athletes. One member of the *I'll Say She Is* ensemble, Mary Carney, gave the *Herald Tribune* a piece of her mind on this subject:

> Let me give you some idea of what is required
> of chorus girls. Every day, during rehearsals,

they are on their feet between 10 a.m. and 1:30 p.m., between 2 and 5 p.m. and between 8 and 11 p.m., and sometimes later. The steps that seem trivial from the front, and that look easy, are so full of aches and pains that the audience can't half appreciate the persistency and endurance they call for. It makes no difference how many charming little ways the chorus girl off the stage may have, when she is on it she must raise her hand, or her toe, or wink her eye just exactly the same way and at the same moment as the girls to her left and right do it. That means work—real, downright hard work, nerve-exhausting work . . . I wonder how many girls in everyday life would be willing to undergo such strenuous labor to win a place in the chorus of a musical comedy revue.

The mania for precision is consistent with Ziegfeld's famous specifications for his Girls, who had to be a certain height, weight, type, and bearing, with every movement predetermined. Through this meticulous austerity, producers like Ziegfeld gave "sophisticated" audiences, who would never dream of attending a burlesque show, permission to ogle half-dressed young women. The experience was safe, because it was depersonalized. It was art, not sex. In burlesque, where there was no need to be safe, performers *wanted* to create a personal experience, by exuding as much distinctive personality as possible. Chorus girls exuded a *collective* personality, a social type, closely aligned (and often overlapping) with that other archetype of young womanhood in the Jazz Age, the flapper.

Chorus girls could be discussed and analyzed as a social phenomenon, a way of talking about sex without really talking about sex. Around the time of *I'll Say She Is*, a catalogue of chorus girl lingo was compiled by none other than Groucho Marx, penning a guest column for one of the New York dailies. In his long experience with chorus girls, Groucho had noted such expressions as "I'll tell the world," "You said it," "Ain't it the truth?," "Butter and egg man," "I got what it takes," "It's all apple sauce," "Ain't you the one dearie?," "Red hot mama," "Sugar papa," "Sweet daddy," "Runnin' wild," "I'm a wow," and "Hot patootie." Groucho assured his readers that "if you learn all these and routine them so that they seem spontaneous, you can't miss. Your telephone bell will ring incessantly. Your room will be a bower of flowers. You will be submerged in chicken a la king and all the girls will be calling you Big Boy, Hey Hey."

Burlesque, in its original meaning, referred to low comedy with elements of parody. This is a reasonably accurate (if incomplete) description of the Marx Brothers, and part of the confusion around the word is in distinguishing between this usage (still common in the twenties) and others.

The Napoleon scene was sometimes described as "a burlesque of Napoleon." Another example of this usage can be found in the notebooks of Mark Twain, who envisioned a version of *Hamlet* in which "a burlesque character" (a modern male wit) wanders through Shakespeare's play making satirical comments. Charlie Chaplin, in 1915, made a two-reeler entitled *A Burlesque on Carmen*, a straightforward parody of the Bizet opera. And even closer to home, in their reviews of *The Cocoanuts* on Broadway, both the *Times* and the *Sun* described "The Tale of the Shirt" as "a burlesque"—also, as it happens, of *Carmen*.

In the early twentieth century, vaudeville emerged as a "clean" alternative to rougher saloon or music hall entertainment. In music halls, the entertainment was an excuse for prodigious alcohol consumption. Women and children were not admitted. Unwelcome on the family-friendly vaudeville stage, this form evolved into American burlesque. It developed in parallel with vaudeville, in its own venues, on its own circuits, or wheels. By the thirties, striptease had become a principal element, though still not *the* principal element; strippers shared the bill with comedians, musical performers, and novelty acts. It borrowed its format from minstrel shows, and mocked the refinements of more sophisticated forms. If vaudeville was a populist alternative to the legitimate stage, burlesque was inescapably, defiantly, low-class. Several important twentieth-century comedians began in burlesque, but in general, they would have preferred to work in vaudeville, films, or on the legitimate stage, and if they were able to make the transition, they did.

The more satirical and suggestive mainstream entertainment became, the less excuse burlesque had for existing. Striptease became the main attraction because it wasn't being done elsewhere. Mayor Fiorello La Guardia, in a rampaging decency campaign, effectively criminalized striptease, and burlesque was pushed into the shadows. When it finally returned to some prominence, in the 1960s, it had forsaken variety entertainment altogether, and it was all striptease and go-go dancing. This strain of burlesque, often spelled *burlesk*, became a prime component of the derelict 42nd Street of the seventies and eighties. After *that* died off, the term was claimed by the neo-burlesque movement, which originated in New York in the 1990s and spread to other cities. The contemporary burlesque scene treats striptease as an art form, often couched in the language of empowerment and self-expression.

When *I'll Say She Is* was referred to as a burlesque show in the twenties, it was *derogatory*, or at least condescending. To call a Broadway revue "the best burlesque show of the season" was like calling a fancy restaurant "the best hot dog stand in town."

The Marx Brothers never worked in burlesque, because they didn't want to and never had to. Even Chico, in his late-career doldrums, never resorted to it (though he and Harpo had both played piano in brothels in the very early days). It's impossible to imagine Groucho, with his somewhat Victorian morals and stated disdain for "dirty entertainment," sharing a stage with strippers and blue comics. (*Variety*'s Sime Silverman once wrote, "It's a rarity in the show business for an ad-libber to be clean—the easy incentive to an extra laugh is ever a cursing temptation; but Groucho never wavers." The same notice concludes that "laughs on Broadway are much more substantial than naked women.")

Another reason why the Marx Brothers never went near burlesque in their early vaudeville years is that they were underage, and their mother was intimately involved with their act. There may be some similarities between Minnie Marx and Mama Rose, but this is not one of them.

IT WAS MINNIE MARX who gave the most dramatic performance on opening night of *I'll Say She Is* on Broadway. The sainted matriarch had been standing on a chair that afternoon, having her dress fitted, when she fell and broke her ankle. So she was carried into the theatre and placed in the box beside Frenchie.

In the vaudeville days, Frenchie had sometimes functioned as a laugh-starter for his sons. He would sit in the audience and laugh loudly and generously at *everything*, with the hope that his laughter would prove infectious. But the night *I'll Say She Is* opened on Broadway, half the audience was laugh-starters. For there were, in 1924, avid, obsessive, die-hard Marx Brothers fans. The journey from the small time to the big time was as real for them as for the Brothers. The Marxists in attendance at the Casino Theatre on May 19, 1924 were like people who'd seen the Beatles at the Cavern in Liverpool, and were now in the crowd at Shea Stadium. They were hysterical. Bursts of applause and cheers greeted all the familiar vaudeville material, like the Theatrical Agency sketch, and the knife-dropping routine. The Napoleon scene absolutely knocked everyone out, leaving a wreckage of an audience gasping in the aisles, faces frozen in ecstasy. There was nothing left to do but hear Nat Martin's band play us off to dreamland. (Unless we're staying for "Beauty's Russian Garden.")

"After the show," wrote Will Johnstone in his diary, "all back stage to congratulate the Marx boys. Their mother had tears of joy in her eyes." Will and Helen accompanied "Julie Marx" and his entourage to a hotel restaurant to drink sodas and read telegrams. "I got one from the *Uncle Tom's Cabin* cast," Will wrote. "Fine. Then to hotel tired but happy." It was typical of Groucho to spend the post-show hours socializing not with the cast but with the writers. (He and Will would remain friendly throughout the twenties, and beyond. It would be at Groucho's request that Will would go west to work on *Monkey Business* in 1931, and their association would continue well into the Hollywood years.)

MIRIAM MARY.
HOLLYWOOD, CAL
Will B. Johnstone
May 23rd 1931

Groucho's daughter Miriam at four. Drawing by Will B. Johnstone, 1931.

Broadway riffraff. Note Harpo's smoke-bubble trick, seen later in Animal Crackers *and elsewhere.*

As Harpo remembered it, he left the theatre after the show and headed home to Long Island, where Minnie and Frenchie had taken a house. (The Marx parents themselves stayed in a hotel in the city that night, due to Minnie's ankle.) The next morning, Harpo was awakened by a phone call from an unusually ebullient Groucho, who had seen the reviews: "They *loved* us. We're a hit!"

ALEXANDER WOOLLCOTT, *New York Sun*: As one of the many who laughed immodestly throughout the greater part of the first performance given by a new musical show, entitled, if memory serves, *I'll Say She Is*, it behooves your correspondent to report at once that that harlequinade has some of the most comical moments vouchsafed to the first nighters in a month of Mondays.

JOHN ANDERSON, *New York Evening Post*: The Marx brothers have left your correspondent too limp with laughter to do more than gasp incoherently at the moment.

BURNS MANTLE, *New York Daily News*: Something of a novelty for the Broadway revue crowd, this glorified Marx Brothers specialty. And sure to be much talked about.

GENE FOWLER, *New York Daily Mirror*: All Broadway track records of this year were shattered last night.

WOOLLCOTT: It is a bright colored and vehement setting for the goings on of those talented cutups, the Four Marx Brothers. In particular, it is a splendacious and reasonably tuneful excuse for going to see that silent brother, that shy, unexpected, magnificent comic among the Marxes, who is recorded somewhere on a birth certificate as Arthur, but who is known to the adoring two-a-day as Harpo Marx.

ANDERSON: His silence, if not dignifiedly golden, is hilariously gold-plated.

ROBERT BENCHLEY, *Life*: The pantomime of Mr. Arthur Marx…is 110 proof artistry. To watch him during the deluge of knives and forks from his coat-sleeve, or in the poker-game (where he wets one thumb and picks the card off with the other), or—oh, well, at any moment during the show, is to feel a glow at being alive in the same generation.

WOOLLCOTT: When by merely leaning against one's brother one can seem richly and irresistibly amusing why should one speak?

BENCHLEY: We will go before any court and swear that two of the four Marxes are two of the funniest men in the world.

ANDERSON: There is a grotesqueness about these fellows…

JOHN CORBIN, *New York Times*: There are four or five people in New York who rarely go to vaudeville and they all write reviews for newspapers and so the boys were discovered again. The next discovery, it is predicted, will be in the July issue of *The American Mercury*, to be followed by a piece in the December *Vanity Fair*.

GEORGE JEAN NATHAN, *The American Mercury*, July: They are gentlemen of infinite jest. And they turn what is intrinsically a ten-cent show into a masterpiece of knock 'em down and drag 'em out humor.

ALEXANDER WOOLLCOTT, *Vanity Fair*, December: The Broadway engagement began and it therefore became the thing to say, when you were

Harpo in 1924

running low of topics, "Well, I suppose you've seen the Marx Brothers."

ROBERT GARLAND, *Variety*: If the Marx Brothers don't watch out Gilbert Seldes will discover them. Then they'll get self-conscious and a little stale.

WOOLLCOTT, *Sun*: In fact, one hesitates to chant the praise of Harpo Marx only through a great fear of seeming too much like Gilbert Seldes, lifting a gracious lorgnette to gaze at the amusements of the poor.

GILBERT SELDES, *The New Republic*: The Marx Brothers, after years in vaudeville, have become the darlings of the local critics, but so far I have seen nothing in their praise which is excessive; they work well together…there is never any question that the three, together, constitute, as a French critic has said, one artist.

NATHAN: Arthur and Julius . . . are especially proficient in the art of falling down upon their so to speaks and kicking each other in the as it weres and will therefore doubtless soon be hailed by the Younger Generation as greater geniuses than Michelangelo and Beethoven.

BENCHLEY: We may be doing them a disservice by boiling over about them like this, but we can't help it if we feel it, can we? Certainly the nifties of Mr. Julius Marx will bear the most captious examination, and even if one in ten is found to be phony, the other nine are worth the slight wince involved at the bad one.

WOOLLCOTT: Julius H., who seems to be the oldest of this household, is a crafty comedian with a rather fresher and more whimsical assortment of quips than is the lot of most refugees from vaudeville.

CORBIN: This was in the course of a hilarious Napoleonic scene—there was, to be sure, no reason why it should have been Napoleonic, but it sufficed to keep the Marxes busy.

WOOLLCOTT: Leonard Marx is more or less suppressed until the property man remembers to leave a piano on the stage. As for Herbert Marx, he is probably the property man.

CHRISTIAN SCIENCE MONITOR: Anyone who has seen the Marx Brothers in vaudeville might ask what they do to be so amusing and it would be as difficult to answer that as to explain what the title, *I'll Say She Is*, has to do with what takes place on the stage of the Casino.

ANDERSON: The fraternal horseplay eludes the heavier touch of description.

CHRISTIAN SCIENCE MONITOR: About all that can be put into words is that here are four remarkably talented clowns who keep an audience in gales of laughter every minute they are on the stage. Their work is not an accident. It is not just talent alone, but talent plus most intelligent preparation.

STEPHEN RATHBUN, *New York Sun*: We had often seen the Marx Brothers in vaudeville, but we had felt always they were funnier than their material. In other words, their potentiality as funmakers waited for an 'open sesame.' They found their opportunity in *I'll Say She Is*, especially Julius.

WOOLLCOTT: The rest of the present extravaganza is much as usual, with the regular allotment of statues coming to life, lithe young gentlemen covered with gold or bluing, and a touching number called "Wall Street Blues," which is sung, for some reason, by a small, shrill young woman wearing blue sateen overalls. It is not known why. Nor greatly cared.

Alexander Woollcott

IT HURTS TO SEE Chico so blithely dismissed, right along with Zeppo. The critics, all through the Marxes' stage career, praised Leonard's piano turn, but rarely even mentioned his comedy or his character. It does seem that his character was less developed than Groucho's and Harpo's, into the twenties. It was Chico who benefited most from the more flamboyant writing the Marxes enjoyed after 1924.

Elsewhere in these pages, I claim much for Johnstone and Timberg that has often been credited to later Marx Brothers writers, particularly George S. Kaufman. Not that Kaufman's contributions weren't enormously important, and brilliant; of course they were. But because he happened to write *The*

Cocoanuts, which is commonly seen as the first "real" Marx Brothers show, he's thought to have invented a few things that were actually presented to him ready-made. This is particularly true of Groucho's character. Similarities between Groucho and Kaufman, in both appearance and manner, added to the confusion—as we shall soon see.

However, I think Kaufman *does* deserve considerable credit for the richness of Chico Marx's comedic character, as it lives on gloriously in the first six Marx Brothers films (and really changes into something different and much less funny thereafter). The pages left behind by Timberg and Johnstone give precious little for Leonard to work with—a few jokes and a chance to play the piano. As always, we can assume expansion in performance. We also know that Groucho was closer with the writers, and more meticulous about material. Read the surviving texts for *On the Mezzanine* and *I'll Say She Is*, and Groucho is *there*; his voice comes off the page. This is less true of Chico, whose role is barely even written in dialect.

Will B. Johnstone was a fine wordsmith, but he was not a virtuoso of puns, like some later Marx writers. To advanced punsters like Kaufman, Ruby, and Perelman, Chico's dialect was an inexhaustible toy. Because of his built-in grammatical quirks, and all the extra *a*-sounds, you could give him puns that would never work for Groucho. Chico's otherness gave him access to dimensions of absurdity Groucho couldn't grapple with—Chico alone can frustrate Groucho, and even outfox him. But these nuances were yet to come, and the Chico of *I'll Say She Is* was still just a charismatic dialect comedian with extraordinary keyboard skills. And—it is not said often enough—absolutely perfect comic timing. Chico Marx, the mathematician of the keyboard and the card table, had perhaps the best comic timing ever recorded. That it was on display in *I'll Say She Is* is easy to presume, even if the character it served was still nascent. Matthew Coniam has observed that Chico "seems to have wandered into the characterization for want of anything else to do, and then simply outlived it, so that by the end he was representative of no comic style other than his own." There is no doubt that he was a dynamic and hilarious presence.

For anyone who knows the Brothers' films, it's not surprising to find that Zeppo had an insignificant role in *I'll Say She Is*, was seen as an extraneous and undefined Marx Brother, and was often ignored or insulted by critics. It *is* surprising to discover the extent to which Harpo was *the* star at this point, as he was throughout much of their vaudeville career. Even critics who went out of their way to praise Groucho were *more* rhapsodic and superlative in their raves for Harpo. (Gilbert Seldes, for example, wrote that although "Groucho's style in the placing of his witty lines is probably unequaled for that sort of thing, there is little doubt that Harpo is the finest of the individual artists.")

It's often been theorized that Groucho's verbal wit made him a *competitor* in the eyes of the Algonquinites, while Harpo's otherworldly silence was something they had no stake in, and could fully celebrate. (It was Harpo, not Groucho, who became a regular at the Round Table, where his willingness to sit and listen was a rare and valuable commodity.) Connected to this explanation is another, which doesn't explain the opening-night reviews, but does help us understand Harpo's continued predominance throughout the Broadway years: Harpo was the particular favorite of New York's tastemakers because Harpo *socialized* with New York's tastemakers, to a much greater extent than his brothers did. Groucho was usually good for a wisecrack when the press called on him, but by nature he was still an introvert, and now he was a husband and father, too. Chico ran with another crowd entirely— gamblers and gangsters. It was Harpo who seemed most in tune with the zeitgeist, because he spent his free time palling around with the people who decided what the tune of the zeitgeist would be. We're so used to thinking of Groucho as the nominal superstar that it's disconcerting to read the *Post*'s review of the Broadway production of *Animal Crackers*, for example, which speaks reverently of Harpo but complains that "there is a little too much" of Groucho.

Jesters of the Jazz Age: Chico, Harpo, Groucho, and Zeppo

Another explanation is that Harpo was simply a more surprising and unusual performer than his younger brother. Broadway audiences were already well acquainted with fast-talking wiseguys. That Groucho was unique among them was less obvious than the fact that nothing like Harpo had ever been seen before. It's long been fashionable to place Harpo in the context of clown and pantomime traditions, and contemporary clowns and mimes are always quick to claim him as a spiritual ancestor. I suppose this is because like clowns and mimes, Harpo dresses funny (though not in the same way), and doesn't speak. I see no further connections. The word *pantomime* is naturally thrown around when describing a comedian who doesn't talk, but in truth, we've rarely seen Harpo do anything that could be accurately described as pantomime. Pantomime is about conjuring illusion. A mime makes you *think* it's windy, or that he's trapped in a box, by behaving as though this is the case. A mime may hand you a flower, but there's no flower there. The emphasis is on the skills of the performer. He makes you believe things that aren't true. Harpo is just the opposite. With him, the gag would be that his coat contains an unlimited supply of *actual* flowers. Harpo makes you believe that what's obviously the case could not possibly be true. His performances, except when he plays the harp, are not showcases for his skills, but for his ideas, his urges.

I don't think Harpo is properly described as a "silent comedian," though silent comedy fans often include him in the ranks among Chaplin, Keaton, et al. Again, it strikes me as an overemphasis on his lack of speech. Imagine for a moment that Harpo *did* speak, that his familiar routines were punctuated with spoken language. I'm not saying this would have been *good*, but imagine it—and *now* does he remind you in any way of Chaplin or Keaton? No, it's an entirely different kind of character, and an entirely different kind of technique. The great silent comedians were silent because they were working in a medium that could not accommodate recorded sound. Harpo may have been a *non-speaking* comedian, but still, most of his comedy was about language. In *Animal Crackers*, when Chico asks him for "the flash" (flashlight), and Harpo obligingly produces from his coat a fish, a flute, a can of Flit, and so forth, he is being a brilliant *verbal* comedian. It's just that his assault on language doesn't happen to involve speaking it. In *Horse Feathers*, when he tries to enter a speakeasy and is asked for the password, he knows it's *swordfish*, but he doesn't pantomime fencing and swimming, the way a clown or a mime would. He pulls a giant fish out of his coat, along with a sword, and plunges the sword into the fish. This may be a sight gag, but that doesn't make it silent comedy.

This, in my opinion, is the most convincing explanation for the spotlight's shift from Harpo to Groucho. On Broadway in 1924, Harpo seemed the most novel of the Marx Brothers, the most fantastic and unusual. When they started making movies, the brand-new, red-hot phenomenon of synchronized speech made Groucho's gift a much greater novelty. Harpo could only be a secondary attraction in a film whose audience was motivated principally by the vogue for talkies. And after *Cocoanuts* came the stock market crash, and attendant changes in the tone of popular entertainment. Groucho's comedy would fully blossom against the gloom and cynicism of the Depression. Harpo, perhaps, had seemed freshest and most relevant in the giddy Jazz Age.

NOW THEY HAD THE big hit they'd wanted. They had topped their Philadelphia success—and in *their* city, in *the* city. They were Broadway stars, rich and happy. They bought a nice house for Minnie and Frenchie in Richmond Hill, Queens. Minnie decided to spend her retirement being a carbonated beverage mogul, and though she fell short of that, she did successfully manufacture, market, and sell bottles of ginger ale branded with the likenesses of her famous family. She continued to participate in the success of her sons, and received even better press than they did. ("Mrs. Marx is the sort of mother that every child would choose if he had a chance to choose at all. She is handsome and brilliant, with the heart of a girl and the wisdom of Solomon." —*Herald Tribune.*) Chico, with his wife Betty and daughter Maxine, also took a house in Richmond Hill. Harpo and Groucho moved to fashionable residential sections of Manhattan—Harpo to an Upper West Side bachelor pad, Groucho with his family to Washington Heights. *I'll Say She Is* settled in for a nice long run at the Casino, and its stars went urgently about the business of indulging their own every whim.

When he first met Alexander Woollcott, backstage at the Casino, Harpo was wary. He was willing to humor an important New York critic, but "then I'd go over to Lindy's and relax," he later wrote, "where nobody ever used words like 'behooves' and 'splendacious' and 'presumptuous.'" But, after an invitation to a poker game with Woollcott's Thanatopsis Literary and Inside Straight Club, Harpo acclimated to the company. "If I had known…that I'd been lured into a den of intellectuals," he recalled, "I would have scrammed out of the joint and run all the way to Lindy's, where my empty seat was still waiting for me."

Soon, though, Harpo was palling around with the literary set almost exclusively. He was either convinced or amused (or both) by their insistence that he was a great artist. A harp recital at Town Hall was announced, probably conceived by Woollcott, who was full of plans for Harpo to do Shakespeare or dance ballet. When Heywood Broun finally saw *I'll Say She Is*, six months after it opened, he lamented that the show "calls on [Harpo] for no more than broad strokes. There is pathos in him and I think it should be brought out more fully if only to savor the fun." The intelligentsia's high regard for Harpo went far enough for an item in the *Sun* to state that Harpo had written the Napoleon scene! Will B. Johnstone sent in a correction: "Since the Napoleonic scene is generally credited with putting the Marx Brothers where they are—on Broadway—it is a great pleasure for me to take an assist in their success and admit that I evolved the Napoleonic scene, which the boys embellished, naturally." The *Post* observed that Harpo "seems to have been accepted in some quarters as the brains of the band," and even that "the other three quarters resent it. They insist that they collectively are the brains of the Marx brothers and have given up cross-word puzzles to read bigger and better literature."

In that lofty spirit, the boys subscribed to the Theatre Guild, donating $100 each toward the construction of the new Guild Theatre on 52nd Street. Harpo, playing his new role for all it was worth, bought two tickets to the first Thursday matinee of every Guild production for the rest of the season. "Now that our most formidable competitors are bondholders in our new theatre," said Guild director Theresa Helburn, "we have nothing to fear." The Brothers posed with Lynn Fontanne for the *New York Times*, and proposed an exchange program between *I'll Say She Is* and *The Guardsman*. Harpo and Alfred Lunt, it was suggested, could switch roles.

Everyone in town with a boldface name wanted to be seen in the company of the Marx Brothers. Mary Pickford and Douglas Fairbanks came to the show and laughed conspicuously throughout the performance. Anne Nichols, author of *Abie's Irish Rose*, had a note passed to the Marxes at intermission, saying she was "enjoying your performance immensely." Nellie Revell, the celebrated actress, writer, and pioneering feminist, had suffered a debilitating spinal injury in 1919; she was now confined to a wheelchair, and had become one of America's most beloved newspaper columnists. She attended *I'll Say She Is* and laughed uproariously when Groucho announced how happy he was that there was at least one person in the audience who couldn't walk out in the middle of the show. After the performance, the Brothers threw a "box party" for Ms. Revell at the theatre. She sang their praises in her column, and told her readers: "I can remember when the four boys first went into vaudeville and it is still a bright spot in my memory to recall how devoted they were to their mother and how enwrapped she was in them."

The Marx Brothers were everywhere, and the city and its press ate up their antics like beggars at a banquet. When the Brothers were frustrated by

All right, now, boys—one serious one...

New York's ever-changing traffic regulations, they decided to avoid parking tickets by roller-skating to the Casino. This caused a sensation on Broadway and in the tabloids. "They went down Broadway," said one account, "dodging automobiles, and shooting around street cars, but obeying all traffic signals and traffic cops." Another reporter added that the boys "had sea or skate-legs during the entire matinee." Then there was the time the Brothers asked Eddie Cantor for four tickets to *Kid Boots*. Cantor was thrilled to give them box seats. That night, Cantor stepped out onstage, looked up at the box, and saw four strange men with full, black beards down to their waists. In June, Beury and the boys announced a "thrill contest," urging audience members to submit essays describing "in not more than 500 words, the most thrilling

...and one funny one.

adventure that one can possibly engage in within the city limits of New York."

The ink-stained wretches of the New York press were apparently ecstatic just to have these guys to write about, these vibrant, hilarious guys whose every remark was quotable, whose every activity was a prank. Like most stage people, the Marxes liked and identified with newspapermen, with whom they formed symbiotic relationships. *I'll Say She Is* was written by newspapermen, and its unofficial first preview audience was the gang at the paper in Allentown. In July, the Brothers demonstrated their affection for the press by appearing in a one-night extravaganza called *The Greatest Show in the World*, organized by the Newspaper Club. The show took place at the Club's headquarters, in a makeshift theatre erected specifically for the occasion by Florenz Ziegfeld. In addition to the Marx Brothers, the all-star bill included Eddie Cantor, Hazel Dawn, Vincent Lopez and his orchestra, Ann Pennington, Will Rogers, and Fred and Dorothy Stone. The Marxes were rewarded with more column inches and more quotable raves.

A certain amount of what was written about them must be taken with a grain of salt, attributed to the imaginations of press agents and journalists. But I am unwilling to doubt that when the *Post*'s theatre columnist went backstage at the Casino and remarked, "This stage isn't as deep as it looks," Groucho shot back, "Neither is the show."

Much less characteristic than this was a long statement attributed to Chico, which ran in numerous papers, on the subject of stage comedy:

> The modern audience is fairly dying for a chance to laugh. All you've got to do is to screw up your face and the audience howls. The trouble these days is finding a space between the laughs to crack the jokes. Now, it was different in the olden days.
>
> Instead of being able to appear in clothes that might once have fitted a human being, and in one's natural complexion, a comedian had to wear clothes

which were supposed to be humorous and either burnt cork or a lavish coating of grease paint. He had to be able to sing, dance, say pieces, do sleight of hand, juggle, take tickets and play the bass drum. Nowadays we comedians come on in a dress suit, like a waiter, wear only a genial smile by way of make-up, and give vent to mild wheezes.

And whereas in the old days—the good old days you read about after you've starved through 'em—the chances were one in one hundred of getting a laugh; nowadays you can't get away from the laughs.

Perhaps the easy laughter Chico observed had less to do with changing times than with the Marxes' changing circumstances. Was "the modern audience" more inclined to laugh, or just more inclined to laugh *at the Marx Brothers*? These, for the first time in the boys' experience, were *Broadway* audiences, eager to display their own cleverness and good taste by laughing generously at the hottest, smartest comedy show in town. In the twenties, there was a high premium on fanciful wit. Columnist Westbrook Pegler called it "the era of wonderful nonsense," and the Marxes' nonsense was the most wonderful of all. As for the declining broadness of comedians' attire, it certainly didn't apply to Groucho or Harpo. But Chico was speaking accurately of himself. From *The Cocoanuts* forward he would wear a wig, and beginning with *Animal Crackers* he added the distinctive hat and corduroy jacket we associate with him, but in *I'll Say She Is* he really was just himself, in a suit.

The Marx Brothers' physical appearances contributed to their fame. They were irresistible subjects for caricaturists, and most New York papers had theatrical caricaturists on staff. Drawings of the Marx Brothers were more ubiquitous than photos of them. John Decker, who published many drawings of the boys in 1924 and beyond, insisted that in their case, the word *caricature* did not apply. "They're such living caricatures themselves," Decker explained, "that all I had to do was draw them from life."

THE BROTHERS HAD WON over New York; they had even won over Percy Hammond. In their Chicago days, Hammond had dismissed the act as "an elaborate disorder of amateur antics said to have been a riot in lesser vaudeville." Now he was a fan and a friend, quoting them in his *Herald Tribune* column ("Oddments and Remainders") and generally associating himself with their acceptance by the city's elite. Hammond sounded proud and not a little bemused when he reported, "Harpo and Julius were to be seen on Tuesday night surrounded by a crowd of eminent New Yorkers outside the stage door of their headquarters, the Casino Theatre," with "many celebrities… clustered about the [Marxes] in attitudes of intimacy." Hammond noted the presence of Alexander Woollcott and Robert Benchley ("calling the Marxes by their first names"), Kelcey Allen, Heywood Broun, Arthur Krock, Dorothy Parker, George S. Kaufman, Marc Connelly, Buggs Baer, Harriette Underhill, Ruth Hale, John Peter Toohey, Beatrice Wilson, and Franklin P. Adams.

In light of the Marxes' career subsequent to *I'll Say She Is*, it's especially significant that George S. Kaufman entered their orbit at this point. Hammond seemed to be pushing them together, by setting up a playful public quarrel. It began with Hammond musing that "Kaufmann [sic]" bore a strong resemblance to "Julius H. Marx, the least beautiful of the Marx Brothers." Shortly thereafter, Hammond received "a sullen communication" from the great playwright:

> Sir, one of our elevator men has called my attention to your article in the *Herald* or *Tribune* or something, in which you declare that Mr. Julius H. Marx, appearing in *I'll Say She Is*, looks like me, and in which you go even further and spell my name with two n's. Now, Mr. Hammond, I happened to be present also at the opening of *I'll Say She Is*, and I want to say that if you think Mr. Marx looks like me then you are even crazier than I have always thought, and I would not like to have my good opinion of you disproved. In the first place, Mr. Marx

is just a wee bit terrible looking, and I have had some very favorable comments on my looks from time to time, not even counting those from people who it turned out afterward were speaking of Mr. S. Jay Kaufman. Also, Mr. Marx wears a black mustache, and you can appoint one person and I will appoint one and together they will pick a third impartial one, and they can search high and low on me without finding a mustache of any color, far less black.

Kaufman went on to suggest that if Hammond was "in any doubt" about "how my name is spelled," he could have gone over to the Winter Garden, "where it is in letters three feet high outside of the building," whereas "your name is not up there at all, Mr. Hammonnnd."

Groucho wrote in next: "I am not sure whether [Kaufman] has a moustache or not, although some authors find it advisable to wear something on the opening night." Another writer chimed in with the argument that Groucho *didn't* look like Kaufman, but rather like the director Frank Tuttle, who did indeed sport glasses, a black moustache, and an air of Grouchocity. "Julius denies that he is copying Frank," reported this conspiracy theorist, "but no one is going to believe that such a startling similarity could be an accident."

Hammond, allowing that "the alleged twin-like resemblance" between Groucho and Kaufman "may seem to be of little public consequence," returned with testimony from Groucho:

> Came a day last week when I met Mr. Kaufman, my image, my counterpart, and I realized with a shudder that there was a resemblance. Not that I looked like him, but he did look a bit like me. He had the same ripe lips and creamy complexion, topped off with tortoise shell glasses and sloping dome, and in a pinch he could pass for me.
>
> What could we do? One face like ours was enough to burden an unhappy world and two would be intolerable. So

we decided to amalgamate our faces and combine and retain the best features of both. We will never be able to launch a thousand ships, but with our merged face we should be able to send one rowboat sliding down the greased ways.

Finally, Karl K. Kitchen of the *World* wrote to assure Hammond that he was onto something. "I was struck with the resemblance the first time I saw the show," Kitchen claimed, "and two succeeding visits served to strengthen the impression. I don't know who is to be complimented by this resemblance—personally I think they ought to pay each other $500." Then Kitchen came out and said it: "Anyway, Julius Marx's material is funny enough to have been written by Kaufman." Not a bad idea.

George S. Kaufman

The Marxes' fiercest advocate in the press was Woollcott, whose own public began chiding him for it. "How much do the Marx Brothers pay you for being their press agent?" one Woollcott reader asked. In his own column, F.P.A. wrote that Woollcott "goes to see *I'll Say She Is* so often that he is becoming known as an expert Marxman." There was no stopping Aleck. In September, he shared with his readers "a terrible nightmare" he had had, in which he "went to see *I'll Say She Is* at the Casino on a night when understudies were taking the places of the Brothers Marx." In October, he reported that he had seen the show five times. In addition to the usual burbling over Harpo, Woollcott spilled some ink in honor of "how fluent and fresh is the humor of Julius Marx, who rewrites his part every night and is as essentially a column conductor as Master Will Rogers." As the months rolled by, Woollcott would get around to praising Chico once in a while. In December, he was even charitable enough to suggest that Zeppo was "like the House of Lords in that he does nothing in particular and does it very well." But despite his love for the Marxes, Woollcott still despised the rest of the show. "One of the several reasons why the Marx Brothers are to be envied," he wrote, "is the fact that they are the only New York family that has never seen the parts of it which they are not in."

Woollcott did have nice things to say about "the abundant Lotta Miles," awarding her "the first prize for cooperation and good sportsmanship" for cheerful, tireless service while "the hilarious brothers have cavorted and gamboled around her." Woollcott revealed that "Miss Miles's real name is as German as that of Frau Schirmer," but that didn't stop the *Sun* from printing erroneous and conflicting items about her name, all through the season, always purporting to set the record straight and usually insisting that her real name was Lotta and she shortened it to Carlotta, or something.

When a newsman came to the Casino to interview the ingénue, the doorman told him, "We have orders to overpower any reporter who comes here to interview Miss Miles and hold him until she sees him, and also the Marx Brothers, all four." Somehow, the fellow avoided this, and found himself in *Carlotta*'s dressing room. "She is what you might call a big peach, to differentiate from the type of girls known as little peaches," he condescendingly reported. "She is a mild, good natured sort of girl, placid and hard to disturb. She sat on a box in her little dressing room, gave up the only chair to the visitor and waited for the agony."

"Why did you change your name?"

"Because people seemed to think it was a joke and kept insinuating that I walked a lot o' miles before I got this job."

"Did you?"

"I should say not. I've only been in the show business about three years and I've been with a success every time…"

"Do you really come from Buffalo?"

"Why not? Grover Cleveland did."

"Do you like being an actress?"

"Pretty good. It's hard work."

"Got any good pictures?"

"A few. Take your pick."

"I don't see any of them in the costumes they are arresting managers for."

"You won't. I'm an actress, not an artist's model. A girl who can't get a job on the stage without posing in the altogether ought to go in for some other employment."

"How can I get out without seeing the Marx Brothers?"

"You'd better go down this fire escape."

During the show's run at the Casino, Miss Miles finalized her divorce from Raymond Anthony Court. She and her attorney, George Mattuck, produced witnesses who testified to Court's infidelity. (He was seen "in company with a 'beautiful young blonde' in an apartment at 666 Lexington

"The abundant Lotta Miles" (Florence Reutti) in 1924

Ave.," reported the *Eagle*, under the headline "BROADWAY STAR ACCUSES 'BLONDE' IN DIVORCE SUIT.") She declined alimony, telling the judge she had already received an unspecified settlement. Shortly thereafter, her sister Henrietta married Henry J. Flohr, in Manhattan. Lotta attended the wedding with two Marx Brothers as her dates.

The boys' desire to conquer new frontiers didn't stay pacified for long, and they were able to use their newfound money and freedom to try different things. As long as they reported to the Casino Theatre a few minutes before curtain eight times a week, they could do whatever amused them. Talk of a film career resumed, and although they wouldn't really have one until sound came to motion pictures five years later, there were baby steps toward the camera. Harpo and Zeppo both took bit parts in silent films, and there was talk of Will B. Johnstone writing scenarios for a series of silent Marx Brothers two-reelers. Mostly, the movies would have to wait. But in July of 1924, the four Marxes did work in a medium that was almost new to them, when they performed excerpts from *I'll Say She Is* on New York's WHN radio. (Let us pause for a moment to weep desperately in the absence of a recording.) Meanwhile, Groucho, always wrongly seeing himself as a businessman, decided to invest in real estate. In July, he bought twenty-four shorefront

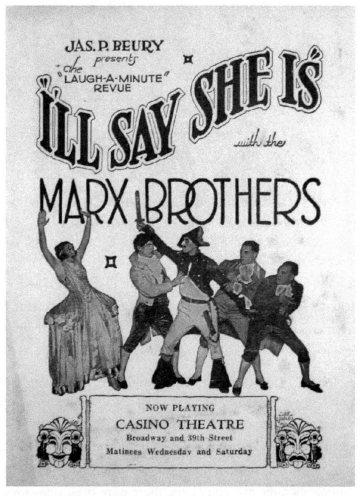

The toast of Broadway

bungalows in Far Rockaway, rented them out, and enjoyed playing landlord for about five minutes before the demands and hassles made him sick with worry. Nevertheless, the Brothers were soon looking to hire a construction company to build them their own 3,000-seat theatre—one of many interesting Marx projects that never materialized.

FIVE WEEKS AFTER the Broadway opening of *I'll Say She Is*, the 1924 Democratic National Convention began at Madison Square Garden. It was a famously contentious convention, the longest in American history, taking a record 103 ballots to nominate a presidential candidate. (John W. Davis lost the general election to the incumbent, Calvin Coolidge, who had succeeded to the Presidency after Harding's death in 1923.) The 1924 convention was also notorious for the presence of the Ku Klux Klan, whose supporters narrowly defeated a measure to condemn the Klan in the Democratic Party's official platform. The hundreds of Klansmen in town for the convention celebrated their victory with a massive rally in New Jersey, known as the Klanbake, which received national attention and squashed any hope for Davis's election.

In the *American Mercury*, George Jean Nathan observed that "the sole concern of the theatrical managers at the present time is the devising of art exhibits that shall meet the taste of the Democratic master minds who are due shortly to flood New York with their supernatural wisdom and intelligence…Four such exhibits have been sent through their preliminary paces. Need I say that they are not Ibsen plays?" Nathan held that "the most amusing of the quartet is *I'll Say She Is*…[which] tops the list by virtue of the Four Marx Brothers," who "cavort with so rich a humor that nothing else matters."

One of Davis's primary opponents was William Gibbs McAdoo, Jr. of California. McAdoo had been Secretary of the Treasury under Woodrow Wilson, and he would later become a United States Senator. While in New York as a presidential candidate, McAdoo—perhaps having read his George

Jean Nathan—happened into the Casino and caught a performance of *I'll Say She Is*. Groucho marked the occasion with an ad lib. In the Theatrical Agency scene, as written, Groucho suggests that Harpo might be crazy, then says he knows how to find out: "Do you want to go on the stage?" Harpo nods. Groucho concludes: "Crazy." On the night the candidate attended, Groucho asked Harpo, "Do you think McAdoo will be nominated?" Harpo nodded. "Crazy." William Gibbs McAdoo, Jr. laughed and applauded along with the rest of the house.

The Marxes found, probably to their supreme delight or frustration, that people enjoyed being insulted by them. When Harpo attended a dinner party given by Jascha Heifetz during the run of *I'll Say She Is*, he heard the great violinist declare, "Since the age of seven I have supported my family by my playing—since the age of seven, mind you. How's that for independence?" Harpo thought it over and remarked, "For six years you were a parasite." Being the subject of a Marxian barb meant you were part of the fun; Dick Cavett would later point out that "an insult from Groucho was only an insult in quotes." The Brothers had a spirit of irony about them, giving audiences the option of laughing at the joke or at the fact that the joke is being made. There was always a lot going on, a true complexity, not of story or character, but of technique. "People do not care whether you are smart or stupid as long as you make them laugh," an unidentified Marx Brother told an interviewer, "and we try to do it both ways, and all kinds of possible ways." One critic sighed, "You can't stabilize these Marxes. They are too volatile and too swift to stand still. Somebody says they were a hit in variety. No wonder. They are variety itself."

What seized New York City in the summer and fall of 1924 was the same fever that had overtaken Philadelphia a year earlier. Life was simply a lot more fun when the Marx Brothers were around, and once exposed to them, you were addicted. ("They are such delightful companions," gushed *Theatre Magazine*, "that everyone in town is making a tremendous fuss over them.") The boys themselves were having fun—more than in many years, presumably, since they had achieved their long-cherished goal of Broadway stardom—and their condition was highly contagious. "All four of them have faith in *I'll Say She Is*, quite obviously," one of the opening-night notices said, "and seem to enjoy their work as much as does their audience."

Nevertheless, when asked to comment on their craft, the Brothers were likely to respond with gravely serious analysis. "Good comedy is not only amusing acting and talking," said Groucho. "It is the ability to keep and hold the attention of hundreds of people because they know that the next move or speech will be more amusing than the last, and the ability to make this true." They spoke not of inspiration or self-expression, but of a rigorous, near-scientific process. When asked to reveal the secret of their success, they replied, "No secret at all about that, we have a real show, not an experiment. We have worked over this show for a whole year, cutting out everything that did not go and putting in new stuff that did catch on instead. That takes time. This show was really built up by the great American public, tried and tested by them before we brought it here." Despite their personal disgust with the road, they would always regard their vaudeville crucible with the pride of battle-scarred veterans. They would never want to go through it again, but Groucho knew it was the only way:

> There is only one school for entertainers in the world, and that is vaudeville. The legitimate actor and the musical comedy actor never learn the secret of entertaining an audience like the vaudeville actor does. The reason is that the reaction of an audience in vaudeville is instant. They tell you as soon as you speak a line in vaudeville just how good you are or how bad you are, and if you are really good that is the only way you will ever come to know it, too, for the agent and the booking office will keep it a dark secret from you in all their conversation. They not only tell you instantly, but they keep on telling you all through your act, in a kind of free and unrestrained way that teaches you something about the reactions of an audience. That is what the legitimate actor misses. Sometimes he misses it

so badly that he even thinks he is good when he is rotten and he never really knows how he stands. There is a lot of hokum about audiences in Carnegie Hall, the Metropolitan Opera House and in legitimate theatres, but in vaudeville everything is on the dead level and you cannot get away with fake stuff a minute. I suppose that is the reason why all the comedians in musical shows these days, and most of the other principals come from vaudeville.

They took their work seriously, and they weren't the only ones. The *Post's* theatre columnist perceived "beautiful ambiguities" in Harpo's head-shaking bit: "When questioned on matters about which there ought not to be two opinions... Harpo manages to shake his head very adroitly in both directions at the same time. He nods 'yes' and the nod turns into a sort of outcurve meaning 'no.' He has invented a symbol for the unsettled brain-pan and caught the very gesture of human fallibility."

Those beautiful ambiguities of Harpo's made him the most rewarding Marx Brother to analyze and interpret. This is why everyone was so tickled over the notion of Harpo as an intellectual, and why that old line about him being "the brains of the band" mutated into a running gag that ran through the city's newspapers for many months. The *New York Review* quoted Harpo's straight-faced opinions on various books (Michael Arlen's *The Green Hat* was "glittering but a trifle ostentatious"), along with his explanation of why it sometimes took him a month to finish one: "I read...in my dressing room while waiting to appear on the stage...There is a great deal of noise going on and, incidentally, my three brothers, who are not studious like I am, interrupt and try to keep me from being the brains of the Four Marx Brothers." In another column, it was asserted that despite Harpo's many musical gifts and literary interests, "most of the time he indulges in no diversion except sitting alone in his study and thinking." A cartoon in the humor magazine *Judge* showed two sophisticates at a cocktail party, with one saying, "She's so dumb she thinks Groucho Marx wrote *Das Kapital*," and the other replying, "Fancy! And everybody knows Harpo is the clever one."

The brains of the Marx Brothers

Groucho, having had just about enough of this, fired off a series of arch complaints to Woollcott:

> First I was accused of looking like George S. Kaufman (a terrific burden for any one man to carry). After that I was branded as a Rockaway bungalow owner. And the crowning insult was when someone on *The Sun* staff wrote that Harpo Marx was the brains of the Marx family. To begin with, there is no brains in the Marx family, and to follow that up, if there was, it most certainly wouldn't be Harpo. I went to school with him, and I know. The year I graduated with high honors he was seriously thinking of marrying his teacher in

the kindergarten, as they had been together for six years.

Then Chico joined in, penning an "Off-Stage Views of Stage People" column for the *Evening World*, in which he proclaimed himself "the only one of the Four Marx Brothers now in *I'll Say She Is* that is handsome. Frankly, the others are so plain in appearance that I can hardly realize they are my brothers…I have the pulchritude. I mentioned that word to Brains Harpo and he thought it meant powdered sugar." Chico then quoted a mash note in which a female fan had supposedly dubbed him "the only flower in the Marx garden." "Just the other day," he added, "I was asked by a film producer if I had time to 'sub' for Valentino."

For the most part, Chico and Zeppo didn't court press attention the way their brothers did. ("Groucho and Harpo need the limelight," Chico once told his wife, Betty. "I just need the act to be good.") But the press did notice that Chico and Zeppo were "the family delegates to New York's night life." One night at the Rendezvous, the emcee began pointing out celebrities in the crowd, and imploring them to come forth and entertain. Some dancers declined, explaining that their skirts were too tight to perform their usual specialties. The emcee's attention then turned to Chico and Zeppo, and when he announced their presence, everyone in the club looked around to see where they were—including Chico and Zeppo, who got laughs by looking around for themselves. But Chico declined to play the piano, telling the emcee, "My pants are too tight."

Zeppo seemingly embraced his role as the Marx Brothers' kid brother. He was only twenty-three years old, and his primary interests were apparently girls and cars. In July, he wound up in traffic court, charged with speeding, and he said to the magistrate, "Your Honor, I'm guilty, but I'd like to have the case adjourned."

"If you're guilty," asked the magistrate, "then what's the idea of an adjournment?"

"Why, I want to hunt up mamma and get some dough," said Zeppo, and if we believe what we read in the *Evening World*, his request was granted.

Not long thereafter, Chico had his own brush with the law, also as the result of a traffic violation. "[Leonard] Marx was arrested Sunday," went the report, "when he told Patrolman Timothy O'Shea to perform some impossible act." Chico was taken to the West 47th Street police station, where, he said, "I got shoved into a room where the cops were holding a motion-picture show." The film was "evidently an educational subject used to show policemen just what and what not may be exhibited outside Earl Carroll's Theatre."

"It was great," Chico enthused. But when the officers in the room realized he wasn't one of them, he was taken to the West 30th Street station and put in the bullpen. This was apparently another great experience. "I got acquainted with a lot of Broadway Highwaymen," Chico raved, "fellows whose acquaintance will do me some good." Chico didn't have much trouble getting $500 for bail, and he was discharged by the magistrate after promising Patrolman O'Shea he would behave himself from now on. Before leaving the station, Chico paid the fines for four fellow prisoners charged with minor offenses.

While Chico and Zeppo were breaking the law, Groucho was fighting crime. One day he was crossing Broadway at 49th Street when he heard cries of, "Stop! Thief!" Groucho saw a man running out of Bert Satz's jewelry store, with a shouting clerk on his tail. Groucho and the clerk, Louis Allisberg, pursued the fleeing thief directly into the arms of a patrolman at Broadway and 50th; he had attempted to make off with a tray of necklaces valued at $42,000.

As for Will B. Johnstone, he now had a Broadway success far beyond *Take it from Me* and *Up in the Clouds*. Presumably, he was even more pleased than usual to play host to his cartoonist colleagues. On October 1, coinciding with an industry convention, "one hundred of America's most noted newspaper cartoonists" attended the evening performance, "occupying the entire upper tier of boxes." The pen-and-ink crowd, in addition to Johnstone himself, included Rube Goldberg, Harry Hershfield, Charles McManus, Windsor

McKay, Cliff Sterrett, Frederick Burr Opper, Rudolph Dirks, Harry Gershfield, and Fay King. In their honor, the Marx Brothers added a special scene to *I'll Say She Is*, in which the four of them stood at easels and faithfully drew some of their guests' creations: Sterrett's Polly and her Pals, Opper's Happy Hooligan, Dirks' Katzenjammer Kids, and Hershfield's Abie the Agent. The boys "revealed surprising talent as cartoonists," according to the *Bulletin*, and "were greeted with a round of applause both by the cartoonists and the rest of the audience." Following the performance, "the artists were the guests of the company at a party held on the stage."

I'll Say She Is was still playing to capacity houses in the fall, when the Brothers presented a gold watch to James Beury in commemoration of their 150th Broadway performance. (It was reported that they "spent several hours at Tiffany's" selecting a suitable timepiece.) The Marxes also bought gifts for themselves: four sealskin dressing gowns, so they could continue holding their intermission receptions outside the stage door when the weather turned cold. In the holiday spirit, Beury threw a lavish midnight supper at the Ritz Carlton for the entire cast, crew, and house staff. Ticket sales sagged slightly in December, then spiked for Christmas.

Old A.W. Bachelder, the company manager, marveled that in more than five hundred performances of *I'll Say She Is* (counting the road), not one cast member had missed a performance. But there was a close call one night when Chico failed to appear for his entrance in the courtroom scene. He had absent-mindedly gone out to move his car, thinking it was intermission. Groucho and Zeppo covered for him, improvising with Harpo an elaboration of the poker scene that threatened to go on forever, until Chico wandered back into the theatre, saw what was going on, went onstage, and took the scene from the top. This episode may have been on Harpo's mind a few weeks later, when an interviewer asked how he killed time during the parts of the show he wasn't in. Do you ever go across the street and get a drink? "Never," Harpo insisted. "We'd kill anyone who thought of trying that across-the-street stuff. Minutes fly at a time like that, and it's ten to one that the show sooner or later would be delayed. That's the unpardonable sin of stagedom."

I'*LL SAY SHE IS* had Broadway patrons rolling in the aisles through February 7, 1925. When the closing date was posted, a despondent tone crept into the coverage. *I'll Say She Is* at the Casino had been an epoch, a gleaming highlight in the life of everyone lucky enough to have been there, and nobody wanted it to end. The Marx Brothers had come to be regarded as a New York City landmark, like the Statue of Liberty, and when the *I'll Say She Is* scenery was carted from the Casino loading dock, it felt like the Lady was climbing down from her pedestal and swimming away. "The clowning antics of Harpo and Julius Marx and their two frères and confreres will be sadly missed," sighed the *Daily News*.

And then, two days later, they were back on the road again.

Their first out-of-town business, as Broadway stars, was to grant Boston one more chance to properly appreciate *I'll Say She Is*. This it did, with *Variety* reporting on March 4 that "the way in which this show has picked up money in the face of very stiff opposition is surprising local showmen ... [it] has clicked consistently since opening here." The *Boston Globe* considered the show much improved since its earlier stay, insisting that "there is not a dull moment in *I'll Say She Is*, for all such moments (and there were plenty of them when the show was here before) have been eliminated." Even the non-Marx elements were a hit; another Boston critic found the opium den scene "a realization of one's most extravagant dreams of what a layout ought to look like." When Coolidge was inaugurated on March 4, his speech was piped into the Majestic Theatre at the matinee, giving the Brothers, presumably, some new straight lines.

Also on March 4, the Richard Dix silent film *Too Many Kisses* opened, with Harpo in a small role which "more than eclipsed all Mr. Dix's heroics," according to the *New York Sun*. The film survives today, and Harpo's appearances in it constitute the earliest known film footage of any Marx Brother. A few weeks later, filmgoers received *A Kiss in the Dark* from Adolphe Menjou, with Zeppo in a small role.

Back in New York, everyone was feeling listless and bereft without their boys around. Needless to say, Woollcott took the Marxes' absence the hardest, writing mournfully in his column:

> *I'll Say She Is* left here for Boston some five or six weeks ago—fearfully revisiting a town where it had failed dismally on its way to New York. And, lo, the foolish Bostonians, with no minds of their own at all, have been flocking to it in such numbers that it is still there and prospering absurdly. The taciturn Marx, that silent old bookworm ... has just resumed communication with this department. On completing the fifth week of the Boston engagement he wired to your correspondent, in whose primitive life a telegram ... is still an event, [and who] tore open the envelope feverishly. The message read: 'ARRIVED SAFE,' Harpo Marx."

After seven smash weeks in Boston, the company moved on to shorter engagements in New Haven, Springfield, and Hartford. Their next stop, Chicago's Apollo Theatre, was intended to be a long stay, but business was slow. *Variety* clucked, "It looks as if they got in all they could on their first appearance." The show hung on for six sluggish weeks, closing on May 30. This Chicago booking was brightened by a visit from Woollcott, who reported to his readers on "a violent scene of internecine strife" backstage at *I'll Say She Is*. Harpo and Chico, according to Woollcott, had just read *The Constant Nymph*, Margaret Kennedy's new romance novel. Harpo was "planning in consequence to drop Heywood Broun socially," because "Broun had said it was the best novel he had read in ten years and Harpo knew that within ten years Broun had read a much better one." But apparently Chico liked it.

By the time Woollcott called upon the Brothers in Chicago, their connection to the Algonquin set was part of their mystique. Groucho had contributed short pieces to several of their columns, and some light verse to *Variety*. Now he was invited to appear in more prestigious print—though its full measure of prestige wouldn't be clear right away. One of Harpo's Round Table comrades was Harold Ross, a lanky tower of a Westerner with a vertical wall of hair, who was famously described by Woollcott as resembling "a dishonest Abe Lincoln." Ross and his wife, Jane Grant, had been nurturing their dream to publish a weekly magazine about New York

Harold Ross

culture, and they were trying to get the whole Table on board. This journal would be aimed at their own crowd of sophisticates, as opposed to "the old lady in Dubuque," whom Ross presumed was the intended audience of most American periodicals. Within weeks of the Broadway closing of *I'll Say She Is*, the first issue went to press, and Ross called it *The New Yorker*, and saw that it was good.

The magazine's seventh issue, published as *I'll Say She Is* left Boston for New Haven, included a piece by Julius H. Marx. It was a dispatch from the road, headlined "Boston Again," and it contained Groucho's report on Boston morality and chorus girls: "Censor Casey made the ladies of our troupe drape their legs with fleshings. I haven't heard so much leg conversation in years and I don't wonder that it was around Boston that the Battle of Legsington was fought." The following week, *The New Yorker* would publish another Julius Marx casual, and soon, another. Harpo was a *social* member of the literary scene, but Groucho was asserting himself as a writer, an assertion he would make with increasing vigor over the years.

NEXT THEY OPENED in Detroit, at the Shubert Theatre, on June 1. This was a far greener pasture. *I'll Say She Is* had been seen in Detroit before, but only for one week, back in October of 1923. It was announced that the show would play an open-ended run, and that this would be the final stop on the post-Broadway tour. Perhaps the company hoped to settle in for another sultry summer. They had enjoyed hot, sticky love affairs with Philadelphia and New York in the summers of 1923 and 1924. For the summer of '25 their conquest was Detroit, and maybe the magic would last until Labor Day.

On the evening of Saturday, June 6, after the Napoleon scene, Groucho and Chico were sitting in their dressing room waiting for the curtain call. It was payday, and they had just been paid. Chico said he wanted to get some air, stood up, and walked off into the night—without his hat, Groucho would tell reporters, and without his car. Chico didn't return for the curtain call, nor for the Sunday show. An understudy went on for him. All the other Marxes, including and especially Chico's wife Betty and their daughter Maxine, were worried sick.

A police search commenced, with officers theorizing to the press that Leonard was suffering from madness or memory loss due to the oppressive heat. The only lead they found was from the proprietor of a leather store near the theatre, who said that a hatless man had come into the store at around 10:45 on Saturday night. "I'm one of the Marx Brothers playing at the Shubert," said the hatless man. He then asked to see some handbags, bought one, and left. (*The New York Times* added that Betty Marx "could offer no explanation.") Betty found a taxicab with "a wise driver," she later said, "and we went to every gambling house in Detroit—and, believe me—there are plenty of them. I had a strong hunch that Leo was gambling again."

The show closed until further notice. For two agonizing days, every effort was made to locate Chico or discover a clue to his whereabouts, and nothing came up. Then, at around 5:00 in the morning on Tuesday, June 9, Betty got a phone call from Cleveland. It was Chico. He was alive, if in Cleveland, and said he'd be back in Detroit that evening. He told Betty that on Saturday night he'd gone from Detroit to Buffalo by boat, and then on to Ohio. "He lost $30,000 in New York shooting craps in the Greek's joint just before the show left there and he had to borrow a lot of money," Betty told *Variety*. "That has been worrying him. He just loves to gamble."

Groucho advanced alternative theories, asserting to the *Detroit Free Press* that Chico was found "sitting on the marble steps of the Cleveland public library awaiting entrance in search of an eight-letter word meaning sleep" and "may have been suffering from a crossword puzzle dementia."

For Betty, this was by no means the first or last time she would forgive Chico for this kind of thing, or worse. We can assume that Groucho and Harpo wanted to kill Chico. This they did not do. But they did kill *I'll Say She Is.*

Variety, June 24, 1925:

> *I'll Say She Is* was supposed to have returned to the
> Casino last week for a repeat Broadway date, but the
> Four Marx Brothers refused to continue longer in
> the show. When it closed at Detroit two weeks ago,
> the attraction had played 107 consecutive weeks.
> The brothers declared they had bankrolls enough
> to last through the summer—except Chicko (Leo),
> who started thinking of the 30 grand he lost shoot-
> ing craps. He figured that it made a difference of
> $60,000 to him. That's why he yearned for a quiet
> journey across the lake to Cleveland.

The Marx Brothers would go on. After all those clamoring years, now
that they had finally really made it, they had to. It had already been reported
that Sam Harris would produce their next Broadway musical, with songs by
Irving Berlin, and it would soon be reported that George S. Kaufman would
write the libretto. Kaufman made a big public show of artificial displeasure
("I'd rather write for the Barbary apes"), and took some ribbing in the press.
Woollcott, supposedly quoting "fellow librettists envious of Mr. Kaufman's
assignment," managed to say in print: "Huh! A soft job. Groucho Marx makes
up his own lines fresh every night and Harpo never says a word." *Variety*,
meanwhile, imagined a writing session between Kaufman and Berlin: "Ever

The Four Marx Brothers in The Cocoanuts *on Broadway, 1925*

see these Marx boys?" "Sure. Know their stuff well." "So do I." "What'll we do for 'em?" "Get 'em on and off." "Okay. See you at rehearsal."

The resulting musical comedy was, of course, *The Cocoanuts*. It didn't run as long as *I'll Say She Is*, but it took place amidst dazzling production values, far beyond the means of Joseph M. Gaites and James P. Beury. Today, with *Cocoanuts* a beloved classic and *I'll Say She Is* more or less forgotten, it's surprising to learn that critical consensus found the Marx Brothers funnier the first time. Their notices were still strong, and the town was still in love with them. But in 1926 there was already a feeling that the authentic Marx Brothers had passed, corrupted by success into something safer, more commercial, and less interesting. Undoubtedly, some of their vaudeville devotees felt that way when they saw *I'll Say She Is*; just as some fans of *Fun in Hi Skule* probably took one look at *Home Again* and said, "I preferred their early stuff!" Beholding the splendor of *The Cocoanuts* on Broadway, the *Times* paid due respect to the "exquisite taste" of the production, but lamented that the Marxes' "blatancy and fury...do not reach the familiar extremes."

> The acceptance of the Marx Brothers into the good society of Broadway (such as it is) costs something in the scope of their humors . . . These are rowdy comedians: their make-up accentuates their natural instincts but moderately. One hopes they will preserve the richness of their slapstick humor in spite of the patronage of so-called discriminating people—in spite of that dangerous and profitable plague.

Marx Brothers fans will recognize this as the essential conflict of their Hollywood career: the wild, poetic Paramount films versus the tamer, more refined, less viscerally funny vision championed by Irving Thalberg at MGM.

With *I'll Say She Is* behind them, the Marx Brothers were big, and were soon to be even bigger. Their story, in some ways, was just beginning. But the story of *I'll Say She Is* ended abruptly, broken down in Detroit, its wreckage the scene of fraternal anger and hurt feelings. Bits and pieces of the show would bubble to the surface in the years to come, either as ideas slipped into later shows and films, or as wholesale imports. In the early thirties they would revive the Napoleon scene on tour, and they filmed the Theatrical Agency sketch for Paramount. But after Chico vanished in Detroit, committing what Harpo had called "the unpardonable sin of stagedom," the Marx Brothers never performed *I'll Say She Is* again.

Ladies and gentlemen, there will now be a ninety-year intermission.

Act Two

I.
JE SUIS MARXISTE,
TENDANCE GROUCHO

With my sister Shayna as Chico and my brother Joe as Harpo, 1989

I BECAME VAGUELY AWARE of the Marx Brothers when I was a small child, not through their films, but through a passion for books. Although I had many books of my own, what I *really* liked to do was explore my parents' bookshelves, which lined the living room walls. Their books were bigger, older, and sometimes vaguely frightening, in their ominous adultness. *A History of Greek Art. The Annotated Huckleberry Finn. The Complete Van Gogh. The Folger Library Shakespeare. T.S. Eliot—The Complete Poems and Plays—1909-1950.*

Then there was a mysterious volume bound in black. On the cover, in silver ink, was a series of mysterious icons: A moustache, nose, and eyeglasses; a harp; a pointy hat; and half the outline of a dapper male head. Hieroglyphics from an ancient civilization. I was drawn to this book first because of its weight, its darkness. This was clearly something substantial, important, Biblical! Inside, it was full of bizarre and fascinating photographs of these strange characters, "the Marx Brothers," as indicated in the book's perplexing title, *Groucho, Harpo, Chico, and Sometimes Zeppo: A History of the Marx Brothers and a Satire on the Rest of the World.* By Joe Adamson.

There was something familiar about the Brothers in these photographs, as though I'd seen them in books by Dr. Seuss or Maurice Sendak; or maybe they were Muppets. They were almost scary—those unforgettable faces, decorated with wigs, hats, and paint, twisted into unsettling hyperboles of normal human emotions. I'd flip through the book quickly and furtively, unready to grapple with the full scope of its power. It would be years before I'd comprehend the *words* in this book, whose early pages offered quotations from James Joyce, James Agee, George Bernard Shaw, and an "anonymous revolutionary in Paris, 1968," who wrote, "I am a Marxist, of the Groucho sort."

As childhood ground on, I remained dimly aware of the Brothers without ever confronting them directly. I looked at Joe Adamson's book once in a while, but I didn't seek out the films, nor were they shown to me. Mom and Dad (that's Cindy Lerner and Steve Diamond to you) weren't big Marx Brothers fans; the Adamson book had been a gift. And it was not easy to see old movies. We didn't have a VCR until I was twelve. We watched *The Wizard of Oz* on television every Thanksgiving. (We eagerly looked forward to the annual opportunity to see *The Wizard of Oz,* with constant commercial interruptions, on a thirteen-inch screen with round corners.) I'm sure that if I'd happened to catch a Marx Brothers movie on television at some point in my early childhood, I would have been mesmerized. But I never did.

Still, those faces popped up now and then, reminding me that I'd get there sooner or later. In the mid-1980s, my father introduced me to *Mad,* the foundational text of American pre-adolescence, which occasionally contained references to the Marxes. I could tell that Groucho Marx was the model for Mr. Kaputnik's doctor, in Dave Berg's *Mad* comics ("The Lighter Side Of…"). Later, I noticed that Les Lye's doctor character on *You Can't Do That On Television* was sort of like Groucho, too.

The words followed me around: MARX BROTHERS. Marx *Brothers*. I always liked the idea of siblings, and I desperately wanted a sister, and then a brother, and my parents obligingly supplied them. As soon as Shayna and Joe could talk, I cast them in little plays and musicals. Our parents divorced, and each remarried, and the three of us would go from one house to the other. We became our own travelling family act. I associated these feelings of indestructible sibling camaraderie with the photographs in Joe Adamson's book.

When I was around ten years old, my friend Dan Truman, who was slightly older than I (and is still, to this day, slightly older than I), showed up at my father's house with a book called *Flywheel, Shyster, and Flywheel*. This was an anthology of exhumed scripts from a 1930s radio program starring Groucho and Chico. Dan and I had a fine time reading those scripts into a Fisher-Price tape recorder, and I was able to read Groucho's lines fluidly, in basically the correct tone and cadence, even though I still had never really heard his voice.

In 1989 I finally started watching the films. This roughly coincided with the introduction of VCRs to our households—though I admit I had to gorge myself on *Star Wars*, *Back to the Future*, *Ghostbusters*, and the entire output of the Henson company before I went black-and-white. My stepfather, Steven Nestler, an actual Marx Brothers fan, brought *Duck Soup* home from the video store one evening, after Groucho's name had come up in conversation at dinner the night before. And that was that. From then on, for me, there was the Marx Brothers, and then there was everything else.

And so it began in earnest, and with urgency. The video store near us also had *A Night at the Opera* and *A Day at the Races*—rented and devoured the next day. Another video store had *Animal Crackers* and *Go West*. The store near my grandmother's house had *Monkey Business*. The library had *The Cocoanuts* and *At the Circus*. I scoured TV listings and eventually nabbed most of the others, and several episodes of Groucho's quiz show. For some reason, *Horse Feathers* was the hardest film to locate, and the last one I saw. I would watch these movies, rewind them, and watch them again. I couldn't get enough. I painstakingly transcribed the dialogue in composition books. I filled sketchpads with drawings of Groucho, Harpo, Chico, and sometimes Zeppo.

And then the research, the endless hours of delicious, meticulous detective work, with no particular goal other than to learn everything possible, to know something inside and out, to possess it. I started, of course, with Adamson. I read it cover to cover, over and over, and I gradually surrounded it with two entire shelves of books and articles by and about the Marx Brothers. I stayed at the library until closing time, squinting at microfiche, poring over film and theatre reviews from the twenties and thirties. I carried home with me, again and again, *Why a Duck?*, *Harpo Speaks*, *The Marx Brothers: Their World of Comedy*.

Watching and reading about the Marx Brothers could only take me so far. The obvious thing was to *be* the Marx Brothers. Inevitably, I identified with, and as, Groucho. I would lock myself in the bathroom and give myself the moustache and eyebrows with my mother's eyebrow pencil. Shayna and Joey were long accustomed to compulsory service as my stock company, obliging me through epic living room productions of *1776* and *Fiddler on the Roof*. That they were now asked to don wigs and hats or speak in vaguely Italian accents or honk bulb horns was taken easily in stride. We were the Marx Brothers for years, at parties, in parades, in talent shows, and just around the house in our spare time.

Out in the cruel world—which is to say, at school—Rufus T. Firefly was less welcome. I told some poor girl that her eyes shined like the pants of a blue serge suit. "That's no reflection on you," I added, wiggling my eyebrows.

"That's on the pants." She didn't know what a blue serge suit was, and neither did I, and that was just the beginning of our problems. Eventually, I had to face the fact that acting like Groucho was not going to help me with girls, so I switched to an ongoing Woody Allen impression, with which I was only moderately more successful.

For the most part, though, I was surprised to find that my peers *liked* the Marx Brothers, if they'd ever heard of them—or at least, they knew that they *should* like them. I've observed this many times: People who have never seen a Marx Brothers movie, who know nothing about them, who cannot even name them, still seem to have good feelings about them. It's rarely a hard sell. The only people who respond negatively to mentions of the Marx Brothers are people who think you're talking about the Three Stooges. The Marxes are just generally understood to be great, like Chaplin, like Shakespeare. I once screened *Duck Soup* for a room full of sixth graders, bracing myself for their scorn, but they *loved* it. They laughed uproariously. The Marx Brothers were cool. By contrast, I had once tried to introduce a group of my schoolmates to another beloved comedy, *The Court Jester*. They hated it, jeered at it, and called Danny Kaye a *faggot*. I'm still angry at them for that, and for all the stupid comedies they like that were released five minutes ago and consist mainly of flatulence.

Well, okay—maybe the Marx Brothers *weren't* cool. But they were funny, more truly and purely funny than anyone else who ever lived. It seemed to me that they were comedy itself, distilled and perfected. They were the Ghosts of Showbiz Past, embodying a whole approach to entertainment. They were aggressive, but whimsical—not Chaplinesque victims, but invincible troublemakers. I think this is what Mel Brooks was getting at when he described them as "the healthiest of all the comics." They joyously break the rules, simply because some fool has gone and made up some rules, and when they're done with those, they break rules it's never occurred to anybody to make up.

I Was a Teenage Groucho:
With Brian Hoffman as Harpo and Corey Moosa as Chico, 1991

I WROTE SONGS and plays, joined an improv troupe, appeared on stage at every opportunity, drew comic strips, made little movies, and filled notebooks. I consumed the work of an expanding gallery of artist-heroes. I got interested in politics. But I always came home to the Marx Brothers. At fifteen, I produced my own makeshift production of *Animal Crackers* at a local theatre—claiming, naturally, the Groucho role of Captain Spalding. Two strangers named Brian Hoffman and Corey Moosa auditioned, and were cast as Harpo and Chico, and we've been brothers ever since.

Shortly after that production, in 1992, my grandmother took us to see a professional *Animal Crackers* at the Goodspeed Opera House, starring Frank Ferrante as Groucho/Spalding, Les Marsden as Harpo, and Robert Michael Baker as Chico. The show made such an impression on me that more than two decades later, I can still remember that Craig Rubano played Zeppo, Celia Tackaberry played Mrs. Rittenhouse, and Charles Repole was the director. What's more, at intermission, my sister Shayna was astonished to meet a real live Marx—Chico's daughter, Maxine—on line for the ladies' room!

It was an exquisite production, and seeing it was a formative experience, packed with revelations. First: *Animal Crackers* is a *Broadway musical!* Of course I had known this, but only academically. (My pirated production had used the screenplay.) On film, *Animal Crackers* feels like a Marx Brothers comedy (the best, in my opinion), but not quite like *musical theatre*—this other thing that I loved almost as much as I loved the Marx Brothers. On stage at Goodspeed, it was both. It was a Marx Brothers musical. There actually *was* a plot, as well as characters and situations which hadn't made it as far as Paramount's Astoria soundstages in 1930. The full Kalmar and Ruby score contained songs I'd never heard before, including the famous (but rarely heard) "Musketeers," a Marx quartet sadly excluded from the film version:

> We're four of the Three Musketeers!
>
> We've been together for years!
>
> Eenie! Meenie! Miney! (Honk!)
>
> Four of the Three Musketeers!

And then there was Frank Ferrante, lithe and vigorous, loping and gliding and corkscrew-kicking his way through the production like a force of nature, or history. He looked and behaved uncannily like Groucho, yet this was inherently a slight variation, a younger and more ingratiating Groucho, playing to the audience—a Groucho of the stage. Ferrante, at the time, was not quite thirty. I had read about his triumph in *Groucho: A Life in Revue* (Off Broadway, 1986), but had never seen him perform. There was real joy laced through the Groucho acidity, and the audience ate it up, especially when he deviated from their expectations. After the "elephant in my pajamas" joke, Ferrante acknowledged its familiarity by turning smugly to the audience and intoning, "Thank you." When the crowd laughed prematurely at a punchline not yet uttered, Ferrante scolded them with mock reproach: "Try to keep time with the jokes." And when Marsden/Harpo doused the cast with knockout juice (as in the movie's finale), Ferrante/Groucho added three words to the

Frank Ferrante, Les Marsden, Craig Rubano, and Robert Michael Baker with Groucho's daughter, Miriam Marx Allen, at Goodspeed Opera House in 1992. Photo by Beverly Sobolewski.

scripted line which brought the house down: "Oh! To think I've got to go, so young…and in Connecticut!"

It all worked. It demonstrated conclusively to me that under the right circumstances, other people could play the Marx Brothers effectively. If they were good, if they were accurate, the experience felt authentic in a way that even the Marx Brothers' films did not. That was the revelation of *Animal Crackers* at Goodspeed: The Marx Brothers were primarily not cinematic artists, but a live act, and the presence of the audience was a key component. I was primed for this lesson. Almost from the beginning, my most intense fascination had been with their Broadway period. The earlier, vaudeville Marxes were irretrievable, too hidden by cobwebs to be understood vividly. The later Marxes, the movie stars of the thirties, were *incredibly* vivid. But it was the Broadway Marx Brothers—the *twenties* Marx Brothers—who were tantalizing to the imagination, just barely out of reach. *Animal Crackers* at Goodspeed seemed to illuminate that darkness.

From that evening forward, I've always loved seeing the Marx Brothers' comedy recreated onstage. If it's being done expertly, so much the better. But even in an amateur or school production, with dubious likenesses and unpolished stagecraft, I still enjoy it immensely, just to sit in an audience and experience a Marx Brothers comedy as *stage* work. I have little patience with the argument that impersonating the Marx Brothers is pointless because "you can always watch the *real* Marx Brothers." Well, of course nobody can ever be as good as the Marx Brothers. But you can't watch *them* in any medium except film. I wouldn't want to see a Hollywood remake of *Horse Feathers*, because the movie exists. But a play ceases to exist until someone puts it on again. If the Marx Brothers were still around, of course you'd rather see *them* in a production of *Cocoanuts* or *Animal Crackers* than anyone else. But due to the problems of the human condition, the boys just aren't available. Does that mean these classics should never be produced on stage again? Whether it's Frank Ferrante or a high school drama club, I'm always thrilled to see this stuff, and it makes me feel closer to my favorite comedy team—the *Broadway* Marx Brothers.

Those Broadway Marx Brothers, in photos, looked *almost* like the movie Brothers. You could recognize their ghosts in the first two films. *Cocoanuts* and *Animal Crackers* belong more to their Broadway period than their

Hollywood period, and were therefore more mysterious and interesting to me than the movies which followed. (They were even filmed in New York; for a while, the boys were doing *Cocoanuts* at Paramount's Astoria studio during the day while performing in *Animal Crackers* on Broadway at night.) I loved the stage more than the screen, and relished the idea of Groucho, Harpo, Chico, and Zeppo as theatre people. As much as I loved the Marx Brothers, I loved musical theatre, and its history; New York, and its history; Broadway; Tin Pan Alley; jazz; the Jazz Age; the Algonquin humorists—things that coalesced around a few golden years in the middle of Manhattan.

And within this favorite chapter of the Marx Brothers saga, *I'll Say She Is* emerged as the subtopic that most obsessed me. In an epoch that was just out of reach, *I'll Say She Is* was the part that was *most* out of reach, since it didn't exist on film, and had never been revived on stage. *The Cocoanuts* and

Broadway on film: The Cocoanuts, *1929*

Animal Crackers had survived not only on film, but as stage properties. I read them. I knew them. But *I'll Say She Is* was represented only by the published Napoleon scene (in *The Groucho Phile*) and the 1931 Theatrical Agency short, which I cherished. Shayna and Joe and I performed it constantly; to this day, I'm sure either of them could recite the entire scene verbatim. But beyond that, *I'll Say She Is* existed only as a handful of anecdotes, reviews, and photographs, found in books and articles about the Marx Brothers.

Every time a new Marx Brothers book fell into my hands, I'd flip to the section dealing with *I'll Say She Is* and read that first. Most of the literature devoted only a few pages to it. *The Marx Bros. Scrapbook* reprinted the entire opening-night playbill from the Casino. I took the *Scrapbook* to the library, where a copying machine was available, 25¢ per page. Using this miraculous tool, scissors, and a stapler, I made my own little copy of the playbill, so I could carry it around as though life was intermission at *I'll Say She Is* and I was waiting to go back in for the second act. From the same book I photocopied a 1924 advertisement for the show, and pinned it to my bedroom wall, surrounded by pictures of the Marx Brothers and other old comedians. I woke up every morning at the center of this constellation.

LIFE GOES ON: I grew up, moved to New York in 1997, wrote, acted, sang, met Amanda Sisk, did a lot of theatre, married Amanda Sisk. I worked as a costumed character, an office drone, a janitor, a tour guide, a box office manager, and a graphic designer. I kept writing and working in the theatre, most visibly (though still not very visibly) on the Nero Fiddled musicals. This was a series of downtown political satires, with titles such as *Moral Value Meal* and *Life After Bush*, which Amanda and I wrote, produced, and appeared in. They were my focus from 2003 to 2008. These musicals (and my performances in them) sometimes showed the influence of the Marx Brothers, but not explicitly. I later realized that the Nero Fiddled shows had a formal similarity to *I'll Say She Is*, occupying a middle ground between revues and book musicals. They were plotted revues, consisting of stand-alone songs and sketches which featured recurring characters and formed a thematic arc.

Occasionally I would throw myself back into the Marx Brothers, revisit the films and books, or work on some Marx-related project. I became Groucho whenever the opportunity arose. The many apartments I lived in over the years included a few on the Upper East Side or in East Harlem, where I enjoyed the proximity to the Marxes' childhood home on East 93rd Street. I'd sometimes walk past the building for encouragement or inspiration, and imagine little Marx Brothers running in and out of its front door a hundred years ago. I got involved with the 93rd Street Beautification Association, which was seeking landmark status for the building, and wanted to make official the block's affectionate nickname: Marx Brothers Place. On behalf of the Association and its co-director, Susan Kathryn Hefti, I made a short film entitled *The Brothers*, a "fantasia" assembled from Marx footage rare and familiar. *The Brothers* was screened at a 93rd Street Beautification Association event at the 96th Street Library.

When I published my book *400 Years in Manhattan*, I used a picture of myself as Groucho for the author photo. (It happens to be a photo of Amanda and me en route to a costume party. Readers of *400 Years in Manhattan* have every right to wonder why the author's photo seems to be a picture of Groucho Marx and Britney Spears.) Later, I designed a faux *New Yorker* cover featuring three versions of the magazine's mascot, Eustace Tilly, made up as Groucho, Harpo, and Chico, and submitted it to the magazine's annual contest. To my immense satisfaction, "Tillo Marx" was printed in *The New Yorker*'s 85th anniversary issue. (It was subsequently used in some of their advertisements, and in one issue it appeared opposite a new Shouts and Murmurs piece by Woody Allen. I began referring to him as "my colleague at *The New Yorker*.") Shortly thereafter, I received a note from a friend of Miriam Marx, explaining that Groucho's daughter would love to have a print of "Tillo" hanging in her home. Arrangements were made, and through Miriam's friend I received a lovely thank-you note from Miriam herself.

The Marx Brothers returned to center stage in my mind after 2008,

"Tillo Marx"

when Sisk and I decided we'd gone as far as we could with the Nero Fiddled musicals. We loved those shows, and we were particularly proud of the last one, *Life After Bush*. It had a very exciting, highly acclaimed run at HERE Arts Center in October and November, culminating in a special Election Night performance where we covered the returns live on stage. And then— it could never be done again! Musical theatre is a tough form for topical satire. Properly writing and developing a musical takes meticulous attention to detail, trial and error, and a great deal of time, but topical satire must be written and presented quickly, because its shelf life is so brief. It was frustrating, pouring immense effort into songs that would be relevant for only a few weeks—or, even worse, rushing material before an audience to take advantage of its timeliness, while knowing it needed more work.

So after several years of getting all my inspiration from political news, I was looking for something else to write about. Maybe there was a big Marx Brothers project in my future, which would be the culmination of my interest in them. It would be fun to play Groucho again, and now I was approaching his actual age during their Broadway period. But I couldn't think of a good vehicle for my enthusiasm. There was no need for my services in a Groucho one-man show; Frank Ferrante was already doing that to perfection. I explored and abandoned an idea called *Groucho at the Movies*, a multimedia show in which I, as Groucho, would interact with footage from classic Hollywood films. That didn't go anywhere. Another idea was *Groucho on the Air*, an anthology of radio material from the 1940s, to be presented in the style of an old-time broadcast. I don't know why it took so long for the obvious to occur to me.

II.
DO IT

IDIDN'T EVEN KNOW what I was working on when I started working on it.

Unsure of what to do in the theatre, I thought I might write a book. I began to write about the Marx Brothers, but I had the sinking feeling that this effort was unnecessary. Their story had already been told. In addition to all the precious volumes I'd grown up with, there were more recent Marx books, including Glenn Mitchell's *Marx Brothers Encyclopedia*, accounts of Groucho's later years by Steve Stoliar and John Ballow, a Groucho biography by Stefan Kanfer, and a landmark group biography by Simon Louvish. My casual research had unearthed some interesting tidbits that were not generally known, but these revelations were neither groundbreaking nor plentiful enough to justify a book.

But on the brink of resignation, I hit my stride when I started to write about *I'll Say She Is*. On this subject, I *did* have fresh things to say, and genuine curiosity. I quickly exhausted the research possibilities of the existing Marx Brothers library, and began poking around in old newspaper and magazine archives again. One of the great advantages of our digital age (besides the ability to watch any Marx Brothers movie any time I feel like it) is how the internet has revolutionized research. What once would have required prohibitively expensive and time-consuming travel could now largely be done from my apartment. Not everything can be found online, and as my research deepened, I did have to chase down some resources in person. But without the fruitfulness of my virtual research trips, I doubt the project would have seemed viable in the first place.

Everything old is new again. Access to history has expanded exponentially since I was ten years old and fell in love with the writing of Mark Twain. I wrote a precocious letter to the Mark Twain House in Hartford, expressing my desire to become that institution's youngest tour guide. I received a charming letter from their director, Constance O'Connell, inviting my father and me to a private tour, including parts of the house and its collection not usually seen by the public. In the Clemens kitchen, Ms. O'Connell told us, "You are about to come as close as possible to hearing the actual voice of Mark Twain." The great man himself had never had his voice recorded, but it was known that his young friend William Gillette did a spot-on Twain impression, and Gillette's impression of Twain *was* recorded. Constance O'Connell played for us a crackling, reel-to-reel recording of Gillette as Twain, reading "The Celebrated Jumping Frog of Calaveras County." This was a profound experience for me, and one I've never stopped talking about. But it's been brought to my attention that the Gillette recording is now readily available on YouTube!

Early in my *I'll Say She Is* web searches, I referred often to Marxology, a thoughtful and well-researched website by the Swedish Marx Brothers scholar Mikael Uhlin. He seemed to know what had happened on stage during *I'll Say She Is*, in more detail than I'd encountered elsewhere. Marxology included excerpts from "the typescript," with actual dialogue from the show, much more than was quoted in Simon Louvish's book. I wrote to Mikael Uhlin, told him I was researching *I'll Say She Is*, and asked if he had a copy of the actual typescript, or knew how I might acquire one. (I assumed it would be easier to contact a stranger in Sweden than to deal with the Library of Congress.) Mikael sent a kind and witty response, and we struck up an instant friendship by correspondence. He shared a lot of his research with me, pointed me in the direction of more research, and even sent me a photocopy of his photocopy of the typescript (which had been provided to him by another Marx scholar, Peter Sprenkle). And there it was, in my hands, just a generation or two away from Will B. Johnstone's typewriter.

The Johnstone typescript, as it entered my life in 2009, was exactly as we left it in 1923—a perplexing and enigmatic document, with flashes of Marxian genius, the occasional cryptic stage direction ("Business with hat"), and the old reed-thin plot about Beauty looking for thrills. It was, as we have noted, quite incomplete. But it did provide a fuller picture of *I'll Say She Is* than I'd ever seen before, and plenty of would-be classic material, totally unknown to audiences. I'd never been so excited to read something in my life.

I kept half-heartedly plugging along at my supposed book, expanding the *I'll Say She Is* chapter. My analysis of the typescript later proved to have been a useful exercise, but I could tell that this prose piece was not going to work. It probably sounds hard to believe—even *I* don't quite believe it—but as I genuinely remember it, I still hadn't given serious thought to the idea of working the show back to the stage. I didn't think there was enough surviving material to call *I'll Say She Is*. I had thirty pages of rough dialogue, plus other, more detailed versions of the Theatrical Agency scene and the Napoleon scene, but little else. At this point, I had only been able to locate the music and lyrics of one song, "Only You."

But as my research doggedly continued, and I amassed a larger and larger collection of news clippings, fragments of *I'll Say She Is* were revealing themselves to me. Critics and columnists frequently quoted Groucho's ad libs, and described impromptu Harpo business, which would otherwise have been lost to history. Often, they described costumes, scenery, and situations not indicated in the typescript. The deeper I dug, the more shards there were to glue back into place. I expanded my research to cover the two proto-*I'll Say She Is* revues, *Love for Sale* and *Gimme a Thrill*, as well as similar Johnstone efforts like *Take It From Me* and *Up in the Clouds*. I discovered more connections with *I'll Say She Is*, and more material that could be imported.

The idea of adapting and reviving *I'll Say She Is* settled in slowly, so that by the time I came to terms with what I was doing, I was already doing it. I quietly abandoned the prose piece, and shifted to transcribing, and then editing, and then polishing, and then expanding, Will B. Johnstone's typescript. There was an advantage in the fragmented material: What better excuse could I have for taking liberties, for improving what existed, and for imagining what didn't? The more I considered it, the more obvious it was. How was it even *possible* that there was a Marx Brothers Broadway Musical that hadn't been seen in almost a century?! It suddenly seemed inevitable that *somebody* would revive *I'll Say She Is*, or would put something on stage and *call* it *I'll Say She Is*. It was a miracle that nobody had done it yet!

MY FIRST DRAFT of *I'll Say She Is* was a gnarled mess of conflicting intentions. I didn't meddle with the Theatrical Agency scene or the Napoleon scene, but I did meddle with everything else. Both acts began with long speeches by Alexander Woollcott, whom I envisioned as a master of ceremonies. I was convinced that the audience wouldn't appreciate *I'll Say She Is* unless they knew all about its historical significance and the circumstances of the original production. Woollcott's opening speech was interminable, explaining everything to death, and it's probably just what Woollcott would have done. It began like this:

> Good evening, friends. This is Woollcott speaking—Alexander Woollcott, of the *Times*, the *Sun*, the *World*, *The New Yorker*, the Algonquin Round Table, and the Thanatopsis Literary and Inside Straight Club. I want to welcome you to the first-ever revival of a certain Broadway revue of 1924—entitled, if memory serves, *I'll Say She Is*. Though not seen on stage in lo these many years, its place in history is assured, for it was in *I'll Say She Is* that Broadway first encountered those talented cutups, the Four Marx Brothers. And tonight, through a special arrangement with the cosmos, you shall see it, and you shall see them.

I dispensed with Johnstone's "rich man, poor man, beggar, thief, doctor,

DO IT

The Morning Moon

THE WEATHER FORECAST
The skies are blue save when we're hoping you'll call when all is grey

THE WEATHER FORECAST
Today the weather's fine let some whimsy I'm calling your dear for a rainy day

NEW YORK CITY, MONDAY, MAY 19, 1924

SOCIETY WOMAN CRAVES EXCITEMENT!

BEAUTIFUL HEIRESS PROMISES HAND, HEART, FORTUNE TO MAN WHO CAN GIVE HER A THRILL

IS VICTIM OF SUPPRESSED DESIRES

A beautiful heiress, who resides in the Mintworth mansion on Park Avenue, with her aunt, Ruby Mintworth, widow of late industrialist Chester Mintworth, craves excitement and is looking for thrills. She promises her hand, her heart, and her fortune to the man who can give her a thrill. It is said that the young lady is a victim of suppressed desires, and has complexes, because she has never been in love.

AGENTS RAID CHINATOWN OPIUM DEN

In the lowest dive of the city, where creatures of the underworld drug their brains with poisonous poppy, the despicable vice, dry agents followed a tip which supposedly led to a rum-running racket. The tip turned out to be cold, but the agents spent several hours investigating, reasoning that the machinery of the brain wasn't planted in the bean for nothing.

SCANDAL AT LONG ISLAND MANOR

There has been increasing concern of curious doings at the famed Long Island showplace Rittenhouse Manor, according to a spokesman for the Long Island Whitehead family, now preparing for a long holiday in Europe.

BACKWARDS CINDERELLA STORY

When shadows fall, and stretch across September, when hope's an ember, then we'll remember, we had a ball, and who could ask for more than the time we spent in 1924? When shadows fall, and all the fun has faded, please don't be jaded; keep the past in sight. We're in love! We're in electric light! Even Broadway's just for us tonight. When shadows fall, and colder winds are blowing, when tears are flowing, we'll wake up knowing we did it all, so darling, don't be still. Let's go find the throngs, the stars, the songs, the thrill. When shadows fall, our love for one another, brother to brother, is bright enough to see. We're alive, and what a thing to be! Baby, Broadway's just for you and me.

NEW RESEARCH REVEALS SECRETS OF NAPOLEON

Surely Napoleon and Josephine are among the most celebrated couples in world history. But new research, conducted by new scholars at new universities, suggests that while Napoleon was off at war, Josephine was not wanting for company. The emperor's advisors, Alphonse, Francois, and Gaston, apparently frequented the royal bedchamber while Napoleon was off, and if he left her with them, he must be off.

HAS COMPLEXES, HAS NEVER BEEN IN LOVE

Dr. Heinrich Gubaduber, a noted expert in women's problems, agrees that the Mintworth heiress "is most likely a victim of suppressed desires." However, Dr. Gubaduber emphasizes that not all victims of suppressed desires have complexes. "Complexes," says Dr. Gubaduber, "are another thing altogether, and although I have not examined the young woman, I believe it is safe to assume that in this case, we are dealing with complexes. I have reached this conclusion based on the fact that she has never been in love." Dr. Gubaduber believes her to be badly in need of thrills.

WALL STREET PAVED WITH GOLD

A lithe young woman covered in gold, who lurks on Wall Street and is said to be the personification of wealth, reported that things move plenty fast on Wall Street, where one may seek the thrill of the high rollers, but may become crushed like a fly in the monstrous web of the Tragedy of Gambling. Oh, the metallic click of the soulless ticker. Dancing over the devil's colors. Playing for gold with red and black. No further details are known.

GALATEA STATUE MISSING

Pygmalion, the famous sculptor, claims that one of his recent works has gone missing. "Her name is Galatea," explained the artist. "I created her, fell in love with her, brought her to life, and then lost her. It all happened so fast, I'm not sure what went on. If anyone can solve this problem, I sure would appreciate it."

My newspaper design for the eventual production.
Photo of Melody Jane by Don Spiro.

lawyer, merchant, chief." I didn't think the nursery rhyme had much currency, and there was no need for eight protagonists. (There's one measure of how Broadway has changed. No contemporary dramatist would ever write, "Eight men enter!") The four Marx Brothers would be the only suitors, and Zeppo would be the romantic lead who ends up with Beauty. I tried to keep the show grounded in 1924, but this Zeppo decision anticipated the early thirties, when the youngest Marx Brother graduated to the role of juvenile love interest in *Monkey Business* and *Horse Feathers*.

I took the liberty of adding a Margaret Dumont dowager character, even though there wasn't one in *I'll Say She Is*. Ms. Dumont herself did not work with the Brothers until *The Cocoanuts*. But the dowager *character* had existed in Marx Brothers comedies long before *I'll Say She Is*. There was a Mrs. Gould in *On the Mezzanine* who was a clear prototype of the Dumont roles in *Cocoanuts*, *Animal Crackers*, and beyond. (Groucho, to Mrs. Gould: "You won't believe it, but from the moment I laid eyes on you there's been something I'm ashamed of, and I think it's you.") The roots of the Groucho/ Dumont dynamic go back even further, to the vaudeville tab *Mr. Green's Reception*. "I did have a big woman in the act to play opposite," Groucho recalled in later years. "I would bounce laughs off of her. Though I never had anyone as good as Margaret Dumont." If this hadn't been the case—if the classic role of the dowager in a Marx Brothers comedy had been created by George S. Kaufman for Margaret Dumont in *The Cocoanuts* in 1925—I would have kept it out of *I'll Say She Is*. But I saw justification for adding a wealthy widow, who is Beauty's guardian. In my first draft she was called Mrs. Gloria Mintworth, and she was the ingénue's mother.

This didn't mean the ingénue was named Beauty Mintworth, though, because I initially chose not to call the ingénue Beauty. In the early drafts I named the character Lotta, in tribute to Lotta Miles, though her name was never spoken in the dialogue. I made a conceptual choice to treat Lotta Miles the same as the Marx Brothers, to use her real stage name, and to proceed as though Lotta Miles is an icon and everyone knows who she is. I envisioned a theatre lobby decorated with old Kelly-Springfield ads. The primitive sexual politics of the plot would require a delicate touch, and giving the female lead a name seemed like a good place to start. Toward the same end, in that first draft, I made Mrs. Mintworth something of a progressive visionary, who wishes Lotta would discover "the thrill of education." I eventually unmade some of these changes, but not all of them.

I kept Johnstone's plot. First an opening number, then the Theatrical Agency sketch, ending with the newspaper ("Society Woman Craves Excitement!") and the title exchange ("Isn't she a beauty?" "I'll say she is!"), which I turned into a song. We then meet the ingénue, her social secretary, her butler, and her mother, and the Marx Brothers show up intending to provide thrills. The original sequence of scenes was streamlined, but mostly left intact—the opium den, the courtroom, Wall Street, intermission. Act Two still began with "The Inception of Drapery," followed by a new scene set in a speakeasy, designed to further the Lotta/Zeppo romance. Then, as in 1924, the Marble Fountain and the Napoleon scene, followed by a Finale in which our heroine realizes that the greatest thrill of all is the thrill of love. I invented a secondary romance between Ruby, the social secretary, and Simpson, the butler. Both of these characters were in the original, but it was my idea to get them together—two lonely domestic workers who discover an urgent longing for one another, after hearing all this talk about thrills and suppressed desires. It was musical comedy tradition to have a primary love story and a secondary, comical one.

And then the show needed a score. It seemed there were two options: I could hunt for obscure songs from the early twenties, or I could write new pastiche numbers. I attempted the latter. Though none of the original music or lyrics were yet available to me (except for "Only You"), the typescript and the playbill gave the *titles* of the songs (and therefore their likely refrain lines), and some narrative context. I knew I needed a number called "Gimme a Thrill," a number called "When Shadows Fall," a number called "I'm Saving You for a Rainy Day."

My first attempt at an opening number was all wrong—it introduced the characters and set up the story! (The original opening, you will recall, had been "Do It," a song-and-dance number for the Agent and the chorus girls.) In later drafts, I made sure that *I'll Say She Is* opened with a diegetic song, characteristic of its period. Later on, when I sought the counsel and collaboration of other theatre people, it was sometimes suggested to me that my earlier impulse had been correct: "Well, don't you see, the opening number should introduce the characters and set up the story, and then after that you need an 'I want' song...." It was a matter of knowing when to follow these postwar gospels and when to ignore them; how to keep the audience engaged without violating the truth of *I'll Say She Is*.

As a matter of fact, there *was* an "I want" song in the original show. I combined what I knew about "Gimme a Thrill" and "The Thrill of Love," and came up with an entrance song for the Lotta Miles character. But in general, the evolution of the modern American musical was something I struggled to ignore. Despite my worship of comedy and popular music from the twenties and thirties, as a writer of musicals I'm a product of the Rodgers and Hammerstein approach, by way of Sondheim. I had to constantly slap my own wrist when I caught myself writing *I'll Say She Is* lyrics which overstepped their historical bounds by moving the plot forward too deliberately, or expressing the internal lives of the characters too knowingly.

Apparently, Groucho Marx did not sing much in the original *I'll Say She Is*, but in my adaptation, a Groucho specialty number was irresistible. The Napoleon scene was the obvious place for one, so I decided to give Groucho's Napoleon the kind of operetta-style entrance song later written by Bert Kalmar and Harry Ruby for Captain Spalding, Rufus T. Firefly, and Dr. Hackenbush.

"When Shadows Fall" had originally been part of the Chinatown sequence, but I moved it to the new speakeasy scene and made it a bittersweet love duet. This number was the one opportunity in *I'll Say She Is* to make a personal statement. By having the two lovers comment on the passage of time and the value of memory, I could speak to the twenty-first-century audience, and communicate something of the love that was going into this project, my feelings about the show, the Marx Brothers, the twenties, the city, love, and life. It's my favorite sentiment: Life is good, so don't forget to enjoy it, because horrific tragedy is inevitable.

> Things are grand today,
> but things won't always be this way.
> Looking back on this, we'll see:
> It was a laugh, a lark, a spree.
> Today it may seem strange
> to think the world will have to change.
> Looking back on this we'll know—
> it was a hell of a show.
> I guess what really counts
> is love in large amounts.
> At least we can say we had a ball,
> when shadows fall.
>
> Life is glam and glee,
> but one day none of this will be.
> Fate will fall—I don't know how—
> but we were here, for this, right now.
> Remember everything.
> We'll need a song to sing.
> At least we can say we did it all,
> when shadows fall.
>
> Feel everything you can feel!
> Why don't we spin the wheel once more?
> We'll laugh at the time we spent
> when it was nineteen twenty-four.
> Sure, everything good goes bad.
> Darling, at least we had each other.
> You're with me until the end
> as friend to friend and brother to brother.

But now the city teems
with stardust-decorated dreams.
Darling, don't be still!
Let's find the throngs, the songs, the thrill!
Today it's hard to hear
that all of this will disappear.
Well, I'll tell you for a fact—
we had a hell of an act.
We're in electric light.
Broadway is ours tonight.
We'll dream of a certain curtain call,
when shadows fall.

III.
ZVBXRPL

DESPITE THE PROBLEMS of that first draft, I was terribly pleased with it. Just to hold a full script in my hands, that went from beginning to end and said *I'll Say She Is* on the cover, was—yes—a thrill. I would leaf through it constantly, scribble alternate jokes in the margins, and read all of Groucho's lines aloud. Whatever my hesitations before, I was now committed. I had to bring *I'll Say She Is* back to the stage.

I still had worlds of research ahead. The time I'd spent digging into the past had revealed tidbits of lost material, but the main lesson of that exercise was that I'd have to put in many more hours, panning for gold. I shared the first draft with one person, Mikael Uhlin, my new friend in Sweden. I knew he'd be interested, and letting him in on the process seemed like a nice way to thank him for his help. Mikael took his time with the script, and responded in detail. Most of his opinions were favorable, or kind; he called it "an excellent and exciting rewrite of the original show," and specifically praised the lyrics and the Woollcott speeches. He regretted my deletion of the "rich man, poor man" motif (though he understood my reasoning), and expressed hope that it could be reinstated in some form, since it was such a prominent element of the original show. He suggested I find a place for "Only You," and any other Johnstone music I could locate. He also offered some shrewd commentary on choices I'd made regarding the Mrs. Mintworth character:

> Since Lotta, the Beauty, is a bored, wealthy—but not underage—heiress, I think it's more effective (and plausible) if Mrs. Mintworth isn't her mother but a former legal guardian, maybe an aunt. I've never imagined Beauty as a Polly Potter [in *The Cocoanuts*], Arabella Rittenhouse [*Animal Crackers*], or Dorothy Gould [*On the Mezzanine*], but a strong

and independent young woman like Connie Bailey [*Horse Feathers*] or Judy Standish [*A Day at the Races*]. In other words, Mrs. Mintworth would be more like the characters Margaret Dumont played in the later Marx films. Mrs. Potter at the Hotel de Cocoanut would never have allowed her daughter Polly to initiate a "give me a thrill" competition, while Mrs. Dukesbury in *At the Circus* just had to accept whatever her nephew did.

In 2010, I think I read more newspapers from 1922-1925 than from 2010. I learned a lot more about the original production of *I'll Say She Is*, and unearthed the occasional nugget that could be used in the script. My second draft was focused on interpolating as much authentic material as possible. I reconciled the various existing texts of the Theatrical Agency and Napoleon scenes, deleted the second Woollcott speech, and cut the first one down by half.

I started to think more seriously about how it might be realized on stage. Sisk and I had proudly self-produced all of our shows, but *I'll Say She Is* seemed much too big to do our way, and the venues we were used to working in were not appropriate for it. This was, for lack of a better term, a Broadway musical. It wouldn't make sense in a blackbox theatre. It needed a proscenium, a curtain, wings, and a large cast. It needed an elaborate physical production. Not only that—the historic importance of *I'll Say She Is* demanded a conspicuous, prestigious event, something that would break through the noise of the New York theatre scene and be written about and talked about. It would need a powerful producer, a first-rate creative team, and, I shuddered to imagine, truckloads of money.

Along with the realization that I might not be able to produce *I'll Say She Is* independently came the fear that I might not be able to appear in it. I had plenty of experience in the role, and supreme confidence that I was the man for the job; my original motivation for working on the show was the search for a Groucho vehicle. But I didn't have the résumé of a professional actor.

Most of my recent performances were in things I'd written for myself. Now I imagined that once *I'll Say She Is* got into the hands of a legitimate producer, he or she would probably want to cast someone with marquee value, some-one more associated with commercial musical theatre. I was prepared for the possibility that one day, it might be in the show's interest for me to surrender the role—but not right off the bat. I felt that playing Groucho in the show was an extension of writing it. Whatever ad libs I came up with on the spot might be closer to Groucho's real ad libs than those I imagined while sitting at my desk. The performance would be part of the adaptation.

Although I had played Groucho many times, it had been a while. With an eye toward burnishing my chops and my credibility, I went back to my old idea for *Groucho on the Air*. I stitched together a bunch of old radio scripts, and created a framing device set in the studios of ZVBXRPL Radio. Amanda played all of the female roles, including Tallulah Bankhead (of whom she does an uncanny impression); a Dumont-like dowager; and a character invented for the show, "ZVBXRPL's Sweetheart of Song, Minnie Shean." Hugh Sinclair (a dear friend, great actor, and true Marx Brothers fan) played Orson Welles, and the announcer, and various heavies. Brian Hoffman, who had memorably lampooned George W. Bush in three of the Nero Fiddled shows, made a special appearance as Chico. (Brian had been Harpo in my teenage *Animal Crackers*, twenty years earlier.) D.J. Thacker, who had worked with us as arranger and musical director on two of the Nero shows, accompanied Amanda on some songbook chestnuts, and me on some signature Groucho numbers. At that time, my brother Joe was a director of the Bushwick Project for the Arts, a now-defunct venue in Brooklyn, where we booked the show for January of 2011. Joe built the set, I designed the poster and the website, and Amanda directed.

In retrospect, the most significant thing about *Groucho on the Air* is that I met Kathy Biehl. I had begun to follow some Marx Brothers blogs, groups, and mailing lists, in an effort to get to know the online community of Marx Brothers fans. These, I figured, were my people, and the crowd most likely to

*With Kathy Biehl at Drew Friedman's "Old Jewish Comedians" show at the
Society of Illustrators (of which Will B. Johnstone was a member), 2014*

be interested in the work I was doing. I had discovered Matthew Coniam's
insightful and beautifully-written Marx Brothers Council blog, where witty
and scholarly discussion ran so thick that Mr. Coniam eventually moved
the conversation over to the Marx Brothers Council of Facebook.[1] It was
through one of these virtual fan gatherings that Kathy Biehl first contacted
me. She was a hardcore Marx Brothers fan, full of heroic tales of the Great
Marx Brothers Renaissance. She had spent time with such luminaries as
Maxine Marx, Paul Wesolowski, Robert Bader, and Frank Ferrante. She'd
had a close relationship with the late Frank Bland, a fan hero who was

---

[1] There, to this very day, he hosts the internet's liveliest and most advanced ongoing Marx Brothers party. He expanded and enhanced the essays from his blog, and
published a delightful and substantial book, *The Annotated Marx Brothers*, in 2015.

responsible for the first Marx Brothers website. Kathy is a fine performer and vocalist, whose credits include the Margaret Dumont role in an independent film called *Horse Phasers*. (The Marx Brothers in *Star Trek* is one idea that somehow hadn't occurred to me when I was casting about for a project.)

By the time she came to see *Groucho on the Air*, we'd had a lively correspondence for weeks. At the show, she presented me with a VHS copy of *Horse Phasers*, and I gave her a print of "Tillo Marx." (She later likened this gift exchange to the moment in *A Night at the Opera* when Harpo and Chico exchange salamis.) Kathy reported back to the Marx Brothers mailing list and said some kind things about my performance. Pretty soon, I decided to tell her about my work on *I'll Say She Is*, and she became the third person to read my script, after Mikael and Amanda.

Kathy was excited about the idea of a resuscitated *I'll Say She Is*, and had comments on the script that were helpful and encouraging. She sent me a fascinating article she'd written for the *Houston Press* magazine in 2000, about a composer, playwright, and researcher named James Doyle. He had developed an obsession with the 1902 stage musical version of *The Wizard of Oz*, starring the vaudeville team of Montgomery and Stone. The 1902 *Oz* was a fanciful extravaganza, bearing little relation to L. Frank Baum's then-recent book, and even less relation to the 1939 MGM film we all adore. No authoritative score or libretto existed, but Doyle threw himself into the research, collected a heap of material, and restored the show to stageworthy form. There were many differences between James Doyle's challenge and mine. But I found his "25-year odyssey," as described by Kathy, to be a major inspiration, and I returned to the article many times while I was working on *I'll Say She Is*.

AS THE WORK continued, my inner circle gradually widened. Mikael Uhlin asked me if he could mention my project to Will B. Johnstone's great-granddaughter, Margaret Farrell. She was an ethnomusicologist at

CUNY, who had conducted her own research into the background of *I'll Say She Is*, and Mikael had corresponded with her when he was working on Marxology. I hesitated. I was aware, of course, that I might eventually have to work out agreements with the Johnstone family as well as the Marx family, but I was hoping not to face them until I had a first-rate script to demonstrate my competence and good intentions.

A few days later, I received an e-mail from Margaret Farrell. She introduced herself as Meg, acknowledged our mutual friend in Sweden, and said she'd heard I was working on her grandfather's play and she would love to meet sometime. She then explained that "Grandpit" (the family's nickname for Will B.) had been a diligent diarist, that his diaries from the 1920s were in her possession, and that they contained revelations about *I'll Say She Is* not to be discovered elsewhere. Meg was then working on a doctoral thesis about Egyptian movie musicals, and was about to leave on a research trip to

The 1924 record of "The Thrill of Love"

Egypt, but we spoke on the phone. She was friendly and encouraging, and seemed enthusiastic about the prospect of an *I'll Say She Is* revival. She did not, alas, possess any surviving sheet music from the show, besides "Only You." But she did have a few Johnstone songs from other shows, which raised the possibility of a Johnstone score, if not the exact songs from the original *I'll Say She Is*.

Then a second *I'll Say She Is* song fell into my lap, when Mikael alerted me to the sale, on eBay, of a 1924 Edison cylinder recording of "The Thrill of Love." A week later, I was holding it in my hands: a beautiful artifact, thick and heavy, with the classic Edison label, and "THE THRILL OF LOVE from 'I'LL SAY SHE IS.'" It was performed by Helen Clark and Joseph Phillips. It turned out to be a pleasant little song, similar in many ways to "Only You"—a simple, romantic melody, with pedestrian lyrics.

Soon after *Groucho on the Air*, I heard from Ira Dolnick, a devoted Marxist based in Chicago, who was looking to buy a print of "Tillo Marx." Ira mentioned that he had a large collection of Marx Brothers books and memorabilia, including a vast archive of vintage sheet music, and asked if there were any obscure items I'd been looking for, which he might be willing to sell, trade, or copy. I assumed that Ira probably had the same sheet music we all knew about (early Chico compositions, the Kalmar and Ruby songbook), but told him that what I was *really* looking for was music from *I'll Say She Is*. I explained that all I'd managed to get my hands on was "Only You," though I knew that at least five songs from the show had been published. Ira wrote back and said something to the effect of, "Yes, I have all five."

IV.
THIS BROADWAY SONG

"Only You" sheet music

THE ENVELOPE FROM CHICAGO arrived and I opened it with a surgeon's care. Inside, there were some unexpected treasures Ira had generously thrown in: An article he'd written about Harpo, and a copy of the original, handwritten sheet music for "Dr. Quackenbush," before it was changed to "Hackenbush" (out of concern, so the story goes, that an unspecified *actual* Dr. Quackenbush might sue).[1] Along with these, there were oversized photocopies of the published versions of "Only You," "The Thrill of Love," "The Wonderful Nile," "I'm Saving You for a Rainy Day," and "When Shadows Fall."[2]

My piano skills are paltry, but I had an effective, painstaking method of getting to know the "new" *I'll Say She Is* music. I transcribed each song, note by note, into a music notation program called Finale. Then I could play them back, and save them as sheet music or MIDI audio files. I could also tinker with the music, transposing songs into different keys, altering musical phrases, or combining elements of different songs into one piece. I had already transcribed "Only You," and now I raced through the other songs as quickly as possible. Then I listened to them, over and over, dizzy with the thought that almost nobody had heard this music in eight or nine decades.

Tom Johnstone's music was much better than I expected it to be. I'd imagined, on the basis of "Only You" and "The Thrill of Love," that it would be pleasantly generic. There was reason to be concerned; *Variety* had said in its Broadway review that "Only You" "has no contender in melody in the score." In Philadelphia, *Variety* had said, "The voices are adequate for the music of Tom Johnstone." The *Brooklyn Eagle* said, "Tom Johnstone wrote the music, much of it, that is, as is not borrowed from the works of more famous and meritorious composers. No one of the songs sounded last night as if it was destined to be a hit." The *Toronto Evening Telegram* agreed that the music in *I'll Say She Is* "was not such as to linger in the memory," while the *Syracuse Journal* took a more thoughtful approach, holding that the show "has no music to get the hoi polloi to whistling. In fact you forget all about the music. Subconsciously you know it is satisfying but it blends in with the

[1] The song was cut from *A Day at the Races*, but Groucho performed it many times on television and radio.

[2] Years later, scans of all four "missing" songs surfaced on the internet.

dances or action as a movie score does into a film story."

So my expectations were lowered by the reviews. But I found Tom's compositions sweet and beguiling—not works of genius; there's a reason why these songs haven't endured alongside the classics of their era. The classics of their era are some of the greatest songs ever written, and to say that Tom Johnstone was not in the same class as Irving Berlin, Jerome Kern, George Gershwin, and Cole Porter is certainly no smear. His music was, in its time, considered ordinary. But what was ordinary in the twenties is utterly charming today. And the other songs turned out to be more interesting than "Only You" and "The Thrill of Love." "The Wonderful Nile" is a slow fox trot with a vaguely Egyptian sound, and funny snake-charmer fills.[3] "I'm Saving You for a Rainy Day" is a lovely piece of kitsch, about two shades bluer than Harry Dacre's "Daisy Bell (Bicycle Built for Two)," which it resembles. I was especially pleased to discover that "When Shadows Fall" was a beautiful and pensive romantic ballad, amazingly close in mood to my own version.

There was one obvious problem that all of these songs had in common. It gives me no pleasure to say it, but I believe it's the truth.

Will B. Johnstone was not a very good lyricist.

The man was protean. He was a brilliant cartoonist, an excellent painter, a great comedy writer, a good prose humorist, a decent librettist, and, let's face it, a mediocre lyricist. My hunch is that he just didn't take lyric-writing very seriously. His cartoons show that he was capable of inventive, finely-crafted work, and his prose shows that he was witty and facile with language. But for whatever reason, he didn't treat song lyrics with the same care. There's the sense that he's just filling out melodic lines as though they are forms. The songs he wrote were decorative, designed primarily as vehicles for the display

---

[3] Its verse is extremely similar to that of an earlier song by Tom and Will B., "How Dry I Am," which was featured in *Up in the Clouds*. This Prohibition blues number shares two lines of lyric and melody ("Nobody knows / How dry I am"), and nothing else, with Irving Berlin's "The Near Future" (from *Ziegfeld Follies of 1919*). Berlin borrowed it from a nineteenth-century hymn. Whether the Johnstones borrowed it from the same place, or from Berlin, is an interesting question. Thanks for asking.

of costumes and stagecraft, in musicals low on narrative or substance. These songs bore no burden of character or content. They had lyrics only because it would have been silly to have the singers going, "Ooooooh, aaaaaaaah, la la la" all the time. I think Grandpit just dashed 'em off and moved on to things he was more interested in.

Some of Will's lyrics seem needlessly awkward, in a way that makes me think Tom wrote the music first. I have no proof that this was their technique, but we *know* Will was a much better writer than his lyrics alone would indicate, and I've got to think that if he was starting from scratch, or collaborating spontaneously with Tom, he would have been more creative. There have been many good poets or prose writers who've proven to be poor lyricists, but their problem is almost always *overwriting*; they're accustomed to forms in which it's possible to pack in more words and ideas without losing the reader. Johnstone's lyrics are underwritten, but generally not with spare elegance; he takes not much of an idea and stretches it beyond reason.

Will was an inspired scenarist, but evidently Tom was the inspired songwriter. Consequently, the music now has antique charm, but the lyrics do not. There is one song from *I'll Say She Is* with music *and* lyrics credited to Tom ("When Shadows Fall"), and I think its lyrics are slightly better— no wit or substance is attempted, but the lines scan better, and are more coherent.

One final point before I leave this and beg forgiveness: Given Will's lack of ambition as a lyricist, a major blow to the overall quality of these songs was Tom's excessive reliance on two melodic devices. Broadly speaking, in his up-tempo or comedy songs, the melodic lines often go back and forth between two notes, and then land, with the result that every other syllable is emphasized. The choruses of his ballads tend to have several long, held notes in a row, making it difficult to set words longer than one syllable. There's nothing wrong with the melodies as melodies, but they pose real challenges to the lyricist, and maybe Will just didn't have the time or the patience. He probably knew that the lyrics would largely be ignored whether he sweated over them or not, and he had a lot of other things to do. And if Will B. was indifferent to songs, he was in excellent company. His successor, George S. Kaufman, famously "hated music," in the words of *Cocoanuts* collaborator Irving Berlin.

I BEGAN TO SEE a new way forward. Now that I had five *I'll Say She Is* songs, I'd have to use them, but half the score was still missing. Clearly, it would now be better to use Johnstone songs from other shows than to compose new ones. My new thinking about the score went like this: *If I'm pulling in songs from other shows, I'll have to rewrite their lyrics. If I'm rewriting those lyrics, I can also polish the others. So there's a missing song called "Wall Street Blues"—I'll find something bluesy by Tom Johnstone, call it "Wall Street Blues,"*

What writing looks like: A rhyming dictionary, a purring cat, and mental anguish

and write a lyric Will B. might have written for it, had he been a slightly better lyricist. So I would *collaborate* with Will B. Johnstone, across the decades, taking his lyrics and prose as his side of the argument, and sometimes letting him win, and sometimes letting myself win. Despite the blandness of his lyrics, taken in sum they do convey a certain attitude—resigned romanticism—and equal parts formal and colloquial language. They are preoccupied, naturally, with birds, kisses, and meteorology. I decided to honor these conventions.

In the major motion picture about how I adapted *I'll Say She Is*, there would be a montage here of a haggard, bewhiskered, thirtysomething maniac searching sheet music archives, skimming through catalogues, calling libraries, writing to Meg Farrell, writing to Ira Dolnick, and poring over hundred-year-old songs at four in the morning. Entering them, note by note, into Finale. Listening to them, singing them, recording them, playing them back, thinking about them, and falling asleep to them. The Finale transcriptions, though tedious and laborious, helped me to get inside the music. I understood the mechanics of these compositions, because I had literally put each note in its place.

The rules were:

1) No songs written after 1924.

2) The music had to be composed by either Tom or Alexander Johnstone.

3) If the original lyric was *not* by Will B. (or Tom), it would be disregarded entirely. When lyrics had to be created from scratch, I would incorporate words, phrases, and ideas from the Johnstone typescript, and from the increasing pile of other Johnstone work I was accumulating, whenever possible.

Over late nights and early mornings, stretching on for months and then years, a set of songs emerged. The arrangements were still only the published Tin Pan Alley versions; I would need an arranger to attend to the music with the same care I was giving to the lyrics. What I printed from Finale toward the end of 2011 was still in rough form, and it would continue to evolve. But it was, there on my desk, a score of *I'll Say She Is*. It was not exactly *the* score of *I'll Say She Is*, as heard in the twenties. But it had a lot of the same material, and other material of the same pedigree. It was a score written by two composers, Tom and Alexander Johnstone, and two lyricists, Will B. Johnstone and me. The four of us worked and reworked, argued and cajoled, and let me tell you, we had some showdowns, but I love those guys. (Incidentally, those Johnstones can *drink!*)

The fact that I had already half-written an alternate score for the show turned out to be a great advantage. After all, the titles and concepts of the songs had not changed. I had already done the most difficult and time-consuming part of the lyric-writing process: Making long lists of rhymes and associated words and phrases, and figuring out what each lyric needed to convey. So, maybe I couldn't use my existing lyric for "Gimme a Thrill," but I had a notebook filled with ideas for that song; uses of the title phrase; phrases with similar meanings or emphases; rhymes for *thrill*; rhymes for synonyms of *thrill*; useful phrases from Will B.'s various writings; and flapper slang copied from Jazz Age books, magazines, and newspapers. All I had to do was find suitable Johnstone music with a workable refrain phrase, and return to the candy store of my notebooks.

Originally, "The Wonderful Nile" had been set late in Act Two, in an Egyptian scene sometimes called "In the Sheik's Tent." The scene, and possibly the song, went back as far as *Love for Sale* in 1919. But before the Broadway opening of *I'll Say She Is*, the Egyptian piece was replaced by the mysterious "Beauty's Russian Garden" sequence. The first piece in this sequence, as listed in the Broadway playbill, was "The Wonderful River," which I suspect was a revision of "The Wonderful Nile." As far as I could tell, there was no connection between *any* of these pieces and the gimme-a-thrill plotline, and I never included any of it in my adaptation. However, I thought that the mock-exotic sound of "The Wonderful Nile" could work nicely in the opium den scene, which needed a song. I rewrote "The Wonderful Nile" as "The Dream Ship," keeping some of Will B.'s lyrics about visions and rivers.

The more straightforward love songs needed only light revision. For "The Thrill of Love" and "Only You," I wrote new lyrics for second choruses, and for "I'm Saving You for a Rainy Day" I clarified the metaphor and added a counterpoint section. The first chorus of "Rainy Day" will serve as an illustration of how I handled Johnstone lyrics that required reworking but not replacement. Here's Will B.'s original lyric:

> I'm saving you, dear, for rainy weather.
> So what if all the skies are gray?
> And what if fate's unkind and storms are brewing?
> I'll always draw the blind and go on wooing.
> Some sun will shine on. My heart's a feather,
> while thunder crash and lightning play.
> When we're together, let come what may.
> I'm saving you, dear, for a rainy day.

And the rewrite:

> I'm saving, you, dear, for rainy weather,
> because you'll turn the clouds away.
> One day it's simply vile, all ice and showers,
> then all at once you smile, and there are flowers.
> The sky is blue, dear, when we're together,
> so I will call when all is gray.
> Today the weather's fine! Let come what may.
> I'm saving you, dear, for a rainy day.

Among my least consequential changes was the deletion of the definite article from a song title. Not "*The* Thrill of Love"—an earthly experience—but "*Thrill* of Love," a philosophical idea. (Actually, I liked it because that's how it appeared in the concisely-rendered 1923 typescript.)

It was safe to assume that the lost opening number, "Do It," was a "welcome to the show" song, a direct statement to the audience, saying what a good time we're all about to have. I had wanted to keep the title "Do It," and use that phrase as the key lyric. I thought I could get a good deal of mileage (i.e., a lotta miles) out of the suggestiveness of the phrase, but I ran into two problems. First, I was working with a limited catalogue of Johnstone compositions. Only a few had the right impact for an opening number, and of these, none had a prominent melodic refrain that could smoothly accommodate the phrase "do it." The other, more severe problem was the long shadow cast by Cole Porter's "Let's Do It (Let's Fall in Love)." I found it impossible to write a twenties pastiche lyric that made playful use of the phrase *do it* without blatantly evoking the Porter song. I couldn't even hide behind the notion that songwriting, then as now, was derivative; the Porter song wasn't written until 1928.

Since the opening was to be a presentational number sung by the chorus, and it couldn't directly reference the story or the characters, I decided to make it a song *about* music, theatre, chorus girls, and nightlife—a *Broadway* song, about the culture and climate of Broadway at the time. It provided context for the show, rather than the story. Thus, "This Broadway Song," a phrase that sat perfectly on the refrain in one of Tom Johnstone's bounciest compositions. (It was originally called "Syncopate," with a lyric by Phil Cook, from the 1922 musical *Molly Darling*.)

The phrase *Broadway song*, like other references to the Big Street throughout the adaptation, was mine. The word *Broadway* does not occur anywhere in Johnstone's typescript, or in any of his surviving lyrics for *I'll Say She Is*. However, he did use it elsewhere (for example, in a song called "Good, Bad, Beautiful Broadway" from *Take it From Me*), as did Groucho Marx, in an *I'll Say She Is* ad lib ("Go ahead and shoot—you're on Broadway").

Broadway itself is the implied milieu of *I'll Say She Is*, and using the word in a Runyonesque manner would tell the contemporary audience something that the 1924 audience didn't need to be told.

> The sweet vernacular of that spectacular
> Broadway sound
> is overtaking us, forever making us
> Broadway bound.
> You can cruise the Caribbean or the Indies—
> we'll be here with all the characters at Lindy's!
> They're serenading us, and it's persuading us—
> this Broadway song.
>
> The fun is heightening beneath the brightening
> Broadway signs!
> When we can run around without the sun around,
> Broadway shines!
> You can keep your old aurora borealis—
> all we know is that she never played the Palace.

There was no title song in the original production. The number performed at the end of the Theatrical Agency scene was called "Pretty Girl," now lost.[4] But the situation is clear: The scene ends with the Agent asking, "Isn't she a beauty?" so everyone else can exclaim, "I'LL SAY SHE IS!" I thought it would be nice to musicalize this moment, so my replacement for "Pretty Girl" is a title song, performed by the Marx Brothers in response to the Agent's question. The music, by Tom Johnstone, comes from *Up in the Clouds*. A large portion of the lyric is by Will B. Johnstone, because I used so many of

---

[4] Incidentally, when I identify songs as "lost," what I mean is that I've been unable to find them. As my experience with *I'll Say She Is* has repeatedly demonstrated, lost things have a way of turning up. When additional songs from the original *I'll Say She Is* come to light, I add them to the adaptation in whatever form possible.

Gimme a Thrill *sheet music*

his words in constructing it—including, happily, a workable inclusion of the old "rich man, poor man" device. I used it as a *reference*, indicating universal consensus, rather than an assignment of roles to eight specific suitors:

> Rich man and poor man,
> beggar man and thief,
> doctor and lawyer,
> merchant and the chief,
> all in agreement—isn't she a whiz?
> Isn't she a beauty?
> I'll say she is!

As soon as I set these words to the music, I got in touch with Mikael and told him that "rich man, poor man" was, in some sense, back in. He was very pleased.

"Gimme a Thrill" was one of the most important missing numbers, because it had to introduce the Lotta Miles character. Theoretically, Beauty is the lead, but she doesn't appear until fifteen minutes into the show, and she walks onto a stage which is already populated by all four Marx Brothers, so her entrance needed a lot of impact. The situation demanded a coy "come and get me" number like "I Wanna Be Loved By You" or "I Want to Be Bad." Alexander Johnstone's catalogue included a piece of music that worked, but its phrasing dictated an intricate rhyme scheme full of short, oddly-emphasized phrases, a real challenge to set smoothly, and a lyric I never stopped tinkering with.[5]

> Good thing you're here, dear.
> Let me make it clear, dear.
> Be a dear, dear—
> Gimme a thrill!
> At our command there
> waits a wonderland there—
> Don't just stand there!
> Gimme a thrill!
> Sir, won't you please attend me,
> then send me the bill?
> Give me laughter that
> lasts and after that,
> give me another thrill!

The Wall Street number, also perpetually rewritten, was difficult to envision. There was some priceless "Tragedy of Gambling" recitative in the

---

[5] Meanwhile, the original song has turned up. Interestingly, the published version on file at the Library of Congress has its printed title, "Give Me a Thrill," corrected by hand to read "Gimme a Thrill."

typescript, which I planned to incorporate into the song, but it was all based on elaborate costumes and carefully-timed entrances and exits, and would obviously have to be developed in rehearsal. I scored it with two separate Alexander Johnstone compositions, edited together, and later condensed all of it in order to accommodate a Tom Johnstone piece that lent itself beautifully to the "Wall Street Blues."

I had the most fun working on "Hail Napoleon," and was pleased to find that some of my earlier Napoleon lyrics fit perfectly into a giddy Tom Johnstone showtune from *Up in the Clouds*. This song was an admitted jump forward in the Marx Brothers timeline, but I put it in because I really, really wanted Groucho/Napoleon to sing a Groucho/Napoleon song, and I was sure that other fans would want the same thing.

> CHORUS: Hail Napoleon! He'll never miss.
> Hail Napoleon! Give him a kiss.
> Look at him seizing power from the Swiss.
> GROUCHO: My hand is freezing!
> I'll have to stand like this.
> *(He puts his hand in his coat, in the classic*
> *Napoleon pose.)*
> CHORUS: Hail Napoleon! Hats will be hurled
> when you conquer the world!
> So dressy, I guess he could be the queen,
> or maybe a baby merchant marine.
> He's neither, so either it's Halloween,
> or it's a Napoleon scene!

In the verse, I indulged in an even more blatant anticipation of Kalmar and Ruby. For *Animal Crackers*, they'd given Groucho "Hello, I must be going / I cannot stay / I came to say / I must be going." In "Dr. Hackenbush," it was "The only reason that I came / is so that I can go." For the new *I'll Say She Is*, I wrote:

Clearly, I'm Napoleon. I've come to stop the show.
I'm very pleased to be here, but I think you ought to
 know,
I only came to tell you that it's time for me to go.

My justification, in case you're wondering, was that the entire Napoleon scene is already about coming and going. Groucho keeps announcing that he's leaving, then leaving, then returning and announcing that he's back, but has to go. It would be reasonable to guess that the Napoleon scene put the "Hello, I must be going" idea into the ether in the first place.

"The Inception of Drapery" wasn't really a *song* in the original show, though I'm sure it involved music. Verbally, it had consisted mostly of Zeppo announcing the various exotic gifts which were presented to Beauty:

Silks from Japan.
Pearls from the South Sea Isles.
Headdress from Zulu.
Fan from Timbuctoo.
Laces from Brittany.
Furs from Russia.
Perfume from Hindustan.

I reassigned the number to Ruby Mintworth, and expanded upon the list of presents, setting it to a lovely Tom Johnstone waltz:

These laces, from enchanted places,
and these brocaded silks from Japan!
Wear your red dress, and a Zulu headdress.
If a fur coat is Russian, there is no discussion.
This fan's new—it's from Timbuktu, too—
made with feathers and leathers from Gao.
Turkish perfumes, frankincense and myrrh fumes—
the inception of drapery is now!

As for "When Shadows Fall," I was pleased and humbled to discover that it was dramatically improved by the Johnstones. Tom wrote a simpler, more emotional, and altogether better melody than the one I had devised, and the title phrase was perfectly, hauntingly set. The rest of the lyric was nothing special, but it would have needed revision anyhow, since I had moved the song from the Chinatown opium den to the speakeasy scene in Act Two, and the existing lyric didn't make sense for that moment in the love story. (Though when I made this case to my imaginary Johnstone brothers, they pointed out that it had made even less sense in the Chinatown scene.)

This is how "When Shadows Fall" ended up, set to Tom's music, and following the design, if few of the actual words, of his lyric:

> Either this is real or it's a beautiful dream.
> We're sitting on a rainbow eating peaches and cream.
> If only the dream would last.
> I'm lighter than a feather, full of get-up-and-go.
> You and me together, that's a heck of a show.
> Next thing you know, it's almost past.
>
> When shadows fall,
> and stretch across September,
> when hope's an ember,
> then we'll remember:
> We had a ball,
> and who could ask for more
> than the time we spent
> in nineteen twenty-four?
> When shadows fall,
> and all the fun has faded,
> please don't be jaded.
> Keep the past in sight.
> We're in love! We're in electric light.
> Even Broadway's just for us tonight.

When shadows fall,
and colder winds are blowing,
when tears are flowing,
we'll wake up knowing
we did it all.
So darling, don't be still!
Let's go find the throngs,
the stars, the songs, the thrill.
When shadows fall,
our love for one another,
brother to brother,
is bright enough to see.
We're alive, and what a thing to be!
Baby, Broadway's just for you and me.

V.
CINDERELLA
BACKWARD

ILIKE TO WORK on one thing at a time. I think the work is better when I'm immersed in it exclusively. And since I'm already balancing my real work with a time-consuming day job, the fight for total focus begins on the mat. Still, I worked on *I'll Say She Is* for so long, without a clear path toward production, that detours were inevitable. Between rewrites, I toyed with an atheist musical called *God for President*, an oratorio based on the films of Georges Méliès, and a *Groucho and Dumont* cabaret act for Kathy and me. I tried to revive my solo show *400 Years in Manhattan*. And, as an exercise, I wrote a screen adaptation of my favorite musical, *Merrily We Roll Along*. None of these projects came to fruition. However, one day I was talking with West Hyler, a dear old friend as well as a hot young director, and he suggested that I pitch *400 Years in Manhattan* to Trav S.D.

I knew who Trav S.D. was. I didn't know him personally, although we had met once, briefly and inauspiciously, when I was the box office manager at HERE Arts Center. I knew that he was a prolific playwright, performer, and producer; that he worked in a style very much to my taste; that he was a modern-day impresario at the forefront of a neo-vaudeville movement, exemplified by his own American Vaudeville Theatre; and that he was an authority on old-time showbiz, having written the acclaimed *No Applause— Just Throw Money: The Book That Made Vaudeville Famous*. I'd been aware of him, and of the feeling that we were kindred comedy spirits, for some time.

West put us in touch, and I met Trav right in the middle of Times Square. He was wearing a wide-brim fedora, unironically. The conversation was pleasant, but it took a while to find its rhythm, as we're both slightly awkward. On stage, we're hammy showmen, but otherwise, we have the sensibilities of writers. I described *400 Years*, and presented Trav with a copy of the book based on the show; he later published a generous review on his widely-read blog, Travalanche. It didn't seem like he had much need for my solo show. But I knew he was a big Marx Brothers fan as well as a comedy historian,[1] and he might be interested to hear about *I'll Say She Is*. At the mention of the title, his eyes lit up, and our conversation sprang to life. He knew all about the original production. At that point, even I didn't know where the project was going, but Trav's enthusiasm was meaningful, and I said I'd be sure to keep him posted.

Reporting back to West on my conversation with Trav, I explained my work on *I'll Say She Is*, which I hadn't mentioned to West before. We've been close since high school, and he directed most of my early plays. In the 1990s, we wrote together, performed in nightclubs together, and co-directed a children's theatre company. (In fact, when we were nineteen, West produced and directed my first full-length musical, which was entitled *The Men in Mabel's Life*, and which bore some thematic and stylistic resemblance to *I'll Say She Is*.) He had since become a rising New York theatre director. West wasn't an avid Marx Brothers fan, but he knew their films through me, and liked them. In a toast given at my wedding in 2010, he offered a list of "Things I Learned from Noah," which included a Marx Brothers reference: "If someone welcomes you with open arms, the proper response is, 'How late do you stay open?'" He thought *I'll Say She Is* sounded interesting, potentially commercial, and well worth pursuing, and offered to read it.

We started meeting regularly to go through the script, talk, and argue. We spent *a year and a half* going through the script, talking, and arguing. These sessions with West were the best thing that could have happened to my writing process, and it was through them that the script approached its

---

[1] Trav would argue here that he is *not* an historian, a humble view he holds out of an abiding respect for those he considers *real* historians. *I* would argue that Trav has written two excellent and authoritative books about history—of vaudeville and silent comedy—and that this makes him an historian.

final shape. Very often, it was improved by following West's suggestions. Occasionally it was improved by *not* following his suggestions, but realizing, through responding to them, what I wanted *I'll Say She Is* to be. Our rapport is fast and easy, like brothers—we've been talking and arguing about theatre since we were kids. West is perceptive, provocative, and wise. He is also stubborn, pontifical, and exhausting—just as stubborn, pontifical, and exhausting as I am. Sometimes I left our meetings dizzy with inspiration and newfound clarity, as though West had cut away all the brush that was obscuring my path. Other times, I left our meetings in a minute and a huff, and performed spiteful rewrites just to show him how wrong he was. Few things are more valuable to an artist than a collaborator who makes you defend your work. If you can't defend it, something is wrong.

West surprised me by championing an approach I called "Back to the Typescript." I had shown him Johnstone's 1923 document, thinking it would help him understand just how many blanks I had had to fill in. Wouldn't you know: West *loved* the typescript. He thought it was practically stageworthy as it was. I attributed this partly to the fact that, oddly enough, West had not memorized every single line of every Marx Brothers film. He wasn't an avid fan, so the comedy gap between the typescript and later Marx efforts was not as apparent to him. Or maybe it was because he was reading it from the perspective of a director, not a writer. Directing for the theatre is an interpretive act, and a show that seems fully-realized on paper can be boring for directors; it's more fun for them to do the realizing themselves. That's why directors love ancient drama, and Shakespeare—in addition to their histrionic splendor, these are public-domain texts that invite interpretation.

Whatever the reasons, after reading the typescript, West became its advocate. He accepted that it needed expansion, but he strongly urged me not to add entire elements that had no basis in the original, like the romantic subplot between the butler and the social secretary. He didn't approve of my addition of Mrs. Mintworth, either. He said that when he read the typescript, he "didn't miss" the dowager character. I assured him that people who loved the Marx Brothers would feel bereft if there was no Dumont figure. He countered that *Horse Feathers*, which we had recently watched together, seemed fine without one.

West also advised me to stick to the notion of suitors courting Beauty, and to take this idea seriously. Here's how he put it, characteristically, in a letter during the summer of 2011:

> The throughline is of course Lotta looking for a thrill, inside of a dramatic structure that is shaped like a 15th century morality play. It has a central character visiting a series of stations and meeting allegorical representations of various ideas ("richman," "poorman," "thief"). During her journey to choose the fate of her life, she tries out several different types of living. And there is a moral conclusion that love for another is more thrilling than the thrill of self-love that comes from money, drugs, or power. That there's one meaning to all lives, whether you are an empress, a beggar, or a criminal, and that meaning is love…I think you need to honor this by keeping Lotta always onstage, by keeping all eight characters attempting to thrill her . . .
>
> I think the joy of the play is the tension created by having these four madmen incorrectly placed in a polite summer revue. Someone once said of *Hamlet* that it would be a simple revenge tragedy if it wasn't for the philosopher inexplicably plunked down in the middle of it. That's sort of what I think about *I'll Say She Is*. But I think you've made the Marx Brothers too big in the show and you've lost something by doing so.

I imagined Johnstone telling the Marx Brothers: "Now, here's what we'll do, boys—we'll mimic the structure of a fifteenth-century morality play!" But West often sees things I don't. Many times, over many years, he has made some pronouncement or some decision which I thought was obviously, insanely wrong—only to realize later, to my embarrassment, that he was brilliantly and inarguably right. So I've learned that his suggestions are usually worth trying, even if they seem wrong to me at the outset. We hadn't worked together since the mid-1990s, but we'd been through the process together on five or six shows, and I knew how this worked. In preparing my next draft, I didn't take *all* of his suggestions, but I took more of them than I instinctively wanted to. The rule I set for this draft was that if West suggested something, and it was not *ruinous*, I would try it.

So, I excised the Ruby/Simpson love story and reassigned their songs (which at this stage included "When Shadows Fall") to other characters. I kept the character of Simpson as the butler, but I cut the social secretary altogether. I kept the dowager, Mrs. Mintworth, but changed her first name to Ruby, and gave her some of Ruby's dialogue from the typescript. In the original show, Ruby the Social Secretary had served as a companion and confidante to the heroine (in one scene, anyway, after which Ruby vanished). It was less of a stretch, then, to simply make Ruby the aunt/guardian; that way, I could keep the dowager, but in a manner more faithful to the original show. I did not revert to Johnstone's eight suitors, nor to the "rich man, poor man" motif (except as referenced in the title song), but I did reinstate two of the non-Marx suitors, bringing the total to six, and removed the Brothers from some of the scenes I'd written them into, like Wall Street and Chinatown.

I gave the typescript a fresh read, and sure enough, there was material in it which I had dismissed too hastily. In places, where my initial reaction had been *This isn't very good—I'll replace it with something else*, I found things to salvage or rework. But more than material, the "Back to the Typescript" fever that overtook the project in the summer of 2011 was about tone. I used the typescript as a style guide, rewriting the material I had added, to make it sound more like the typescript. There were, of course, plenty of Johnstone lines I had recognized as gems and kept verbatim. But there were others I had needlessly tinkered with. My adaptation was overwritten.

At the same time, my ongoing research was revealing more and more of what Johnstone had written. The archives of the *New York Morning World*, to which Johnstone was a regular contributor, were a particular treasure trove. I spent several weeks combing through as much Johnstone prose as I could gather, clipping useful words, phrases, jokes, and ideas, and finding places for them in *I'll Say She Is*. None of these interpolations had a substantial individual effect on the show's content, but collectively, they brought more of the original librettist's mind into the script, and enhanced its overall texture and authenticity.

I added material from surviving fragments of the Marxes' earlier vaudeville tabloids, particularly *On the Mezzanine*. The Theatrical Agency sketch had, of course, been part of *I'll Say She Is* from the beginning. I now imported some Groucho / Mrs. Gould dialogue and gave it to Groucho and Ruby Mintworth (who in effect became the secondary romantic couple Ruby and Simpson had been in my earlier drafts), as well as the reincorporation of the Agent and the Timbergian rhyming dialogue at the end of the show. These had recurred at the end of *On the Mezzanine*, and I borrowed them, with some revision, for the new *I'll Say She Is* finale. Other tidbits from *Mezzanine* wound up in the Cinderella Backward scene.

EVENTUALLY, I HAD a draft sound enough to share with a few more people. At the top of my list was Meg Farrell. We had been in regular communication; Meg, Mikael, and I had had an enjoyable *I'll Say She Is* research-and-revelation e-mail thread going for months. But I was still nervous about showing her the work I'd done on Grandpit's lyrics and libretto. I was afraid she would disapprove of the liberties I'd taken, and I didn't want to proceed without Meg's approval. But it was time. I wanted her to read it, and I wanted to meet her in person, and I felt emboldened by the rewrites. I e-mailed the script to her, perhaps with more caveats than necessary, and a few days later we met for coffee in midtown.

I had nothing to worry about. Meg liked the script and lyrics, and offered no criticism, just expressions of faith in my abilities and intentions. She said she was glad someone was taking on this challenge, that it was my project, and she didn't want to hover over my shoulder. She said she would be happy to offer whatever permission or support I needed. She was anything but defensive about the material, and pointed out that my rewriting of lyrics and interpolation of songs was perfectly in line with tradition. Just as *Love for Sale* had become *Gimme a Thrill*, and *Gimme a Thrill* had become *I'll Say She Is*, now *I'll Say She Is* was entering its next iteration.

And then she said: "Do you want to see the diaries?"

I gasped, first at the thought that she was about to reveal some precious secrets of the Johnstone journals, and then at the thought that she was about to pull a precious, hundred-year-old artifact out of her backpack in a diner. Meg saw all of this going on in my mind, laughed, and said, "They're photocopies."

So they were—and there they were!—pages of hurried semi-script, set down by Will B. Johnstone in concise, dated entries, one brisk paragraph per day. Meg read them aloud and scanned each line with a capped pen as she read, because the handwriting was tricky. Sitting there, listening to Johnstone's great-granddaughter read unpublished words he had written in the 1920s, about how he met and worked with the Marx Brothers, was one of the great "I love New York" moments of my life. The words had travelled ninety years, and about nine blocks. I scolded myself for not keeping a diary. It really is a good thing to do, for the benefit of any future writers who may want to adapt your work.

Meg and I always have lively conversations. We're quite well-matched for being granularly aware of obscure corners of musical theatre history. Especially at this stage of my immersion in *I'll Say She Is*, it was an indescribable relief to spend time with someone who could appreciate an offhand joke about Joseph M. Gaites.

Sometimes I felt that *I'll Say She Is* was a charmed project, because the lucky breaks kept piling up. I was lucky to meet Meg, and I was lucky that Meg was Meg; I was lucky to cross paths with Mikael and Kathy and Ira; I was lucky to spend all those hours talking through the show with West. In another remarkable piece of luck, one day West happened to be talking to his agent, Barbara Hogenson, about a show he was directing. To illustrate a point about the problems of a large cast, he said, "For instance, my friend is working on this adaptation of a Marx Brothers show called *I'll Say She Is*, and ideally it needs a cast of twenty or thirty, but . . . "

But Barbara's eyes had lit up at the mention of the show's title, in such a way that derailed whatever West had been talking about, and instantly changed the subject to *I'll Say She Is*.

"I didn't know this before, but Barbara and her family are *huge* Marx Brothers fans," West told me on the phone. "She knows all about *I'll Say She Is*. Not only that—she represents the authorship for new productions of *Cocoanuts* and *Animal Crackers*, and she wants to meet you."

Shortly thereafter, West and I spent an uproarious evening with Barbara Hogenson; her husband, film writer Jeffrey Couchman; and their daughter Ella. Barbara, Jeffrey, and I gleefully exchanged Marxian obscurities while West and Ella stared at us like puzzled sociologists. I talked about my work on *I'll Say She Is*, my lifelong Marx Brothers obsession, and my experiences playing Groucho. Jeffrey showed me his autographed copy of *Groucho and Me*, and in a terrible unthinking moment, I put my hand on the page and touched the signature. It was an instinct, to touch the ink that had been inside the pen that had been held in the hand of Julius Henry Marx, on the chance that some fraction of his greatness might find its way from the curve of his capital G to my own synapses. I don't know much about autograph collecting, but it occurred to me a half-second too late that autograph collectors probably don't want you touching their autographs. I imaged that the oils in my skin would cause the ink, the signature, and the entire page to instantly disintegrate.

"I'm so sorry," I said, pulling my hand away, but Jeffrey laughed and said, "It's okay, I understand."

I'll Say She Is was accumulating important allies left and right, but there was still no indication that it would be produced, no real leads toward money or opportunity. West was interested in directing it, but we felt stymied by the show's bigness. Could it be effectively workshopped, or would we need a full production just to convey what the show was? I knew how to self-produce indie theatre, but West was biting at the ankles of Broadway, and it wasn't hard to get romantic about the notion that Broadway was where *I'll Say She Is* belonged. Uncertainty pervaded, and momentum slowed. I felt powerless to move the thing forward. Occasionally West or I would pitch the show somewhere, and we had a smattering of talks with prospective producers or collaborators. But nothing took. I kept working on the script and lyrics, but West was a working director, always running off to direct an opera in Germany or a circus in Brazil,[2] and could not be expected to focus full-time on my labor of love.

I'd continued to share successive drafts of the script with Kathy Biehl. By e-mail, she introduced me to her friend Robert S. Bader, whose name I knew well. Bader is one of the world's leading Marx Brothers scholars and researchers, and the editor of *Groucho Marx and Other Short Stories and Tall Tales*, an anthology of lost Groucho prose. The first time Bader and I spoke on the phone, he answered with, "So you're the *I'll Say She Is* guy!" We spent an pleasant half hour comparing research and discussing miscellany. He had compiled a spreadsheet which identified the date, city, and venue of every performance of *I'll Say She Is*, from Allentown through Detroit, which he generously shared with me. He said he had spreadsheets like this for *all* of the Marx Brothers' stage efforts—reference tools he'd painstakingly created while he worked on a comprehensive chronicle of their stage career. As he described things he'd discovered about *I'll Say She Is*, many of which were

---

[2] West would tell you that he's never actually directed an opera in Germany or a circus in Brazil. This is a simple matter of his word against mine.

new to me, Robert would occasionally pause and quiz me.

"Of course, the show flopped in Boston right after it left the Walnut. You know what happened to them in Boston?"

"Yeah, it was respectfully reviewed, but there were a lot of musicals in town, and especially the Ziegfeld road show. . ."

"Starring...?"

"Gallagher and Shean?"

"Very good."

It was a very good conversation, and we hung up saying we'd speak again soon.

Around the same time, I had an e-mail correspondence with Paul G. Wesolowski, a legendary figure among Marx Brothers fans. Wesolowski, known fondly as Wesso, had been the editor and publisher of *The Freedonia Gazette* (1978-1991). This was a groundbreaking publication, which expanded Marx fans' knowledge of the boys, and awareness of each other. Paul used to travel around to libraries, and leave little cards stuck in books about the Marxes, so that fans who checked out the books would also learn about the *Gazette*, and about Paul's annual gatherings. Besides his vast archive of research materials, he's the owner of the world's largest collection of Marx Brothers artifacts and memorabilia. A large part of this collection is displayed in his home in New Hope, Pennsylvania, where he holds annual Open Houses attended by Marx Brothers fans, insiders, and subscribers to the *Gazette*. I had only dreamed of attending such an event, but I'd read about them, and I knew Wesso's name from the acknowledgments page of almost every book written about the Marx Brothers. I thought he was someone I should talk to about *I'll Say She Is*, but I wasn't sure what to ask him. I just wanted him to know about my project. I asked if he was aware of any earlier attempts to revive *I'll Say She Is* since 1925. I received a friendly response from Paul, saying that it sounded like a very interesting project, and as far as he knew, nobody else had yet taken it on.

These exchanges with Robert Bader and Paul Wesolowski gave me the feeling that I was getting close to the heart of Marxism, that I was moving among the Marxerati. The feeling was reinforced in March of 2012, when I received a letter from Kevin Fitzpatrick, inviting me to serve on the planning committee for a citywide Marx Brothers festival planned for 2014. I knew Kevin as "the Dorothy Parker guy," who led walking tours of landmarks relevant to Parker and her Algonquin cohorts. Kevin had written a book I admired, *A Journey into Dorothy Parker's New York*. He was also a friend of Kathy's. She and I joined a wacky gang assembled by Kevin for occasional meetings, usually in moody midtown Manhattan locations, to plan the festival.

But the idea that I might find myself standing in the wings of a New York theatre, made up as Groucho, prepared to step into the light and deliver *I'll Say She Is* to its first audience in ninety years—that still felt like a distant cigardream.

BETWEEN THE SUMMERS of 2012 and 2013, I worked on two unexpected projects, both of which had lasting consequences for *I'll Say She Is*.

First, Trav S.D. re-entered the picture, and invited me to appear in *Travesties of 2012*. This latest incarnation of his American Vaudeville Theatre show was being presented at the 45th Street Theatre[3] as part of the New York Musical Theatre Festival, an annual showcase rather seductively known as NYMF. That show was a much-needed break from writing; it was a pleasure and a relief to perform in front of an audience, which I hadn't done since *Groucho on the Air*, more than a year before. It was also surprisingly nice, after co-writing and co-producing all those agitprop shows, to be responsible only for my performance.

---

[3] Now the Davenport Theatre.

And it was good to work with Trav. Other than our tentative chat in the middle of Times Square, we hadn't spent any time together, though I can't say we got to know each other well during *Travesties* either. But we did have some good conversations, talked comedy, and occasionally talked *I'll Say She Is*. I was still researching and tinkering with the script, incorporating newly-discovered nuggets, and refining lyrics. When scraps of *I'll Say She Is* were floating around in my brain, I sometimes shared them with Trav, knowing he was part of the very small crowd that knew about my project and was interested.

It was fun to observe Trav, an enigmatic figure who presented himself as a link to old showbiz. His stage persona wore greasepaint glasses as well as a greasepaint moustache, and even in real life, he was often seen wearing a pith helmet. He carried a handkerchief. He played the ukulele and bellowed original songs with titles like "Buy My Book." At the same time, he was an accomplished playwright whose works covered a wide range of styles and subjects. The author of *No Applause—Just Throw Money* was also the author of a rock musical about Charles Manson. Although he often seemed to have just arrived from 1912, he was still unmistakably a figure of the contemporary downtown theatre scene, an exponent of Charles Ludlam and Charles Busch. That's the dichotomy I related to, the idea that it was possible to have one foot in the world of the Marx Brothers and the other in the world I'd been knocking around in. The imaginary walls between historical periods collapsed when Trav was around. He seemed to have the whole twentieth century flowing through him.

Like earlier editions of Trav's vaudeville project, *Travesties of 2012* was a variety show, crammed with self-contained acts—singers, dancers, comedians, storytellers, a contortionist, a roper, an impressionist, a mentalist—all recruited by Trav, who presided as master of ceremonies. There were also comedy sketches and musical numbers, written by Trav and directed by John Hurley, performed by a "core cast." I was part of the core cast, and I also had a solo vaudeville turn, performing my "United Nations Song" (a lightning-fast,

Danny-Kaye-via-Tom-Lehrer patter song which lists all of the member states of the U.N.). My favorite part of *Travesties* was a Trav sketch, in verse, entitled "The Crime of the Rhyme." It owed something to Herman Timberg and the Theatrical Agency scene, and I was cast in what was essentially the Groucho role (though for variety, I performed it at about 50% Gleason).

I had been away from the theatre too long, sweating in solitude over jokes and lyrics, without the roar, the smell, the stardust, the tinsel. It was the first time I'd performed in the theatre district, not in a Village blackbox but up among the glittering marquees of Times Square. I'd arrive at the theatre amid eccentrically-clad artists doing vocal warmups, rehearsing snatches of Irving Berlin and Friedrich Hollaender; a cowboy practicing with his lariat; dancers stretching; comedians schticking. It was like being backstage at *The Muppet Show*. It was a reminder that archival digging and surgical rewriting were not ends unto themselves, but small steps toward the true goal of putting on a show.

I loved walking around Times Square every day, after three years saturated with research about 1920s Broadway. I spent a lot of time on the corner of Broadway and 39th, staring incredulously at the dreadful office building which occupies the former site of the Casino Theatre, and I hunted down the addresses of Texas Guinan's speakeasies, and other such ghosts. My research had given me a wealth of information about Jazz Age New York that had no direct place in *I'll Say She Is*, and during the summer of *Travesties* I began to envision another musical, built partly of these leftover findings. I called it *Broadway Memory*, and quickly finished a rough draft and a handful of songs. But I was distressed to realize that this was another musical with the same problem as *I'll Say She Is*—too damn big. *Broadway Memory* took place in spectacular locations, over fifty years, and had about fifty characters, including several who were seen in both youth and old age. I didn't want to clog up the pipeline by trying to make this ambitious show happen, with *I'll Say She Is* still awaiting production.

But *I'll Say She Is* was in suspended animation, and after *Travesties* I wanted to stay productive. So I decided to turn *Broadway Memory* into a newspaper-style daily comic strip, titled *Love Marches On*. I published one installment per day—black and white strips on weekdays and Saturdays, color "broadsheets" on Sundays. The story unfolded over the course of 188 strips, presented online from January 1 to July 7, 2013. *Love Marches On* usurped *I'll Say She Is* as my primary focus during these months, but it was full of *I'll Say She Is* references, and felt to me like a parallel work. It also turned out to be the most serious and personal thing I'd ever written for public consumption.[4]

DURING THE MONTHS that I spent with *Love Marches On*, meetings for Kevin Fitzpatrick's Marx Brothers festival continued. By the summer, we had the outlines of a plan for what was now called Marxfest. Of the dozen or so who had attended the early meetings, a group of six remained to form the Marxfest Committee. Kevin was our President and Founder, and the rest of us were the Freedonia Chamber of Deputies:

Brett Leveridge, devoted Marxist and acclaimed humorist, author of *Men My Mother Dated and Other Mostly True Tales*, a gentleman of witty tongue and natty attire.

Jonny Porkpie, impresario, bon vivant, and self-appointed Burlesque Mayor of New York, whose Pinchbottom Burlesque company combines striptease with narrative theatre.

The aforementioned Kathy Biehl.

The aforementioned Trav S.D.

And me.

We planned a month-long festival, to occur in May of 2014, in locations all over the city. There would be at least one event in each of the five boroughs.

---

[4] Why, yes, there *is* a *Love Marches On* book—thanks for asking! It contains the entire run of comic strips, along with much additional material. If you want to go read *Love Marches On* before continuing, go ahead; I'll wait here.

Kevin had been inspired by Bill Marx, son of Harpo, who'd declared that May 15, 2014 would be an International Day of Laughter. The date was the likely centennial of the day Leonard, Arthur, Julius, and Milton were assigned their famous nicknames by monologist Art Fisher, during that mythic poker game in Galesburg, Illinois. In addition to the May 15 holiday, Bill Marx's CGH Society (Chico, Groucho, Harpo) had announced a two-day Marx Brothers convention, to be held in Rancho Mirage, California, in March. Kevin thought that since New York was the Brothers' hometown, and the site of many of their greatest triumphs, there should be some equivalent New York celebration in May.

From there, Marxfest grew into a sprawling and ambitious undertaking. We forged a few helpful partnerships, and the Museum of Modern Art agreed to screen their beautiful print of *Duck Soup*. But Marxfest was a thoroughly self-produced, fan-driven phenomenon. Each member of the Committee produced his or her own Marx-related events, and we promoted them all together, our joint coffers enhanced only by a $5,000 Kickstarter campaign. Kevin hired a press agent, Ron Lasko, at his own expense. By the time Marxfest took place, there were more than two dozen events on the official calendar, including film screenings, lectures, parties, performances, and more than one life-changing experience.

It was obvious to me that *I'll Say She Is* had to be part of Marxfest somehow. For one thing, it could not possibly have a better or more appreciative audience. For another, history plainly demanded it: May 2014 was not just the centennial of the stage names, but also the ninetieth anniversary of the Broadway opening of *I'll Say She Is*. I resolved that my adaptation must be put before an audience, one way or another, in May. How to make that happen was, as always, a perplexing question.

Then, in his puckish way, West Hyler suddenly bounded forward with a genuine opportunity and a clear, decisive plan. He had convinced the director of a prominent Off Broadway theatre to include *I'll Say She Is*, under West's direction, in its 2014 season—conveniently enough, in May—as part of its annual series of staged readings. West thought this would be the perfect developmental first step for a Broadway-bound revival. And in an instant, there it was: a chance to present *I'll Say She Is* to a New York audience, near the anniversary of the original, and coinciding with a great convergence of Marx Brothers fans upon the city.

There were only a million problems.

West was brilliant with the script. But when we discussed a production, it was increasingly clear that we didn't have the same vision for the show. The current draft represented a series of small compromises and an impasse or two, but I think we could have navigated these if not for a major conceptual disagreement. I wanted to present *I'll Say She Is* as though it *is* 1924 (with period-appropriate stagecraft), and these *are* the Marx Brothers. West envisioned a straightforward modern revival, with four actors playing not the Marx Brothers but *the roles the Marx Brothers played*. He was staunchly opposed to "impersonations," and felt that the familiar voices and mannerisms should merely be suggested. In my equally unswervable opinion, the four actors cast as Groucho, Harpo, Chico, and Zeppo must resemble the real Marx Brothers *as closely as possible*, and must try to sound and behave exactly like the real thing. The job of these four actors is to *be* the Marx Brothers, to understand on an innate level the way Marx Brothers move and talk and think. They should be performers who have played the roles before, who revere the Marxes, who grew up watching their movies, who…no, I'm not thinking of anyone in particular…why?

Yes, it was clear that if West took the reins, I would not be playing Groucho. The show would be cast, as all shows in this series were, with emerging Broadway talent. Two rehearsals and an Equity staged reading.

I simply could not take this chance, with the first public hearing of the Napoleon scene in two generations, and invite the Marxfest audience to see it. This seemed irreconcilable, and not just because I wanted the role and believed in my rightness for it. I could imagine a compelling reason to let someone else play Groucho, but I would certainly want that person to play

Groucho. I'm not normally opposed to the reinterpretation of classic characters or beloved works. In fact, I'm strongly in favor of it, especially in the theatre, where it's been keeping familiar stories interesting for centuries. I wouldn't even say that *Cocoanuts* and *Animal Crackers* are too sacred for reinterpretation. But this was different. *This* project, this first presentation of *I'll Say She Is* since the Marx Brothers themselves hung it up, had to be done in their honor. They *were* the show and always would be. This meant not only that the actors playing the Brothers should replicate their presence faithfully, but that decisions made on this project must be motivated first by love for the Marx Brothers and a desire to honor and perpetuate their work.

I'd been going along with the understanding that West knew how to get to Broadway, and *I'll Say She Is* belonged there. It was fine to be uncompromising about my other work, which was self-produced and relatively inexpensive, but this was something *big*, this was *the Marx Brothers*, and my role was to guide *their* work back to the public spotlight. But the special nature of the project was the reason I *couldn't* go along with an approach that didn't feel right. This was the Marx Brothers, my heroes, the greatest comedy act of all time. To attempt to recreate their work was to assume an awesome responsibility. My role was to protect the work, not just to promote it. If I had just written an original play, and someone had a plan to get it to Broadway, I might submit to the corresponding vision, even with misgivings; the worst possible outcome would be having my name on something I don't like. But to take the same gamble with the names of my greatest heroes would be unacceptable.

This was all painful. Around this time, I suffered a repetitive stress injury from too many sleepless hours of intense writing, drawing, and piano-pounding. My right hand was in a brace, useless for several weeks. I have memories of wandering around Washington Heights at all hours, cradling my aching hand and trying to balance my phone on my shoulder, having emotional conversations with West, as we tried to find a harmonious way forward.

We couldn't quite do this, and it was heartbreaking. I had come to

251

equate our creative reunion with the return of *I'll Say She Is*, and the reanimated brotherhood it implied. One day West and I will do a show together, and it will be wonderful. It was not to be *I'll Say She Is*. But was *I'll Say She Is* to be?

VI.
UP IN THE CLOUDS

I HAD WALKED AWAY from a major opportunity, and now I was lost at sea. The future of *I'll Say She Is* was less certain. Self-producing it was financially impossible, and even if an effective fundraising campaign could be waged, or a grant could be obtained, there was so little time. It was October of 2013, and Marxfest was just eight months away. Now my insistence that *I'll Say She Is* be a central feature of Marxfest was suddenly a liability. We'd been touting the festival as including the historic return of a lost masterpiece, and now what if I couldn't deliver it?

I was standing at the base of a mountain, with no hope of scaling it alone. As strange as it was not to be working with West, it was even stranger not to be working with Amanda. Except for the anomaly of *Love Marches On*, all of my creative efforts since 2001 had been not just my work but *ours*; she staged and schemed the Nero Fiddled shows, while I coached the comedy. In 2007 she directed me in *400 Years in Manhattan*. She's my creative partner as well as my life partner—an outstanding artist, thinker, and leader, besides being the person I love and trust more than anyone else on the planet. But Amanda officially joining me on *I'll Say She Is* was not a viable notion at the time. She had just started a demanding new job in the ad biz, and was throwing herself into it with characteristic zeal and vigor. She followed my *I'll Say She Is* exploits with interest, but there didn't seem to be room in her life for an enormous theatrical project. And unlike the shows we'd created together, *I'll Say She Is* was always going to be more mine than ours. Amanda loves the Marx Brothers—in fact, at the time of this writing, I would say she is a true, devoted, and unusually knowledgeable fan. But in 2013, it seemed clear that she loved them through me; it wasn't quite her thing.

I wrote some desperate letters to people I knew who had some status in show business and might point me toward some resources, but that didn't go anywhere. I needed help.

There was one person I could think of who had the right combination of producing experience and an abiding love for the Marx Brothers, and that was Trav S.D. He was also a member of the Marxfest Committee, though he hadn't been attending meetings up to that point, preoccupied with other projects. I hesitated. I liked Trav a lot, but I didn't know him very well, and asking him to be my partner in such a precious and personal venture would be a leap of faith. I knew that Trav was accustomed to being at the center of his own theatrical world, often as writer, producer, director, and star. I wasn't sure if he'd want to be my co-pilot. I thought maybe it was presumptuous to ask him.

When I did ask him, he said, "Why, you little worm! How dare you ask that I, Trav S.D., sully my good name by associating myself with this—"

No, no, he was thrilled, and eager to get to work.

We started meeting regularly for lunch at the Waverly Restaurant in Greenwich Village. This spot was chosen because it was an approximate midway point between Trav's headquarters in Brooklyn and mine in Washington Heights. But it was also a lucky and familiar location for me. I've spent hundreds of hours at the Waverly, over two decades in New York. In 2008, when Brian Hoffman organized a reunion of our old high school improv group, after the show we wound up at the Waverly. This gave it official continuity, not only with five generations of Greenwich Village artists, but with the diners we haunted as stage-struck kids.

Trav and I soon found our footing together, and a plan emerged. We decided that in May, at Marxfest, we would present a staged reading—but a staged reading that felt like a show, with simple costumes and props, and with enough rehearsal to deliver the comedy effectively. This reading would be the first step toward a larger production, to take place later in the year.

The reading would get us some press, prestige, and attention, and would put us in a stronger position to attract enthusiasm and funds for the production. We agreed that I would play Groucho; that Kathy Biehl would at least get to audition for Ruby Mintworth; that we'd use a cast drawn partly from the neo-burlesque scene; that Trav would direct the staged reading as well as the ensuing production; and that if a commercial production resulted from these efforts, we'd hire a commercial director to take the helm. For the larger production later in the year, we decided to submit the show to the New York International Fringe Festival. If accepted, we'd present *I'll Say She Is* at the Fringe in August. If not, we'd produce it at another theatre in the fall.

At first I was skeptical about whether the Fringe was right for the show. The festival had been the origin of some legitimate successes, including *Urinetown*, a witty musical satire that made it all the way to Broadway and won Tony Awards for best score and best book. But, partly because of this breakthrough, the Fringe was closely associated with experimental, offbeat theatre, not classic showbiz. Even on Broadway, *Urinetown* didn't feel like a Broadway musical in the classic sense. It felt, in its own way, more like *A Chorus Line* or *Rent*—shows which unmistakably bore the stamp of their downtown origins, and were successful on Broadway partly for their "authenticity," for the unusual Main Stem presence of distinctive personal visions. The Broadway musicals that *I'll Say She Is* seemed to have the most in common with—*The Producers, Anything Goes, No No Nanette*—certainly would have looked out of place at the Fringe Festival.

I thought through this problem, discussed it with Trav, discussed it with Amanda, and concluded that the advantages of a Fringe production outweighed my concerns. These advantages included built-in conspicuousness, the guarantee of a production with minimal administrative needs, the services of a press agent, and the certainty that the show would be noticed and written about. Best of all, the Fringe Festival represented a chance to present *I'll Say She Is* free of commercial pressures.

The disadvantages, besides the question of appropriateness, had to do with the lightweight style of production required by the festival. A Fringe show can't have much in the way of scenery, special lighting, or physical production. You share a venue with dozens of other shows, and you arrive thirty minutes before curtain with all of your props and costumes in bags. You set up, put on the show, and then pack it all up to be out of the theatre again minutes later, while another show's army stormed the gates and began to urgently set up for *their* Fringe production. If *I'll Say She Is* was accepted, it would be an unusually large production for the festival, but it would still be a severely pared-down version. And only five performances. On the plus side, all of these things were a foregone conclusion to the Fringe audience. One attends a Fringe show knowing that it's essentially a workshop, a rough, bargain-basement version of something that generally needs more rehearsal, more production, and more money to really come across.

As I pondered all of this, I came to an important realization that altered some of my earlier thinking: *I'll Say She Is*, even in 1924, *was* in many ways a downtown show, in the sense that we now use the word. It was not the *Ziegfeld Follies*. It was a scrappy, quirky, ramshackle revue, independently produced, starring vaudevillians; it was a low-class interloper on Broadway. Today, we assume that any 1924 Broadway musical must be the opposite of the arty, self-consciously experimental downtown theatre scene. But the assumption is wrong, at least in the case of *I'll Say She Is* and its ilk. As we've seen, Broadway revues of the period *were* willfully artistic. And what could be more consciously experimental than the comedy of the Marx Brothers, a team famous for going out there and trying things, startling the audience with their fearlessness and spontaneity? If we hesitate to call them *experimental*, it's only because they're so much more entertaining than anything experimental is expected to be. They arrived on Broadway in a vehicle that was offbeat, idiosyncratic, and in some ways distinctly third-rate, but which they elevated to the level of great art.

I'll Say She Is was a Broadway musical, but it was a Broadway musical of a distant age, and a distant Broadway. It had less in common with the

Broadway fare of our own time than with the satire and burlesque that thrived below 14ᵗʰ Street.

THE STAGED READINGS were scheduled near the end of Marxfest, May 23 and 25. We chose the dates for their proximity to the ninetieth anniversary. The May 25 reading would be followed by a panel discussion about the show and its history.

Trav and I worked on the script together much the way West and I had. Trav had his own notes and suggestions. He contributed some new dialogue leading into "I'm Saving You for a Rainy Day," and suggested moving the speakeasy scene (and "When Shadows Fall') outdoors. We excised the two extra suitors, bringing it back down to the Four Marx Brothers, with additional thrills provided by Ruby (as in my earlier drafts, leading "The Inception of Drapery") and the Hop Merchant, who now introduced himself to Beauty after "When Shadows Fall," and led the way to the Chinatown opium den. The Thief was subsumed into the character of the Hop Merchant, much the way Chief had been subsumed into Zeppo.

The most radical of Trav's suggestions involved moving the Napoleon scene from the end of Act Two to the end of Act One, and moving the Chinatown and Courtroom scenes to Act Two. It was radical because one of the few widely-known facts about *I'll Say She Is* was that the Napoleon scene came at the end. Yet Trav's argument was quite sound: Since the Napoleon scene is framed as a fantasy sequence, and has nothing to do with the plotline, it doesn't belong in a climactic spot, late in the evening. The Chinatown/ Courtroom section placed the characters in the greatest peril, and made a fitting denouement. There was also a practical argument: Since the fans in the audience would be waiting for the Napoleon scene from the moment they entered the theatre, we might as well give it to them early, end Act One with a bang, and move on to other thrills.

And so, Wall Street became the first "thrill," followed by a scene with

Beauty and Zeppo in front of a marble fountain in Central Park ("I'm Saving You for a Rainy Day"). After our heroine sends Zeppo on his sad way, she encounters Chico. He's fishing in the marble fountain, and he reels in a 150-pound Harpo. What follows is essentially the original Marble Fountain scene, reassigned to Chico and Beauty, combined with some Beauty/Chief dialogue from an earlier scene. Discussion of Pygmalion and Galatea cues the Pygmalion ballet, which cues the Tramp Ballet. I decided to give the Tramp Ballet to Harpo and Chico, as part of an overall effort to expand Chico's role. From the Tramp Ballet, Chico goes right back into his conversation: "There, see what I mean?" She doesn't. She implores him to give her a thrill. "Well, lady, I tella you what I do. I am a hypnotist." (I bet you forgot Chico was a hypnotist.) The old hypnosis scene ensues, leading, as ever, into the Napoleon scene. End of Act One.

Act Two begins as in the original, with "The Inception of Drapery" (now preceded by some dialogue between a reproachful Ruby and her yet-unthrilled niece). Ruby and the chorus leave, with all their draperies, and, as before, Beauty longs for poverty and is visited by Groucho in Fairy Godmother drag ("Yoo-hoo! Here I am!"). Johnstone gave Groucho a line about "one of my assistant fairies," which I took as a cue to add Chico to the scene ("He's the head of our billing department, and that'll give you an idea of our billing department."). Groucho admires Beauty's dancing abilities ("Hot cole slaw!") and Chico leads her away to meet Prince Charming. Groucho gets a few moments with Ruby, and some jokes from *On the Mezzanine*. Then Harpo's rope gag. The Broadway scene, which used to be the speakeasy scene, has Beauty and Zeppo falling in love and singing "When Shadows Fall," but after the song she realizes that she is still not quite thrilled. The Hop Merchant lurches her way with the entreaties originally spoken by the Thief, and whisks her away to Chinatown. Opium den; courtroom; "Only You"; the greatest thrill of all is the thrill of love!

I reluctantly cut one beautiful number, "Up in the Clouds." I think it's Tom and Will B.'s best song, and I'd imported it mostly unaltered from their earlier musical. It was a song Meg remembered from her childhood—it had lived on as a lullaby in her family, and she remembered her mother singing it. The first time Meg and I met in person, in fact, we had talked about "Up in the Clouds," and she sang some of it, right there in the diner:

> We're dreaming daydreams, up in the clouds,
> far, far away dreams, up in the clouds . . .

So I was sorry to lose it. I'd incorporated it into the Cinderella Backwards scene, but it seemed to slow down the second act, and we had one too many chorus numbers.

I deleted, once and for all, the Alexander Woollcott speech, and the entire conceit of Woollcott as a presence in the show. It had never been necessary. Using Alexander Woollcott as a way into the Marx Brothers didn't make much sense, because audiences were more likely to be familiar with the Marxes than with Woollcott—leaving us no choice but to begin with *Groucho*, explaining who Woollcott is. No, whatever was being said in the Woollcott speech would be more appropriate as a note in the playbill.

Another small but fundamental change, implemented around this time, was the decision to stop calling the ingénue Lotta and revert to the character's original name, Beauty. This didn't change any of the material, as the character is never addressed by name in the show. But it reflected a change in approach. Whoever we cast in that role was not *really* going to be playing Lotta Miles, the way I'd be playing Groucho Marx. There was no Lotta Miles to play, since no audio or video of her existed. The prospect of asking an actress to play this role made me set aside my reservations about the character name, to clarify the performer's job.

I rewrote the finale. I had intended for "Only You" to transition into a simple reprise of the opening number. But now that we ended with Beauty's release from the clutches of the law, narrowly escaping a bum rap for murder, I thought a cheekier and more celebratory finale was needed. I recalled

Joe Adamson's description of a typical 1920s revue, which ended with the chorus singing, "It was nice having you to see our show, but now we're afraid it's time to go, tra la la, the end!" With this in mind, I crafted a reprise of the title song, with new lyrics:

> Folks, it's what you've waited for—
> the ending of the show!
> Sure, it's been spectacular,
> but now you'd like to go.
> May the thrill continue when this presentation ends,
> and may you run right out and tell your friends:
> *I'll Say She Is*—the winner in revue!
> *I'll Say She Is*—the start of something new!
> Take to the rooftops, shout it from above:
> *I'LL SAY SHE IS—*
> THE THRILL—
> OF—
> *LOOOOOOOOOOOOOVE!!!*

Once in a rare while, I write a line that catches me emotionally, that gives me goosebumps and throatlumps every time I think about it. "*I'll Say She Is*—the start of something new" has been one of those lines, from the moment it occurred to me, and every time I've heard it since.

SUDDENLY THE PROJECT was decisively moving forward. Casting was an immediate challenge, and Trav and I saw scores of performers before discovering the remarkable group that would bring the show back to life. Two key roles, which should have been among the most difficult to cast, fell right into place.

Robert Pinnock, an old friend and longtime collaborator of Trav's, did a wonderful Chico impression, capturing the eldest Marx Brother's insolence and vehemence. I heard him read a few lines and was instantly sold, and relieved. (The evidence, in every Marx Brothers recreation I've ever seen, suggests that Chico is the most difficult Marx Brother to impersonate.) Kathy Biehl was also an immediate yes, as soon as she read and sang for us. I was especially happy to have Kathy aboard. She'd known about my *I'll Say She Is* dream longer than almost anyone, and by this time she was a good friend as well as an esteemed Marxfest Committee colleague.

The most remarkable audition was Seth Shelden's, for the role of Harpo. Neither Trav nor I had met Seth before, and after his audition, we still hadn't. He arrived in costume and in character as Harpo, and never spoke a word. He gave us his leg, and he alternated hysterical silent laughter with abrupt stony indifference. He played the piano, as well as other musical instruments he had concealed on his person. When Trav finally implored him to open the violin case he'd brought with him, it turned out to contain ping pong balls

Seth Shelden as Harpo, with Aristotle Stamat and Bob Homeyer.
Photo by Jim R. Moore.

and paddles—a gag which, I later realized, was a reference to an anecdote about Arnold Schoenberg in *Harpo Speaks*. Seth was also the first man ever to sit on my lap at an audition—though this had nothing to do with him getting the part. Amanda was helping us run the audition, and she later told me that she'd spoken with Seth outside the room (proving that Seth Shelden can talk in real life). He'd impressed her as a passionate Marx Brothers fan who dearly wanted to play Harpo, and also as a mass of anxiety over whether he'd properly embodied his hero.

Robert, Kathy, and Seth were exactly what I'd been hoping for—a talented cast motivated by love of the Marx Brothers. They knew Chico, Dumont, and Harpo with the same intimacy that I had with Groucho. The first time I met Robert, we ended up doing pages and pages of Groucho and Chico dialogue, from *Animal Crackers, Duck Soup,* and *A Night at the Opera,* from memory. I was in heaven. I couldn't wait to play with these kids.

Surprisingly, Zeppo was by far the hardest Marx Brother to cast. This Zeppo had to be a credible romantic leading man, who could sing, dance, and do comedy; *and* who bore some general resemblance to Zeppo Marx. No matter what you may have heard, Zeppo Marxes are not a dime a dozen. We had all but given up when at last Trav discovered Matthew Curiano—a credible romantic leading man, who can sing, dance, and do comedy, and bears some general resemblance to Zeppo Marx! I quickly learned that Matthew also had a brash and mischievous sense of humor which was very much in the spirit of things.

The part for which we saw the most contenders was the Lotta Miles role, now known again as Beauty. Dozens of women, about equally representative of the worlds of musical theatre and burlesque, sang and read for the role. (We were aware that the chorus girls would be drawn from the same pool.) It was a tricky part to cast. New York has no shortage of pretty actresses with good singing voices, but the necessity of a convincing 1920s sound, both in song and dialogue, eliminated many. The style of *I'll Say She Is* is in many ways the antithesis of what an aspiring musical theatre performer learns in acting school. Moreover, just as important as charm and singing ability, it was crucial that we find someone with great comedic chops. She had to hold her own on stage with the Marx Brothers. She had to carry the Napoleon scene. It's a delicate balance, a role that must be played with just enough winking irony to make the audience comfortable. At the same time, Beauty has to take her search for thrills seriously. She can't appear to be mocking the proceedings—that's the Marxes' job. Beauty has to be both naïve and knowing, funny and earnest.

We found everything we were looking for in Melody Jane, a burlesque performer and performance artist with a background in musical theatre, who established herself in the role from the moment she entered the room. Melody's vocal sound was lovely and unusual, with operetta diction and trilly sustains. Her line readings had just the right amount of vintage declamation and knowing humor. There was something uncanny about how well Melody fit the part, and although I have no way of verifying this, I'm convinced that her interpretation is very close to Lotta Miles. Even her stage name seemed to fit nicely with the ambience of the project. Lotta Miles—Melody Jane—it all seemed compellingly right.

The rest of the ensemble cast, for the readings, was Bob Homeyer, Dan Hermann, and the acclaimed circus performer and PBS star Glen Heroy, who would become a great friend and ally of the *I'll Say She Is* project. Our miniature chorus consisted of burlesque performers Ivory Fox and Grace Gotham. Trav would read the stage directions, and narrate.

Around the time we were holding auditions, an important new collaborator joined us. Ever since I'd started working on *I'll Say She Is*, I'd been longing for a musical collaborator. I had had tentative conversations with several prospective arrangers. (One even created new piano arrangements for three of the songs, for a series of demos recorded with West in 2011.) Then Trav was introduced to Sabrina Chap, a brilliant songwriter and performer who worked in a bluesy, vaudevillian style. Sabrina's experience included plenty of musicals, and she was conversant with early jazz and the

Melody Jane in I'll Say She Is

Great American Songbook. I listened to her albums, *Oompa!* and *We Are the Parade*, and was deeply impressed. I met Sabrina and talked with her and was even more impressed. When we talked about the music in *I'll Say She Is*, she finished my sentences, which was a good thing, because Sabrina Chap is not only fluent, but hyper-articulate, in a language most of us can only dream of understanding.

WHILE THESE PLANS were falling into place, plans for Marxfest were rumbling along too. I was working twenty hours a day—eight on my day job, twelve on the Marx Brothers. For Marxfest, besides my work on *I'll Say She Is*, I produced two additional events, lectured at one, performed at three others, built and maintained the festival's website, and attended to its graphic design needs. As May approached, momentum gathered and excitement mounted. Information about the festival had begun to appear in the *Times*, the *Journal*, and *The New Yorker*, and we on the Marxfest Committee found ourselves giving interviews to the press and appearing on radio shows and podcasts, extolling the Brothers and plugging the festival. Trav, Kevin, and I were all guests on *The Halli Casser-Jayne Show*, along with Bill Marx and Dick Cavett, which was astonishing. Cavett's segment, and Bill's, had been recorded earlier, and none of us were ever in the room with them, but it was still thrilling to hear a promo touting appearances by Dick Cavett, Bill Marx, and my friends and me! "I felt the earth move," as Mr. Cavett once said in reference to something else. My adaptation of *I'll Say She Is* had gone from a carefully-guarded secret to something I spoke about on the radio. I kept telling myself: *Don't forget to enjoy this. Don't forget how recently this was all just a dream.*

One of my favorite Marxfest projects was RadioMarx, an online radio station which streamed Marx Brothers-related music twenty-four hours a day. This was managed and curated by Brett Leveridge, whose Cladrite Radio enterprise had been delivering well-chosen golden-age gems for years. In the spring of 2014, I had RadioMarx playing at my desk almost constantly, giving the lucky woman who married me hundreds of opportunities to ponder the subtleties of "Love Me and the World is Mine" and "The Monkey Doodle Doo."

The latter song, from *The Cocoanuts*, became household shorthand for the season's madness. One of the tentpole events of Marxfest was *Music of the Marx Brothers*, a concert at 54 Below ("Broadway's Supper Club"), produced by Kevin. The emcee, pianist, and creative director of the event was Bill Zeffiro, cabaret titan and creator of the twenties pastiche musical *The Road to Ruin*. In addition to performing in the concert as Groucho, I helped Bill choose songs and locate sheet music. One night, Bill called me in a panic. He was on his way to a rehearsal with Rebekah Lowin, when he realized that he had made a terrible mistake: He had acquired the music for "The Monkey Doodle Doo," a novelty song Irving Berlin wrote in 1915, as opposed to "The Monkey Doodle Doo," the completely unrelated number he wrote for *The Cocoanuts* in 1925! Hasn't this happened to all of us? When you write as many songs as Irving Berlin did, it's inevitable that you'll write at least two with this title, and if you give Shakespeare a typewriter, he'll eventually do the Monkey Doodle Doo. I located the correct song and sent it to Bill, but when the phone rang ten minutes later, I interrupted Amanda mid-sentence, exclaiming, "I'M SORRY, BABY, I HAVE TO TAKE THIS! *IT'S ABOUT 'THE MONKEY DOODLE DOO!'*" From that moment onward, anything that required my immediate attention was "about 'The Monkey Doodle Doo.'"

ONE OF THE GREAT pleasures of planning the festival was that I got to speak, correspond, and spend time with people who were close to the Marx Brothers' world in one way or another.

Howie Heller, nephew of Harry Ruby, told me stories I'd never heard about his uncle, and shared some rare photographs and artifacts. Howie is rightfully proud of his uncle's contributions to popular culture, and I was happy to see him at numerous Marxfest events. I also enjoyed talking with Hank Rosenfeld, the "as told to" of *The Wicked Wit of the West*, a lively memoir by Marx Brothers screenwriter Irving Brecher. In the past, I'd had pleasant written exchanges with Steve Stoliar, who had been Groucho's secretary in the later years, and documented his experiences in a beautiful book, *Raised Eyebrows*. I enjoyed a friendly correspondence with Andy Marx, grandson of Groucho. And I was aware, through my participation in the Marx Brothers Council of Facebook, that even Joe Adamson was friendly and accessible. But most of these guys were on the west coast. I regretted that Marxfest didn't have a bigger budget, and couldn't offer travel, lodging, and resources to people we otherwise would have invited to participate. I envisioned a future Marxfest, more inclusive, more robust, more money; I still envision it.

But we did pretty well. Kathy had secured the invaluable participation of Robert Bader, who would present two evenings of stories and rare film clips—and one of these evenings would include an onstage conversation between Mr. Bader and Mr. Dick Cavett. Kathy kept telling us this was going to happen, but we somehow didn't believe it—not that we doubted Kathy, but it was difficult to conceive of a world so glorious that we plan a Marx Brothers festival and DICK CAVETT SHOWS UP! It was also through Bader that Kathy got in touch with Bill Marx. As all Marx Brothers fans know, Harpo's son is every bit the kind and lovely gentleman his father was. He and Kathy became pen pals, and he was warmly supportive of *I'll Say She Is* and the whole Marxfest effort. Bill was too busy with musical

The logo I designed for Marxfest contains at least one
visual reference to each Marx Brothers movie.
The image of the Marxes is from a 1925 caricature by Victor Bobritsky.

commitments to join us in New York in May, but he expressed love and gratitude for what we were doing, and cheerfully agreed to headline a *virtual* Marxfest event. And he signed "Official Unofficial Nickname Certificates" for our crowdfunding donors, bestowing upon each of them a unique Marx-styled "O-name."

And then there was the one, the only, Frank Ferrante, the performer most associated with Groucho's character, post-Groucho. Since that 1992 *Animal Crackers* at Goodspeed, I had continued to follow his career. In 2001, his performance in *Groucho: A Life in Revue* was preserved as a PBS special, which I watched many times. I had a back issue of *American Theatre* magazine with Frank as Groucho on the cover, and I'd had a couple of pleasant Facebook interactions with him. One day at a Marxfest meeting, Kevin told me that Ferrante's *Evening with Groucho* tour happened to have two performances scheduled in the New York area in May, one on Long Island and one on Staten Island. Perhaps we could incorporate these into Marxfest, as Frank might welcome the promotional boost, and it also would solve our problem of not having any events planned for Staten Island. And since he was in the area, maybe he'd be interested in some of the other Marxfest events, too.

I volunteered to get in touch with Frank, and we had several telephone conversations in the months leading up to the festival. Our first conversation was particularly memorable, a long, personal exchange about our feelings for the Marx Brothers, and how they had changed our lives. I shared my memories of Goodspeed in 1992. "It may be that I saw it through a child's eyes," I said, "but I was just dazzled by it." Frank said it was indeed exceptional, and that the director, Charles Repole, understood the Marx Brothers' comedy. He also told me that he had recently visited Miriam Marx, and that she cherished my "Tillo Marx" print. That was touching—not only that Miriam still had the print, and loved it, but that Frank knew it was mine. He said he'd be seeing Miriam again soon and would give her my regards.

He talked about his long friendship with Groucho's son Arthur, who had died in 2011. It was Arthur Marx who "discovered" Frank Ferrante,

Miriam Marx with Frank Ferrante and the 1992 cast of Animal Crackers
at Goodspeed Opera House. Photo by Beverly Sobolewski.

when the latter quixotically invited the Son of Groucho to an early version
of *An Evening with Groucho*—Ferrante's senior project in college. Then and
there, Arthur said something like, "I'm going to write a play about my father,
and I want you to play him." *Groucho: A Life in Revue*, by Arthur Marx and
Robert Fisher, starring Frank Ferrante, had a sensational Off Broadway run
at the Lucille Lortel Theatre in 1986. Someone should write a play about
the relationship between Arthur Marx and Frank Ferrante. Arthur once said
that Frank was both his father and his son.

WORKING "WITH" THE MARX BROTHERS so intensely in the
buildup to Marxfest, I was frequently moved to tears. Some little
aspect of the Marx mythos, or something said about them, or some new
tidbit of evidence of their time on Earth, or a lessening of the degrees of
separation between them and me, would get to me, and I began to reflect on
the central paradox of the Marx Brothers fan.

The Marx Brothers were willfully unsentimental artists. In their great works, they never ask for our sympathy. Yet we who love the Marx Brothers love them sentimentally, emotionally, with all our hearts. We find their work not only funny but profound—and not, or not only, because of whatever critical or satirical value it may have. The sound of their voices, the sight of their faces, the movement of their bodies, and the interplay of their minds are collectively one of the greatest works of art our species has ever conceived. Without even intending to, Groucho, Harpo, Chico, and sometimes Zeppo, and sometimes Gummo, have made us care. They have moved us, and touched our lives with an artistry comparable to that of Picasso or Stravinsky, to whom Woody Allen memorably compared them. We identify with them, and associate them with truth, goodness, and joy; they are our heroes. We feel as if they're family: our Brothers.

IN THE MONTHS before Marxfest, I was so preoccupied with planning events, designing programs, writing lectures, meeting people, and trying desperately to hang onto my day job, that I nearly forgot about the other task ahead: Playing Groucho. *I'll Say She Is* was first on my mind, of course, but it was clear that Marxfest would present other opportunities.

I generally make no great claims for myself as a performer, but I'd been saying for years that I thought I could play this one particular role as well as anyone. Now this claim was to be conspicuously tested, and I felt nervous. It was humbling to consider the example of Frank Ferrante, not to mention the example of Groucho Marx. Just by stepping on stage in that makeup, you're telling the audience, "I am the greatest comedian who ever lived!" Despite my experience in the role, Marxfest and *I'll Say She Is* seemed to comprise a sort of debut, and I felt rusty. I started to run the films endlessly and play Groucho right along with him, doing everything I could think of to make sure I was as sharp as possible in the role.

I'd always felt confident in my *vocal* likeness to Groucho, but I fretted about my physical performance. As comedian/impressionist George Bettinger has often noted, Groucho felt that people who impersonate him "have to move well." It's one thing to imitate the walk and all the signature moves, and another to instinctively move through space the way Groucho did. His physical performances are probably the most overlooked aspect of his art. Because the sound of his voice and his use of language were so exhilarating, and because his brother Harpo was such a gifted physical comedian, Groucho's idiosyncratic grace is rarely noted. He has an odd combination of lightness and heaviness that's unmistakably his, and challenging to imitate. He's sometimes manic, but never spastic. In general, Groucho is stiller and slower than you may recall. There's a smoothness to his motions, but they're frequently clumsy or imprecise. His body, like his eyes and eyebrows, often seems to be floating. I spent a lot of time in March and April fine-tuning my physical Groucho.

The highly distinctive corkscrew kicks, as seen in *Animal Crackers* and *Horse Feathers*, had always eluded me. I had a way of faking it, by doing a sort of side kick with a wiggle, but the fans would recognize it as counterfeit. I thought it would be lovely if, at the *I'll Say She Is* reading, during the first chorus of "Hail Napoleon," I could execute a series of authentic Captain Spalding corkscrews. I worked on it, watched Groucho in slow motion, and tried, but I could never quite replicate it. The matter required an intervention from Amanda Sisk, who found me sobbing in despair over my corkscrews one evening, and sat down with me and *Animal Crackers* and the remote control and the mirror and said, "We're going to figure this out tonight." She is much more choreographically inclined than I am. She somehow broke through whatever was clogging up my technique. It's possible that she even tolerated a snit. Thanks to my wife, I was now doing corkscrew kicks all day long. I was corkscrew kicking down the street.

On April 26, four days before the beginning of Marxfest, Trav and I received notice that *I'll Say She Is* had been accepted to the New York Fringe Festival.

VII.
SELECTIONS FROM
THE MARXFEST DIARIES

The Marxfest Committee
(Noah Diamond, Trav S.D., Kathy Biehl,
Jonny Porkpie, Kevin Fitzpatrick, Brett Leveridge)
performs a ribbon-cutting ceremony at the Algonquin Hotel, May 1, 2014

DURING THE MONTH of Marxfest, I published regular reports and commentary on the festival's official blog. The immediacy of those dispatches conveys the spirit of May 2014 more effectively than I can convey it in retrospect, so this chapter will consist largely of selections from the Marxfest Diaries.

APRIL 30

'Twas the night before Marxfest,

without waxing wroth.

Not a creature was stirring—

not even a left-handed moth.

MAY 1

Technically, the first Marxfest event was a matinee screening of *A Night at the Opera* at the Epiphany Library on 23rd Street. Nevertheless, the festival *began* hours later, in the Blue Bar at the Algonquin Hotel, with The Party of the First Part. (Credit Jonny Porkpie with the name—actually, credit Kaufman and Ryskind. Jonny Porkpie will get additional credit in the *Academy Bulletin*.) At 7:40 pm, the Marxfest Committee stood around the Algonquin Round Table (go with it) and held a very, very official Ribbon-Cutting Ceremony. Kathy Biehl cut a ribbon in two, and we were off to the races, the opera, Casablanca, Freedonia, and Cocoanut Beach . . .

MAY 2

. . . and Coney Island, for Trav S.D.'s presentation "From Angels to Anarchists: The Evolution of the Marx Brothers." Trav delivered an excellent discussion of the origins of the Brothers' act. The event took place a couple of blocks from the site of Henderson's, where Harpo appeared on stage for the first time, pissing or shitting himself. (Trav touched on that, but don't worry, he washed his hands.) "From Angels to Anarchists" was complemented by the presence of an angel, Sarah Moskowitz (our host seizing the opportunity to exclaim, "O-KAY, Ms. Moskowitz!!"). She performed three selections from the early Marx repertoire. It was wonderful to hear these ancient numbers performed live, and Ms. Moskowitz's sincerity unburdened them of cobwebs. The revelation, believe it or not, was "Peasie Weasie."

I love the *idea* of "Peasie Weasie," how Minnie bought it for $27, and how it incessantly followed the Brothers through vaudeville and beyond, and I love Groucho's impish glee as he performs the song with Dinah Shore on television. But I've always found the song itself insipid to the point of embarrassment. Guess what—it *killed* at Coney Island tonight. I've completely misjudged "Peasie Weasie" all these years. It's a fine piece of showbiz.

Shortly thereafter came *An Evening with Groucho* in Freeport, followed by my onstage conversation with its star. I was prepared for the interview, having seen the show in March, and I'd given much thought to the questions I might ask. But I was a little anxious, bouncing along the Belt Parkway toward Long Island with my esteemed Marxfest Committee colleague Jonny Porkpie and my esteemed wife Amanda Sisk. When we arrived at the venue, we were greeted by none other than Paul Wesolowski, whom I immediately recognized from photographs. We fell right into a pleasant conversation about various Marx matters, and I followed him down a hallway to a dressing room. There, in a white button-down, Groucho hair parted perfectly in the middle, and no pants, was Frank Ferrante. Thirty minutes before showtime he was completely relaxed, and he put me at ease right away, with a warm and friendly greeting, and a conversation that quickly travelled numerous byways of Marxian arcana.

While chatting with Paul and me, Frank did some stretching exercises and limbered up for his performance. "So that's the secret, huh?" I asked, and he laughed. I asked if there was any particular technique by which he captured Groucho's physicality, because it seemed so effortless. "I just throw myself through the air and trust that I'll be okay," he said.

We were in Freeport, the town in which a very young Harpo had briefly been employed as a piano player in a brothel, and Paul had some fresh research findings to share on that subject. That afternoon, he had tracked down the former location of the brothel, and taken some pictures. I couldn't believe I was there. I still felt like the fifteen-year-old fan, *reading* about Paul Wesolowski, and watching Frank Ferrante from a distance; yet here I was, holding my own among them! I had been looking forward to Frank's performance and our interview, but now I wished this pre-show period would go on forever.

MAY 3

. . . It should surprise no one to hear that Mr. Wesolowski has unearthed enough material on Mrs. Schang and her gang[1] for a miniseries. (My suggested title: *Schang Hide*.) It should surprise even fewer to hear that Frank's tour de force performance as Groucho is sharper than ever, or that spending time with this most distinguished graduate of Huxley College has been among the highlights of my Marxfest experience. To meet him is to know that the legacy of history's greatest comedian could not be in better, more caring hands.

The interview after the show went well, despite a couple of moments when I became uncharacteristically tongue-tied. Frank answered questions, mine and the audience's, with thoughtfulness and eloquence. He talked about being a shy young boy, growing up in Sierra Madre, California, and how his imagination burst to life when he encountered the Marx Brothers on television in *A Day at the Races*. Groucho, Frank said during our Freeport conversation, "was an alter ego for a lot of the shy kids. He was saying things you should never say. He was doing things you should never do. And it was exhilarating. I was taught by nuns, and I think I wanted to treat the nuns the way Groucho treated Margaret Dumont. He was a suit of armor, for so many of us." When it was over, Frank and Paul and I said goodnight, and our conversation continued the following evening after the next big Marxfest event, "The Marx Brothers on Television."

1 The Schang gang was a minor crime family with whom young Harpo became involved when he took a job tickling the ivories (and, apparently, little else) in that Freeport brothel.

With Frank Ferrante onstage in Freeport

One thing that never came up, in these conversations with Frank, was the fact that I, too, sometimes performed as Groucho. I was somewhat relieved that it never came up, though I was reasonably sure that he knew. The night after the Freeport show we talked a little about *I'll Say She Is*, but I discussed it in terms of my work on the book and lyrics, not as a member of the cast. There was a part of me that was eager to discuss technique with him, ask him what kind of greasepaint he uses, and so on. But I was a bit embarrassed. I felt like a kid who played Hamlet in high school, meeting Olivier. And I was sensitive to the possibility that this might not be a subject Frank was eager to address. I was sure that people approached him all the time saying, "You know, Frank, it so happens I do a halfway decent Groucho myself! *How he got in my pajamas I'll never know! That's the most ridiculous thing I ever hoid!* Hey, whadaya think, Frank? Have I got it?"

After the "Marx Brothers on Television" event, a bunch of us were hanging around on MacDougal Street. We were all taking pictures with our phones, and someone suggested a photo of "the three Grouchos," meaning Frank, Jonny Porkpie, and me. (Jonny was playing a Groucho-like character in his own Marxfest event, a Marx Brothers-inspired burlesque show.) Acute embarrassment! *This is Frank Ferrante! Morrie Ryskind said he was the only*

With Frank Ferrante and Jonny Porkpie on MacDougal Street

actor besides Groucho to say the lines right! He's in a class by himself—please don't ask him to acknowledge us as Grouchos! But I do love the photo.

I was sorry that Frank couldn't stick around to attend other Marxfest events throughout the month, particularly *I'll Say She Is*. But the road was calling, and his schedule was thick with *Evening with Groucho* bookings, plus appearances as his original comic creation, The Caesar, with the Seattle-based "cirque/comedy/cabaret" company Teatro Zinzanni. The Groucho show soon took him as far as Australia (a continent Groucho himself never played) as well as most of the United States. I pictured him as a gleeful missionary, spreading the gospel, keeping the spirit of Groucho alive by doing exactly what Groucho had done with his brothers: crisscrossing the country, descending on small towns and big cities, bringing laughter to the masses. But it was great to begin the festival on such a high note, with Frank's participation and encouragement. He even donated to our Kickstarter campaign to help make Marxfest possible.

MAY 4

Day Four of Marxfest can be conveyed only by adjectives such as *magical, unforgettable,* and *oh my god, that's Dick Cavett!*

When the Marxfest Committee began, we were almost afraid to say out loud that we wanted Groucho's friend Dick Cavett, a comedy legend in his own right, to be involved. A Cavett appearance seemed too good, too big, and too unlikely to hope for. Last night at "The Marx Brothers on Television," the dream that we dared to dream really did come true, through the great efforts of many—but especially Kathy Biehl and Robert S. Bader.

Mr. Bader hosted the event, sharing some prize revelations from his vast research—including a selection of extremely rare Marx Brothers television clips, many of which have not been seen since their original broadcasts (and all to be included in the upcoming Shout Factory DVD set, compiled by Mr. Bader). Then he welcomed to the stage his good friend, whom we all think of as our good friend. The great man shared Groucho

Amanda Sisk and Dick Cavett at "The Marx Brothers on Television"

anecdotes both familiar and rare, and with Bader, engaged in the kind of sparkling conversation that reminds you of *The Dick Cavett Show*. At program's end, Mr. Cavett drew whoops of laughter and applause when he performed Michael Jackson's moonwalk.

Under any circumstances, it would be beyond thrilling to see footage of the Marx Brothers we'd never seen before. But what I'll remember from last night, even more than the excitement of the clips or the presence of a living legend, was all the love in the room. There we were on MacDougal Street, steps from where Mr. Cavett first shook the hand of Mr. Woody Allen in 1961—the Marxfest Committee, fans, friends, family, Ferrante, Wesolowski, Bader, Cavett and many more—all together for a night at the theatre, watching the Marx Brothers.

MAY 5

While Kathy Biehl, Kelley Loftus, Jonny Porkpie, Richard Taylor Pearson, and I enjoyed a German meal which surely would have pleased Lafe and Fanny, Robert Bader shared further morsels of his research. We wound up walking around the city and talking long into the night about obscure corners of the Brothers' story, with an emphasis on *I'll Say She Is*.

My Manhattan midnight stroll with Robert Bader was memorable. Besides having as complete a knowledge of the Marx Brothers as anyone on Earth, he is a highly engaging storyteller, with a comic's gift for timing and irony, and a fountain of anecdotes. He has Marx Brothers stories that nobody has ever heard before. He talked about his friendships with Bill Marx and the late Maxine Marx. He said that his research was always turning up new examples of Chico's gambling, womanizing, and legal trouble, to the point where Maxine would greet him with, "Hello, Robert, now what terrible thing are you going to tell me about my father today?"

He told me more about the book he was working on, the complete chronicle of the Marx Brothers' stage career. A lot of what he told me that night I can't tell you here, because it's in his book, and it's his to tell you. I believe that the publication of that book will be the beginning of a new era in our knowledge and understanding of what the Marx Brothers did and who they were. The monumental *Marx Brothers TV Collection*, from which Bader shared clips at these two Marxfest events, was released by Shout Factory in August of 2014.

MAY 7

For some reason I've been craving cigars lately. Having arrived in the Village much too early, I treated myself to a two-dollar stogie and loped around Minetta Lane, puffing and mugging.

"Marxes in Manhattan" included twenty minutes of Marx family home movies, deftly edited by Bader and narrated by Bill Marx. This "family Marx Brothers movie" includes the earliest known footage of Groucho, previously unseen in public. There was also a multimedia presentation by Bader; performances of "Alone" and "Everyone Says I Love You" by Rob Schwimmer on the theremin; and recreations of early vaudeville material.

Who ever thought we'd be watching a faithful recreation of the Leroy Trio? As directed by Kathy Biehl, the boys—Richard Taylor Pearson as Gene Leroy, Kit Russoniello as Johnnie Morris, and Zachary Catron as Julius Marx—were completely convincing. They performed "I Wonder What's the Matter with the Mail," one of those ghostly song titles encountered in Marx Brothers literature. Mr. Catron returned to the stage twice, to perform early Julius Marx specialties "Somebody's Sweetheart I Want to Be" and "Hello Mr. Stein." According to Bader, Minnie purchased "Hello Mr. Stein" in 1907, and it was in the Brothers' act for many years. Mr. Catron's performance of "Hello Mr. Stein" was likely the song's first public hearing in a century, and the resulting video, available on YouTube, is the song's first-ever recording.

It was especially fascinating to see this ancient material recreated. Robert, Kathy, and the young men onstage were doing with early Marx Brothers vaudeville material what I was trying to do with *I'll Say She Is*. Just as I wanted to give audiences the illusion that they were sitting in the Casino Theatre in 1924, the vaudeville portions of "Marxes in Manhattan" took me to Cripple Creek, Colorado in 1905; and to the May 4, 1906 Metropolitan Opera House benefit for the survivors of the San Francisco earthquake, at which young Julius performed "Somebody's Sweetheart." Robert had explained to me that a familiar photograph of the vaudeville Marxes on stage holding beer steins was in fact a picture of them performing "Hello, Mr. Stein."

> I wrapped up the night at the Washington Square Restaurant with Biehl, Bader, Wesso, Meg Farrell, and even Mr. Herbert G. Goldman, masterful biographer of Jolson, Cantor, and Brice. As we partook of moussaka, tuna melts, pizza burgers, and pie, we traveled more uncharted byways of Marx Brothers history. Mr. Bader showed us a true color photograph of the boys in costume in 1928. I now know the exact color of Harpo's red stage wig. Marxfest continues to exceed my wildest expectations, and my expectations are plenty wild.

That night at the diner, Robert Bader and Herbert Goldman told us about how they used to run into each other in libraries and newspaper morgues. Bader was hunting down everything that could possibly be known about the Marx Brothers, and Goldman was doing the same for Jolson. Now and then Goldman would stumble upon a Marx Brothers revelation and send it along to Bader, or Bader would inadvertently find some Jolson tidbit and give it to Goldman. It reminded me of something I'd once heard on a TV documentary about the *Titanic*. An oceanographer on Robert Ballard's team said that while they were exploring the *Titanic* shipwreck, species of fish were swimming by that were completely unknown to science. But it wasn't time to discover new species of fish; it was time to explore the *Titanic* shipwreck.

That's what these granular research missions are like. You're exploring the Marx Brothers, and you have to stay focused, but there's Al Jolson swimming by, and ooh, look, Jack Benny!

MAY 9

There was something in the air on Friday, besides mist, but the mist didn't hurt. I was early for the soundcheck, so I wandered around Broadway in the mist and did something I've never done before: I bought the *Wall Street Journal*. Its arts page included a nice mention of *I'll Say She Is*, which Trav fears they may retract after they see our Wall Street number. When Bill Zeffiro, Kevin Fitzpatrick, and I were admitted to 54 Below, they escorted us to our dressing room, and guess what it said on the door: THE MARX BROTHERS.

54 Below is a great room, and the show was spectacular—owing largely, like other Marxfest events, to the rollicking enthusiasm of the audience. Imagine a crowd that breaks into cheers and applause when they hear the opening notes of "The Monkey Doodle Doo!" Roughly halfway through the show, Bill Zeffiro announced that there was a very special guest in the house who probably needed no introduction. Then a familiar voice was heard, yammering from a corner — *"Well, a worse-looking audience I've never seen!"*—and a strange figure darted through the room and onto the stage. Once there, he casually insulted Zeffiro, the venue, and the audience, and between jokes he warbled "There's a Place Called Omaha, Nebraska."

Performing at 54 Below was a big deal for me. It's a beautiful, world-class venue that evokes a past era of New York nightclub entertainment. The other performers on Zeffiro's bill were the cream of the city's cabaret scene: Steve Ross (a haunting "Love Me and the World is Mine"), Marissa Mulder (a heart-melting "Always"), Rebekah Lowin ("THE MONKEY DOODLE DOO!"); opera singer Tonna Miller ("Alone," of course); and an all-Marx

Performing as Groucho at 54 Below, with Bill Zeffiro at the piano

Brothers set by my favorite musical act in the city, the husband-and-wife vaudeville team of Gelber and Manning. Dandy Wellington was the emcee.

It was my first Groucho performance at Marxfest. It had not been publicized, other than some hints about a special guest, so the entrance had a lot of impact. During that performance, and while mingling with the crowd in character afterward, I had a revelation. I was always so preoccupied with whether I looked, sounded, and moved *accurately* as Groucho. Fine. But the audience, I suddenly realized, isn't concerned about these things at all! They're not studying the performance for inaccuracies; they want to be entertained. What's more, they *want* to accept me as Groucho! Just as much as I want to be him, they want to *see* him. My policy was, *Don't do anything as Groucho that Groucho wouldn't do.* But Groucho was not predictable! You didn't always know what he was going to do. So I'd been limiting myself not to what he *would* do, but to what he *had done*—what I had seen him do. At 54 Below I realized that I could be more creative. Shortly thereafter, Trav S.D. made a sagacious observation, which has been part of my approach ever since: "Groucho didn't always *do* Groucho."

MAY 15

To mark the International Day of Laughter, Marxfest hosted an online conversation with Bill Marx and a virtual gathering of fans from around the world. "My dad said, 'I never would have made it without my brothers,'" he told us. He talked about playing the piano for Allan Sherman's debut performance (attended by all *five* Marx Brothers), shared memories of Harpo's innate wisdom and decency, and described, then imitated, his father's speaking voice. The hour flew by, and at the end, Bill said, to all Marx Brothers fans everywhere: "I want to tell you that I love you." He thanked all of us for loving the Marx Brothers and keeping their comedy alive.

Immediately following the Bill Marx shindig, Kathy Biehl and I high-tailed it to the Players to catch the second performance of Pinchbottom Burlesque's *The Pinch Brothers in "The Bawdy House."* We had a fine time spotting the many classic Marx references which Jonny Porkpie has cleverly woven throughout his original libretto.

MAY 17

On a beautiful morning in Yorkville, I briefly met up with the Barx Brothers Dog Walk crowd, on the steps of the Brothers' childhood home. Then to the 96th Street Library for my own presentation, "The Marxes of Yorkville." I spoke for about thirty minutes, telling the story of the Brothers' early years, accompanied by photographs and artifacts projected on a screen behind me. It was so much fun, I wanted to keep going and cover their whole career. Next on the bill were Dan Truman and Seth Shelden, reading excerpts from *Groucho and Me* and *Harpo Speaks*. (Seth, who plays Harpo in *I'll Say She Is* this week, told me that it was very helpful having heard Bill Marx's description of Harpo's voice.) Third was Susan Kathryn Hefti, co-director of the 93rd Street Beautification Association, who spoke about the "Save Marx Brothers Place" movement.

MAY 19

There were no public Marxfest events on Monday, but it was nevertheless an important day. It was the actual ninetieth anniversary of the opening night of *I'll Say She Is* at the Casino Theatre. Their ninety-year-old vehicle is still "a masterpiece of knock 'em down and drag 'em out humor" (George Jean Nathan), and you can be part of the first audience to enjoy this work since the original production closed, and all you have to do is buy tickets right now.

MAY 20

At the Party of the Second Part at Kabin, thrown by Kevin Fitzpatrick for the festival's Kickstarter backers, many familiar names were finally given faces. I was especially glad to meet Ira Dolnick in person, a man who played an important role in my early stumblings with *I'll Say She Is*, and to shake his hand at last. Other highlights of the Party of the Second Part included Marx Brothers cupcakes, conceived and prepared by modern-day flapper and *pâtissière* Dandy Dillinger; and Jonny Porkpie and I performed our own version of the Gallagher and Shean theme song.

MAY 22

Tonight *Duck Soup* was screened at no less a venue than the Museum of Modern Art! Far too rarely have I had the experience of watching the boys on the big screen, with a big audience. Far too rarely have I laughed so sincerely at something so familiar.

MAY 23 & 25

My adaptation of *I'll Say She Is* was publicly presented for the first time. It's difficult to write about the *I'll Say She Is* readings the way I've been writing about other Marxfest events. The whole festival has been a dream, but this show is exceptional for me, even in this month of exceptions. I can only marvel at Trav S.D. and the beautiful group of people who've brought the show back to life. There hasn't been a cast of *I'll Say She Is* since 1925. Let's hear it for 'em!

The readings included a scoop, announced with characteristic flair and showmanship by Trav during his opening speech: *I'll Say She Is* will be presented in full at the New York International Fringe Festival in August of this year. But it may never have as appreciative an audience as the glorious crowd who attended the Marxfest readings. I could live forever on those laughs. It was a tribute to the Marx Brothers, to the Johnstone brothers, to the family on stage and the family in the audience.

MAY 24

One of my favorite sidebars to the saga of the Marx Brothers is Groucho's unlikely friendship with T.S. Eliot. My next Marxfest event, "The Love Song of J. Cheever Loophole," consisted of readings: First of the Groucho/Eliot correspondence as published in *The Groucho Letters*, and then of thematically-linked selections from both men's work. The Eliot selections were read by Hugh Sinclair. I could listen to him all day. May is the kindest month.

MAY 26

There were no public Marxfest events on Memorial Day. I spent a lovely afternoon with my lovely mother, who was in town for the *I'll Say She Is* reading and the Eliot event. We even found time to discuss things other than the Marx Brothers! I'd forgotten there was anything else. Thanks, Mom!

MAY 27

When the Theatre Museum asked Trav S.D. to organize and host a variety program for its awards gala, did they know that the redoubtable Mr. S.D. would inject their ritzy soiree with a stiff shot of Marxian anarchy? Milling about the Players Club (distinct from the Players *Theatre*, scene of past triumphs) with the cast of *I'll Say She Is*, it felt like we *were* the Marx Brothers, crashing Mrs. Rittenhouse's party.

MAY 31

All good things must come to an end. The end began where the beginning ended, at the Algonquin Hotel. In the very spot where the legends of the Round Table once lunched, stood our leader, Kevin Fitzpatrick. Today, Kevin's Algonquin Round Table walking tour was punctuated with references to the Marx Brothers, and Kevin was even kind enough to call on me for an anecdote or two. It was as lovely a day as New York has had this year, and it was a huge, spirited crowd—the largest he'd ever had on the tour, Kevin told us.

One of the pleasures of Marxfest has been seeing so many of the same faces from event to event. I think it's clear that Marx Brothers fans are the best people in the world. I'd pit us point for point against the children of any other obsession. In the past month I've made many friends, struck up correspondences, met people whose books I've read, met people whose books I'm *going* to read, and in general, expanded my world far more than I ever thought I would by obsessing about one comedy team from a hundred years ago.

And so . . .

For the last night of Marxfest, friend-of-the-festival Don Spiro of Wit's End threw a spectacular speakeasy party at Flute Midtown (which was once Texas Guinan's Club Intime). This magical night was the perfect chaser to the big drink of Marxfest. It was attended by old friends, new friends, and many of the people who have made this month the time of our lives.

I spent most of the party as Groucho. (Walking to Flute, a pedestrian saw me in costume and shouted, "Hey, Charlie!" Which is a little better than the time I was dressed as Groucho on the subway and some kids shouted, "Hey, Borat!") Groucho hobnobbed, Groucho posed for a caricature by Adriano Moraes, Groucho danced with my wife. Groucho was even permitted to perform a couple of songs with Gelber and Manning and their band. We all laughed, talked, sang, and danced into the night, and then we all said goodbye and went home. Marxfest, ladies and gentlemen.

A question that's come up a lot lately is: Are you going to do it again? There have even been references to "next year's Marxfest" as though it were sure as Christmas. Well, here and now, I can give you the official answer: We don't know!

Some of us are turning our attention to *I'll Say She Is*, which you will see at the Fringe Festival in August. It seems impossible that there *won't* be another Marxfest, but it also seems impossible to start planning it now. All we can do is tell you to watch this space, keep playing with us on Facebook and Twitter, and stay tuned.

It's not goodbye—it's hello, we must be going.

As always, I remain

YOURS IN MARX,

NOAH

With Amanda Sisk on the last night of Marxfest

VIII.
THAT FROG

Trav S.D. emcees the I'll Say She Is *readings at Marxfest.*
Photo by Jonathan Melvin Smith.

IF YOU'RE PLANNING on killing me, right now would be an excellent time," Trav S. D. said cheerfully to the audience in his speech prior to the *I'll Say She Is* readings. He was describing the "veritable Shangri-la" that was Marxfest, an entire month when it had been unnecessary to waste time on "all that boring shit people talk about that has nothing to *do* with the Marx Brothers."

Here's how Trav set the reading up for the audience:

> Though the mysterious artifact you're about to
> encounter might be new to many of you, to the
> hardcore center of the faithful, it is part of the lore.
> It is one of the Holy Grails of classic comedy. It is
> quite literally legendary, in that people know *of* it,
> but they don't know *it*.
>
> I want you to know, ladies and gentlemen, that
> people have travelled not only from other states to
> be here tonight, but from other countries. People
> have come from England, from the Caribbean; and
> I've just heard from one of our cast members that
> someone who was in Mexico yesterday is here this
> evening . . .
>
> What we have for you tonight is a reconstruction.
> If you remember *Jurassic Park*, the way they did the
> dinosaurs—eighty or ninety percent of the DNA
> is real dinosaur DNA, and the rest is from frogs.
> Ladies and gentlemen, Noah Diamond is that frog.
> But as Warner Brothers cartoons have taught us,
> sometimes a frog can sing like Jolson.

Trav didn't know this at the time, but I've always been a frog. From the age of two or three, I identified with, and was identified with, Kermit the Frog—my first and truest hero, and surely one of the greatest entertainers of the twentieth century. In high school I made a movie called *My Life as a Frog*. When Amanda and I got married, we put on our wedding mix that immortal couplet: "Because you share a love so big / I now pronounce you frog and pig." The reception, at Amanda's parents' home in Memphis, Tennessee, was graced by little statuettes of a frog and a pig, tastefully placed among the flowers by Amanda's mother, Ginny.

Trav continued:

> I first learned about this show thirty years ago, but

I learned about Noah's project a couple of years ago. He doesn't know it, but when he mentioned it to me, I was privately willing to be the *I'll Say She Is* janitor, I was so excited to hear about it. And as the person who's reading the stage directions tonight, I practically *am* . . .

We thank you for coming tonight and helping to make this revival possible. And now, without further ado, we give you, for the first time in ninety years, the Marx Brothers' *I'll Say She Is*.

I listened to these words from a vantage point I'd been imagining for five years, or thirty. I was backstage at *I'll Say She Is*. It was ninety years, almost to the day, since Groucho Himself first stood in the wings at the Casino, dressed just like this, waiting to go on. That was the first New York debut of *I'll Say She Is*, and this was the second. But of course, it wasn't *really* an opening or a premiere. It was a staged reading, preceded by one week of rehearsal. Later, we would downplay the historicity of the readings, in order to emphasize that our subsequent effort was the first *production* of the show in ninety years. (And later still, we would downplay *that* effort in order to emphasize

I'll Say She Is *in 1924 and 2014*

the show's next, even fuller, incarnation.) But the Marxfest readings seemed auspicious in their own way, and have never quite been matched for the sheer amount of electricity in the room. It felt like we already had a smash, before we'd even truly gone into rehearsal.

At the talkback session following the May 25 reading, Meg and Trav and I spoke about the history of *I'll Say She Is*, and Meg spoke about the Johnstones, and I spoke about my research and writing process. We took questions from the audience—informed, thoughtful questions about what was original and what had been added, and how *I'll Say She Is* fit into the context of the Marx Brothers' career. I would have been happy if that talkback lasted forever. But eventually Trav announced that there was time for one more question. The final questioner began by saying, "Noah, we're so impressed with your portrayal of Groucho," which caused the room to break into applause, and my eyes to moisten. He asked about my experiences and my technique, and a familiar voice in the audience threw in a follow-up question about how I'd managed those corkscrew kicks.

On the subject of playing Groucho, I began, "It's amazing—if you just concentrate on something for thirty or forty years ..." Then I talked about my early infatuation with the Marxes, my sense of identification with Groucho, and how it was easier to play him now than it used to be. On the subject of the corkscrews, I gave all the credit to Amanda (and not just because she had been the one asking the question). I explained that the move had eluded me, "and then my wife, Amanda, not only improved my corkscrew kick technique, by breaking it down with me and teaching me how to do it, and being very patient with me—I am not a choreographer's dream—but she also curled my hair, and got it looking much closer to Groucho's than it's ever been before. If there are any single men here who love the Marx Brothers, I hope you find a beautiful woman who will teach you how to dance like Groucho."

By the end of Marxfest, I felt like I'd walked a million miles. I was gratified, overwhelmed, and profoundly exhausted. I not only hadn't slept in weeks; I had no memory of what sleep was like, or if I'd be able to remember how it was done, if the opportunity ever again presented itself. But there wasn't much chance of that, because when Marxfest was over, the Fringe Festival was eight weeks away.

FIRST, THERE WERE REWRITES—there are always rewrites. The audience response at the readings had been loving and generous, but it still pointed to a few things that needed fixing. There were jokes that didn't land, and there were pacing problems in Act One. There were sections which would rely heavily on movement or spectacle, which were omitted for the readings, and now needed attention.

The Wall Street number had landed with a thud at Marxfest, at least in part because I'd packed it too full of dense, tricky lyrics, when a simpler statement was called for. I thoroughly rewrote it for the Fringe. "Gimme a Thrill" was in good shape, thanks to Melody's performance and a newer, bluer arrangement by Sabrina. The two of them improved the song so much, the lyric now felt unsubstantial. We eventually built it up with a dance break and an extended ending, and I reworked the second chorus and wrote some new lyrics. Similar surgery was performed on the opening number. Then there was dance music to consider, for both the Apache number and the Pygmalion ballet. My old favorite "Up in the Clouds" found its way back into the score, as an instrumental piece, when Trav decided we needed a dance specialty after the Wall Street sequence.

We snapped back into casting, filling up the chorus and the ensemble, and once again, desperately seeking Zeppo. Matthew Curiano had been terrific in the reading, but we knew at the outset that he was booked elsewhere in August. Trying to find a good Zeppo was, once again, a comedic enterprise in its own right: Two guys sitting with their notebooks, watching one handsome young man after another sing a song and tell a joke, and after each hopeful

The I'll Say She Is *chorus, 2014. Clockwise from center: Emily Turner Marsland, Alexis Thomason, Kita St. Cyr, Francine Daveta, Amber Bloom, Melissa Roth, and Lefty Lucy*

leaves the room, they look at each other and say, "Well, he's pretty good, but he's no Zeppo Marx!" Then we found the deep and dashing Aristotle Stamat. Aristotle is an old movie buff, a history buff, and a Marx Brothers buff. (He is also very buff.) In fact, he had attended some Marxfest events, including one of the *I'll Say She Is* readings. As with Seth, Robert, and Kathy, here was someone who already spoke the language. Ari knew exactly how to talk and behave as Zeppo, because Ari is a fine actor who has been watching Marx Brothers movies all his life.

The hilarious and magnetic C.L. Weatherstone, who had been in *Travesties of 2012*, joined the cast at this point. So, gradually, did a dazzling bevy of musical theatre, dance, and burlesque performers, the first *I'll Say She Is* chorus since 1925: Amber Bloom, Francine Daveta, Lefty Lucy, Emily Turner Marsland, Melissa Roth, Kita St. Cyr, Alexis Thomason,

Foxy Vermouth, and Jamie C. Wells. Trav recruited Helen Burkett, of the Pontani Sisters burlesque act, to choreograph the chorus dances, and the astonishingly resourceful Juliann Kroboth to design costumes and props.

I decided to be the calm center of this storm. I did my best to set the general tone, but left most of the production decisions to Trav, and deferred to him in rehearsal. There was an understanding that I had veto power if I thought something was egregiously wrong, but I was comfortable allowing it to be a Trav S.D. production. I wanted him to feel that it was. It wouldn't have been fair to seek the collaboration of someone of Trav's caliber, and then retain all the creative authority for myself. Moreover, the grander version of my vision for *I'll Say She Is*—a large physical production, designed and constructed in emulation of the original, with details plucked from my reams of research—would not have been feasible in a Fringe production anyway. The goal for August was simply to present the material effectively. The hope, as with most festival shows, was that we would attract the interest of producers or backers who would help take it to the next level.

The summer of 2014 was an unusually mild one for New York, and I spent it dashing from day job to rehearsal to meeting to interview, working at a manic clip, and repeating to myself the refrain that had helped me all throughout Marxfest: *Don't forget to enjoy this. Don't forget how recently this was all just a dream.* Now here we were: *I'll Say She Is* was in rehearsal! When not in rehearsal, I might be at Seth's apartment in the West Village, helping him figure out how to build the perfect Harpo horn, or walking around midtown with Melody, running lines for the Napoleon scene. Melody's distinctive performance was making Beauty a much funnier and more interesting character than she seemed on paper, and this prompted some revisions to the lyrics. On one glorious afternoon, Sabrina and I played and sang through the entire score, fixing many small problems, and enhancing the Wall Street sequence with some fantastic variations Sabrina had improvised for the readings.

Many aspects of the show would have to wait for its next iteration.

Some of the revue elements would be excised for the Fringe Festival, and it was generally light on musical staging. Toward the end of rehearsals, we reluctantly cut the Apache and Pygmalion dances, and the Tramp Ballet, for practical reasons. This was unfortunate, not only because the Fringe audience was denied the excellent work of the cast in those dances, but because without them the show felt less like a revue.

Now that *I'll Say She Is* was more than a theory, Trav and I found the need for more shuffling of the sequence. The Chico/Harpo poker game had always been part of the courtroom scene, but the courtroom scene had always been in the first act. Now that it was the climactic scene, stopping for the poker routine was a drag. Trav found a way to "cut" from the middle of Act One, Scene Two (Beauty's Reception Room) to a reconfigured poker routine, cued by Beauty's suggestion that the boys "go into the parlor and draw lots." Groucho was added to the poker game, making acerbic remarks. We worked out the scene by improvising in rehearsal, and in performance it retained a loose, off-the-cuff quality that helped the audience believe that we were the Marx Brothers and were capable of anything at any moment.

Even with the minimal staging and the absence of scenery, the production had a certain lavishness, due to the contributions of Juliann Kroboth. Julz, as she is affectionately known, managed to costume the show with heart-stopping beauty, on a shoestring. Some of the more elaborate chorus girl costumes, as well as the sartorial splendor of the Napoleon scene, were enhanced by the Theatre Development Fund Costume Collection. There were costumes in *I'll Say She Is* that were recognizable from other shows—a tailcoat from the Broadway production of *Beauty and the Beast*, for example. This felt nicely continuous with the original production, and its scenery from Kane's Warehouse. Other aspects of the *I'll Say She Is* wardrobe sprang entirely from Julz's fertile mind. She designed hilarious costumes for the "Tragedy of Gambling" dancers, for Emily Turner Marsland as the Fairy of Wall Street, and for the international women of "The Inception of Drapery."

Julz attended ingeniously to the many special demands of Seth's Harpo coat. She sewed large hidden pockets into the interior, so Seth had a trick coat just like Harpo's. She engineered a long, thick tube which made it easy to fill Seth's sleeve with "enough cutlery to stock five automats" (Gene Fowler, *New York Daily Mirror*). This, of course, would come crashing out in perfect time when Trav, in a cameo appearance as the Detective, shook Seth's hand.

With Trav in the director's chair, and such capable collaborators as Sabrina, Julz, and Helen seeing to many of the production details, I concentrated on Groucho. I stuck to a daily exercise regimen, including ten minutes of corkscrew kicks, and run-throughs of the dance routine for the Napoleon number. It was a catalogue of Groucho moves, and I had to drill it extensively, not only to get it right, but to make sure that by the end of the song I wasn't too winded for the Napoleon scene which immediately followed—a workout in itself. As is often the case in rehearsal for a demanding musical, I seemed to wake up every morning a couple of pounds lighter than the day before.

Noah Diamond, Aristotle Stamat, Seth Shelden, and Robert Pinnock.
Photo by Kathy Biehl.

In rehearsal, I was ad-libbing all over the show, partly to keep things interesting for myself and get into the right Groucho mood, and partly to amuse my castmates. I genuinely liked everyone in the show, and felt grateful to them, and, I think, they to me; everyone seemed to feel that this was a special project. Everyone was happy to be involved. Largely due to all these warm feelings, I felt comfortable enough with the cast to fail in front of them. This is an essential condition for good improvisation. Also bad improvisation. In rehearsal, I allowed myself to descend ever lower into the depths of contrived puns and unprovoked nonsense. Trav at one point had to pull me aside to talk about it. He allowed that this ad-libbing rampage seemed to have reinvigorated me, but carefully expressed that he felt some of my impromptu additions were not up to Groucho standards. I assured him that I knew this was true, that I was giving myself a wide range to try anything that came to mind in rehearsal, but that in the show itself I would exhibit greater fidelity to both script and character.

A S WITH MARXFEST, the weeks leading up to the Fringe Festival opening were filled with heady interviews, a press conference, and promotional appearances. I made the rounds, telling the story of how I'd researched and reconstructed *I'll Say She Is*, and singing the praises of the cast and company. I was having the time of my life, and I sound downright giddy in some of those interviews. Darnelle Radford, of the Rep Radio podcast, asked what inspired me to recreate *I'll Say She Is*, and this was my answer:

> It's love! It's love and joy. I love the Marx Brothers with all my heart, and like anyone who's really evangelical about a passion, I want to spread the gospel. This is a classic that nobody knows...The idea that there's this forgotten Marx Brothers masterpiece, and that I might play some role in putting it back before the public—it's missionary work, as far as I'm concerned.

True to Trav's prediction, *I'll Say She Is* was being heavily touted as a highlight of the upcoming festival. Thanks to its promise of laughs, its historic nature, and Don Spiro's vivid photographs of the cast in costume, the show was prominently featured in most of the advance press coverage. On August 5, the *Wall Street Journal* ran our photograph under the headline, "The Return of the Marx Brothers." On August 8, the theatre page of the *New York*

Don Spiro's photo of Melody Jane and me, in character, which led the New York Daily News' *coverage of the 2014 Fringe Festival.*

Daily News was dominated by an enormous photo of me as Groucho and Melody as Beauty, next to the headline "HIGH MARX." That day, the entire Fringe run of *I'll Say She Is* sold out at the box office.

On the day the *Daily News* piece landed, Amanda rose early, and went running across the street to the nearest bodega to scoop up a few copies of the paper. Right there, at the Ideal Mini Mart on 174th and Broadway, she flipped eagerly through the *Daily News* until she found the theatre page. Too excited not to share immediately, she exclaimed to the man behind the counter, "*Look!* This is my husband!" The man skeptically glanced at the photo, nodded his head in a cautious kind of way, and perhaps took some mental note about whatever he thought was happening to the neighborhood. Amanda and I thought she should go back the next day, buy another paper, and point to a photo of President Obama: "Look! My husband!"

I HAD BEEN making an effort to stay out of Trav's way, to assist him in any way possible when asked, but to let him lead. Trav was doing top-drawer work, but he was doing the work of ten men, and here I was, only doing the work of five or six. In the home stretch, I took on more, and it seemed to help get us over the finish line. The comedy scenes, on which we had lavished great love and attention, were in good shape, but there were musical numbers that hadn't been touched. I'd had a concept in mind for the staging of "When Shadows Fall," and I was in the middle of explaining it to Trav when he said, "Why don't you just stage it?" I stayed up all night mapping the number out on paper, and walked the cast through it the next day.

The number took place "on Broadway," with Beauty and Zeppo walking the streets ("Broadway at night! The bright lights, the excitement!") and falling in love. It was the emotional center of the show, and I wanted it to feel like a big production number. In the absence of scenery, the best way to achieve some spectacle was to get the whole cast on stage, in colorful and amusing costumes. So Melody and Aristotle, the young lovers, strolled through a Runyonesque Times Square populated by a flower seller; a street sweeper; a fortune teller; the Statue of Liberty; a nun; a newsboy; the Marx Brothers; chorus girls holding up Broadway signs reading LOVE, BROAD-WAY, and THRILLS; and the devious Hop Merchant who later escorts Beauty to the Chinatown opium den.

Our first performance was to be on Sunday, August 10. On the preceding Friday (the day of the *Daily News* piece), in a rehearsal studio in Brooklyn, the cast performed its first complete run-through. That was the first time we performed the Napoleon scene in costume. Following the rehearsal, I went to a studio in Queens, where Julz and her assistant, Tina McCartney, had set up shop, frantically assembling costumes and props that were needed on stage in less than forty-eight hours. I was there until dawn, painting Broadway signs for the "When Shadows Fall" number, helping Julz with assorted crafts emergencies, and having a fine, long talk about the theatre. By the time I climbed wearily into the sunlight from the 175th Street subway station and stumbled toward home, I had four hours to sleep before the dress rehearsal, and I had lost my voice.

I looked at myself in the mirror. I looked, as my mother once said in

Painting signs on the eve of the dress rehearsal

criticism of a haircut I wanted, like Mr. Weird. I was thin and bedraggled, with hollow cheeks and deep, dark bags under my bloodshot eyes. My hair was wild.

My natural hair, to my ongoing disappointment, is not nearly as curly or frizzy as Groucho's. For recent Groucho appearances, I'd been putting little curlers in my hair for several hours before showtime, as Amanda had taught me; this technique, in combination with numerous sprays and fixatives, gave me convincing Groucho hair. But it would only last for an evening, if that, and it could be undone by moisture or too much handling. It was also a lot of work, best done a full day in advance. There were times during Marxfest when I was going about my day, all over New York, with my hair in curlers

The author getting a perm, as all authors must.
Author's perm courtesy of Amanda Sisk.

and a bandana. And so, to avoid this humiliation, my wife gave me a perm. We did a test perm in July, and another one in August. It was a tremendous success, not only for my likeness to Groucho, but in giving me the frizzy head of unruly, vertical hair I'd always wanted. I made it a point to mention my perm as often as possible, and predicted I would be elected Homecoming Queen. But on this particular morning, after my long day and night, it was no longer combed and parted, a la Groucho. The mop of wild curls above my exhausted, skeletal face was like an illustration of my head exploding.

Seemingly moments later, I was back on the subway, heading back to Brooklyn for the dress rehearsal. At least Amanda was with me now, to discourage me from falling down or bumping into things. I was amazed to see Julz at the studio, bright and chipper, with the Broadway signs and all the costumes that had seemed far from ready just hours ago. I was extremely worried about my voice. The combination of fatigue and over-exertion in rehearsal had reduced it to a raspy burr; and at the dress rehearsal I sounded more like Joan Rivers than Groucho Marx. In one further annoyance, I misplaced my round wire-rimmed glasses, and had to do the rehearsal without them, which made me feel even less like Groucho.

It was a low point. At home, I'd had a kind of despair-tantrum. *So this was it!* This is what the cruel universe had in store! Years of working on this project, dreaming of playing this role, and now robbed of the gift of speech! Why couldn't *Seth* lose his voice—he didn't need it now, I did! Amanda reminded me that psychosomatic or fatigue-induced voice loss was not an uncommon syndrome for me in the days before an opening, and that I had had similar problems on the eve of the first Marxfest reading, not three months ago. She reassured me that when it was time for the first performance, my voice would be there, as it always was when I needed it. She made me tea as thick as soup, and told me to stop talking. A directive more fun to make than to follow.

Except for my own deficiencies, the dress rehearsal was pretty solid. I thought we were in great shape—if only we had another two weeks. But that's how it always is. "Then out of the hat, it's that big first night." And despite some rough edges, *I'll Say She Is* was now real. It wasn't just a play anymore; now it was a production, a thing that a group of people got up and *did*. It was spectacular. When we got to the end, and the small invited audience applauded, I asked Trav if I could say a few words before he and Sabrina and Helen gave their notes to the cast.

"I just want to say, don't worry about my glasses or my voice—I will find both," I told the company. "And I want to tell you how full of love and admiration I am for everyone in this room. I can't thank you enough…" I was planning to say more, but they drowned me out with applause.

O N SUNDAY, THIRTY MINUTES before showtime, I arrived at the beautiful Loretto Auditorium, at the newly-opened Sheen Center on Bleecker Street. The Loretto was a former concert hall, and although it had been dramatically renovated, it retained some of the details and grandeur of its nineteenth-century origins. Venues are the luck of the draw in the Fringe Festival; you tell them what you need and they do their best to accommodate you. The Loretto was just about perfect: a large, traditional proscenium space, with a sense of history.

Amanda was right about my voice. After Slippery Elm and sleep, I rose on Sunday fully restored and ready to join my hero on a list of the two people in history who have played Groucho in *I'll Say She Is*. Normally, on the evening of the first performance of a new work, I would have been at the theatre hours early, sitting in the seats, wandering around backstage, and kicking the tires. But under Fringe conditions, there was no time to soak up the mood. This feeling of rushed intensity characterized the entire process, and its effects were largely positive. But as a result of it, the emotional aspect of the experience caught up with me later, after we'd opened and there was an occasional moment to reflect. I don't remember thinking, in rehearsal, *Oh! We're working on the Napoleon scene!* I remember thinking, *We have to work on the Napoleon scene.*

There were no tickets left, but people were still trying to get them. I was informed of a cancellation line that went around the block, and that a few people with tickets were out there trying to resell them. That first audience included Paul Wesolowski and Marx Brothers scholar Robert Moulton (both of whom generously helped Seth repair his malfunctioning Harpo horn after the performance); and our old friend Kevin Fitzpatrick; as well as familiar names from the New York theatre and burlesque scenes, and a lot of friends. Amanda was there, of course, along with my brother Joe, Joe's girlfriend Margaret Aldredge, and my father, who'd purchased a ticket for every performance. Shayna, Mom, and Steve would arrive in New York, and see the show, the following week. Also, toward the end of the run, I had the pleasure of finally meeting Mikael Uhlin. My e-mail to him, years ago, had been the origin of this project, and he came all the way from Sweden to see it. I have a prized photograph of Mikael, Meg, and me, looking invigorated after a performance of *I'll Say She Is*.

With Meg Farrell and Mikael Uhlin following the last performance of I'll Say She Is *at the 2014 New York International Fringe Festival*

But all of that, and much more, was to come later. Now it was time to begin.

Amid a flurry of frenzied backstage preparations, Trav gathered the company in a circle. He thanked everyone for their dedication and hard work, and said a few words about the special nature of the project and the significance of what we were about to do. His voice grew thick with emotion when he said, "You are making history," and his eyes welled up and he was unable to continue. The company applauded Trav, hugged, and dispersed—a moment of exquisite tenderness immediately dissolved into the dash and hustle of a show nearing its first curtain.

"Can you believe this?" I said to Kathy Biehl.

"Yes, I can," Kathy said.

I made my way past the women's dressing room, bursting with chorus girls in elaborate art deco headpieces, and entered the men's dressing room. There were Seth, Robert, and Aristotle, at mirrors surrounded by lights, in various stages of Marxian costume and makeup.

"Well, boys," I said, "I guess we're home again."

I sat down, opened my makeup kit, and met my own delirious gaze in the mirror as I smeared a black stripe of greasepaint across my face.

Aristotle Stamat, Noah Diamond, Robert Pinnock, and Seth Shelden in I'll Say She Is. *Photo by Don Spiro.*

ENCORE

I'*LL SAY SHE IS*," wrote Martin Denton in his opening-night review, "is sheer delight, a clear and obvious landmark of the 2014 FringeNYC festival, and an absolute triumph for all involved." History News Network began its review, "The Marx Brothers are back!" and called the show "a restored treasure, overflowing with comic gold." Trav was praised for his "graciously tumultuous" direction, intended "not to re-enact the Marx Brothers' shtick so much as create it for the first time all over again." The reviews, in almost every case, were everything we could have hoped for, extolling the show's entertainment value as well as its historical significance. Several predicted, or expressed hope for, a Broadway production.

The entire cast drew raves. Melody Jane was compared with Lillian Roth and Thelma Todd, a "pert, forthright, zany heroine" who "would have been a fan favorite in any Marx Brothers movie." Kathy Biehl was "an ideal Margaret Dumont" with "a golden voice." There was praise all around for the "drily uproarious" Robert Pinnock as Chico, and the "subtly grandstanding," "sturdily handsome" Aristotle Stamat as Zeppo. As in 1924, the silent, noisy brother was the subject of much celebration: The "fabulously funny," "wondrously alive" Seth Shelden, "charming yet quietly troubling as Harpo," "steals the show" with "a meta, masterly performance." And my performance as Groucho was unanimously lauded: "Uncanny and hilarious"; "Sensational...a wonder"; "Miraculous, tapping the source of that comedian's anarchic essence"; "The absolute stunner of the night...I feel as if I saw Groucho himself perform live on stage, and what a treat that was. Diamond had the look, feel, timing and connection to the audience that made Groucho so special. He ad-libbed and cracked wise in ways that would've made Groucho proud. Diamond has apparently dedicated a good portion of his life to his love for and performance of the comic genius, and

Kathy Biehl as Ruby Mintworth, displaying pictures of the rest of the principal cast of I'll Say She Is, *2014. Photos by Don Spiro.*

to very noble effect."

The few critical tsk-tsks had to do with parts of the show seeming messy or under-rehearsed. That was fair enough. It had been an ambitious undertaking for the Fringe, and if we fell short of the polish that a revival of a hit Broadway musical would suggest, it was now clear that there would be opportunities to further develop those aspects of the show.

At the stage door after one of the Fringe performances, a gentleman approached me and introduced himself as the son of Russell O. "Busse" Heycock, who'd been a trumpet player in Nat Martin's *I'll Say She Is* orchestra. He presented me with a laminated newspaper article in which his father shared memories of Groucho. The younger Mr. Heycock told me he was ninety-three years old, and as a toddler he had attended performances of *I'll Say She Is* at the Casino Theatre. He had met Groucho backstage, and had vague childhood memories of the show. Now, he and his wife had journeyed to New York from their home in Wilkes-Barre, Pennsylvania, to see its first-ever revival. Mr. Heycock is the only person in the world who has seen both productions.

As a result of the Fringe show, I received invitations to play Groucho in various contexts, or to write about the Marxes and the *I'll Say She Is* experience. I continued to hear from Marx Brothers fans around the world, expressing support or gratitude for my efforts, and wanting to know when an *I'll Say She Is* touring company might make its way to their cities.

The Fringe production was a real moment. But the moment passed, and I went back to work. The Wall Street number needed another rewrite, and I had recently discovered a "new" piece of Tom Johnstone music that I thought I could use as an improved "Wall Street Blues." The show had run short at the Fringe—less than ninety minutes—so there would be room in the future, not only for the deleted dance sequences, but for more songs and specialty material. One example was "Glimpses of the Moon," a lovely *I'll Say She Is* original which I hadn't been able to locate before; I would rework it as a comic duet for Groucho and Ruby in Act Two.

As I write this, the next production of *I'll Say She Is* is being contemplated, and after it there will be others. I'd still love for the show to return to the Big Street. But when presented with opportunities to fast-track it commercially, I thought that the circumstances weren't right. In the fall of 2014, I felt as though I'd spent a lifetime on *I'll Say She Is*, but in fact, it had only had two staged readings and five workshop performances. A number of industry people who saw the Fringe production didn't grasp that the show was a revue, and made suggestions about how to transform it into a Rodgers and Hammerstein-style book musical. Others felt that the entire score should be discarded in favor of familiar 1920s hits—a Marx Brothers jukebox musical, or perhaps a Victrola musical. These suggestions made some sense, from a commercial perspective, but I knew they were wrong for *I'll Say She Is*. I started to contemplate another independent production, downtown but on a larger scale, to more fully demonstrate what *I'll Say She Is* was, is, and should be. The Marxes and the Johnstones worked on this show in front of hundreds of audiences before bringing it to Broadway. If it's ever to be seen there again, it should be as the result of an equally arduous process.

A T THE CASINO THEATRE on February 7, 1925 (which, incidentally, would have been my birthday had I been born fifty-two years earlier), *I'll Say She Is* played its final Broadway performance. After the curtain call, Harpo Marx departed to his new hangout, the Algonquin Hotel. Woollcott, Kaufman, Parker, Benchley, Ross, F. P. A., and the rest of the gang were waiting to celebrate the Marx Brothers' dazzling success. It was an ending and also a beginning: *I'll Say She Is* still had a four-month tour ahead, which was to culminate in Chico's disappearance and the abrupt closing in Detroit. Then there would be two more glorious Broadway hits, and twenty years of Marx Brothers movies.

Some of the friendships Harpo kindled around the Round Table would last a lifetime, enduring testament to the epochal power of *I'll Say She Is*. Some of these stories would end in despair or tragedy, like the Jazz Age itself, which petered out into depression. In the years ahead, the Marx Brothers would play an important role in making depression tolerable.

But let's leave them here, in 1925, sitting on a rainbow, eating peaches and cream. Julius can't help but smile, smug and self-satisfied, as he wipes away the greasepaint with cold cream. Leonard and Herbert are itching to strike out into the electric New York night, in pursuit of their own favorite kinds of action. Arthur is at the Algonquin and life is but a dream. As the silent partner remembered, decades later:

> When I shook hands with F.P.A. he said nothing, but a hotel knife dropped out of his sleeve and clattered onto the lobby floor. I think that was the exact moment I knew, without any reservations, that I belonged to the world of Woollcott and his friends—and to no other.
>
> I never did get back to Lindy's.

PHOTO CREDITS

All photos and images are from the author's personal collection, and/or the public domain, unless otherwise indicated here.

Photos by Don Spiro: iv, 207, 266, 295, 303, 312, 314

Courtesy of Margaret Farrell: 23

Courtesy of Rodney Stewart Hillel Tryster: 29

Bain Collection, Library of Congress: 36

Courtesy of Frank Ferrante / The Groucho Marx Collection: 57, 72, 73, 118, 131, 134, 147, 160, 161, 183, 317

Billy Rose Theatre Division, New York Public Library: 65

Collection of Robert Moulton: 81

Courtesy of Pau Medrano Bigas: 82

Courtesy of Miriam Marx Allen: 145

Photos by Beverly Sobolewski: 194, 269

Photos by Amanda Sisk: 225, 306

Photo by Kathy Biehl: 301

Photo by Jim R. Moore: 263

Courtesy of the Freeport Concert Association: 279

Photo by Jonathan Melvin Smith: 293

All graphic design associated with the I'll Say She Is *revival is by the author. "The* I'll Say She Is *curve design," seen at the top of this page, elsewhere throughout this book, and in publicity and scenic design materials for the* I'll Say She Is *revival, is adapted by the author from a design element in the 1924 Broadway production, evident in photos such as the one on page 139.*

NOTES and SOURCES

Books are identified first by title and author, and by author only for subsequent references. Periodicals whose titles and dates are already included in the main text are usually not cited again here.

Frequently cited:

Adamson, Joe: *Groucho, Harpo, Chico, and Sometimes Zeppo*

Arce, Hector: *Groucho*

Chandler, Charlotte: *Hello, I Must Be Going: Groucho and His Friends*

Coniam, Matthew: *The Annotated Marx Brothers*

Crichton, Kyle: *The Marx Brothers*

Farrell, Margaret: "*I'll Say She Is*: The 'Laugh-a-Minute Revue' that Made the Marx Brothers," *Studies in Musical Theatre*, vol. 7, no. 1

Louvish, Simon: *Monkey Business: The Lives and Legends of the Marx Brothers*

Marx, Groucho: *Groucho and Me*

Marx, Groucho: *The Groucho Phile*

Marx, Groucho and Richard J. Anobile: *The Marx Bros. Scrapbook*

Marx, Harpo and Rowland Barber: *Harpo Speaks*

Mitchell, Glenn: *The Marx Brothers Encyclopedia*

S.D., Trav: *No Applause—Just Throw Money: The Book That Made Vaudeville Famous*

Stoliar, Steve: *Raised Eyebrows: My Years Inside Groucho's House*

Uhlin, Mikael: Marxology (marx-brothers.org/marxology)

A word about the Smithsonian's Groucho Marx Collection: Some of the newspaper and magazine content cited here was found in two *I'll Say She Is* scrapbooks kept by Groucho during the show's run. These scrapbooks are now housed in the Groucho Marx Collection at the Smithsonian's National Museum of American History Archives Center. Many of the clippings in Groucho's scrapbooks are identified and dated, but many are not. When I've been able to cite the exact date, newspaper, city, and/or author of a clipping from the scrapbooks, I indicate it here as I would any article in a periodical. When information is missing, my notes will say something to the effect of, "Unidentified clipping in the Smithsonian's Groucho Marx Collection," or simply "Groucho Marx Collection." In every case, Smithsonian items quoted here can be found in one of Groucho's two *I'll Say She Is* scrapbooks, his *Cocoanuts* scrapbook, or an additional file of loose clippings connected with *Co-*

coanuts. For more information about the Groucho Marx Collection and the Archives Center, visit americanhistory.si.edu/archives.

A word about the index: Major references and digressions in these Notes do appear in the index at the end of this book, but not *every* reference in the following pages is included in the index; that would be crazy. Scholars and completists should read these notes in their entirety, twice every day.

Act One

I. BROTHERS

The story of the Marx Brothers' childhoods and early years in show business has been told many times, often very nicely, and sometimes accurately. To avoid redundancy, I haven't provided much pre-1920 background in these pages, but if you're new to these parts, a world of Marx Brothers literature awaits you. *Every* book about the Marx Brothers is worth reading. The most accurate accounts of the early years are in Simon Louvish, *Monkey Business: The Lives and Legends of the Marx Brothers*; and Hector Arce, *Groucho*; the most poetic and evocative are in Harpo Marx and Rowland Barber, *Harpo Speaks*. As noted elsewhere, Robert S. Bader's forthcoming work on the Marxes' stage years is likely to redefine our understanding of this period.

Marx family background: Arce, Louvish. That Harpo never actually played Fanny's harp is stated by the man himself in *Harpo Speaks*, and further explored by Louvish. The misconception that Harpo learned on Fanny's harp is widespread. The description of Frenchie as "the most incompetent tailor…" is from Groucho Marx, *Groucho and Me*. Groucho's earliest vaudevillian stumblings are chronicled in Arce; Louvish; Charlotte Chandler, *Hello, I Must Be Going*; Groucho's own *Groucho and Me* and *The Groucho Phile*; and Groucho's interviews in *The Marx Bros. Scrapbook*. The team's association with Ned Wayburn is from Louvish.

Nicknames: Robert S. Bader says the Galesburg incident took place on May 14, 15, or 16, 1914. Groucho's reference to Manfred's death of "old age" can be found in Chandler, *Hello, I Must Be Going*, as well as Steve Stoliar, *Raised Eyebrows: My Years Inside Groucho's House*. Stoliar also tells the story in the 2003 documentary *Inside the Marx Brothers*. Chico joining the act: *Harpo Speaks*. It happened in Waukegan, according to Harpo, and the violin player was Benjamin Kubelsky, later known as Jack Benny. Gus Mager: Contrary to some Marx biographies which describe Groucho the Monk as a peripheral character in Mager's world, the character had his very own *Groucho the Monk* strip for years. Hans Pumpernickel: See "Six Mascots" ads in *Variety* throughout April 1910. "Somewhat Original School Act": *Variety*, April 15, 1911. For general impressions of vaudeville, explanations of vaudeville terms, and a tapestry of anecdotes, see Trav S.D., *No Applause—Just Throw Money: The Book That Made Vaudeville Famous*. "Grueling and tiresome": *Harpo Speaks*. "The hardened artery" was Walter Winchell's term for Broadway. "The 'revue' in vaudeville now amounts to...": *Variety*, January 16, 1920. "An effort is being made...": *New York Clipper*, November 15, 1916. "In their frantic search...": *Billboard*, June 21, 1919. "Begin a career": *Chicago Daily Tribune*, September 22, 1918. "Forsaken the varieties": *Billboard*, September 23, 1918. Zeppo's debut: *Variety*, November 6, 1918.

The Street Cinderella was directed by Al Shean, and written by Jo Swerling, Egbert Van Alstyne, and Gus Kahn. Swerling would later write *Humor Risk* for the Marxes; much later, he would write the original book for *Guys and Dolls* (which was then substantially rewritten by Abe Burrows). Gus Kahn, in the distant future, would become a member of the family when his daughter married Groucho's son, and...well, no need going into that here. Sources for *The Street Cinderella*: Adamson, Louvish; also Mikael Uhlin, marx-brothers.org/marxology; *Chicago Tribune*, September 22, 1918; *Billboard*, September 23, 1918; and *New York Clipper*, September 25 and October 2, 1918.

The Marxes sign with Dillingham: *Variety*, November 19, 1919; also, an advertisement run in *Variety* throughout early 1920. Kyle Crichton, in *The Marx Brothers*, says that Dillingham later made the insulting Montgomery and Stone offer; in Crichton's telling, Chico wants to take the job and the money, but Minnie talks him out of it. Dillingham and Aaron Hoffman: *Sunday News*, May 25, 1924. *N'Everything*: See Louvish. "A thousand per cent beyond": *Variety*, June 18, 1920. "More people were talking about Marx Brothers...": *Variety*, August 20, 1920. "Were forced to respond...": *Billboard*, October 2, 1920. Arce and Louvish cover the Zeppo-Ruth-Groucho love triangle.

Herman Timberg introducing "School Days": Steve Sullivan, *Encyclopedia of Great Popular Song Recordings*. The review of *Fun in Hi Skule* which mentions Timberg is reprinted in *The Marx Bros. Scrapbook*. Timberg's early success and upbringing: *Syracuse Herald*, November 10, 1929. *Chicken Chow Mein*: *National Glass Budget*, October 25, 1919, and *Pittsburgh Gazette Times*, October 28, 1919. *Herman Timberg in Three Acts*: *Theatre Magazine*, April 1920. "Larry Fine idolized Herman Timberg": Morris Moe Feinberg and G. P. Skratz, *My Brother Larry: The Stooge in the Middle*. "Successors to the Marx Brothers": Jeff Lenburg, Joan Howard Maurer, and Greg Lenburg, *The Three Stooges Scrapbook*. Timberg's "Monkey Business": *Brooklyn Eagle*, October 16, 1927. After the success of *I'll Say She Is*, Timberg went out of his way to emphasize his connection with the Marxes, letting it be known that he had written "much of the material that was used...in their big Broadway success" (*Brooklyn Daily Eagle*, June 21, 1925), and even declaring himself "discoverer of the Marx Brothers" (*New York American*, August 30, 1924). The remarkable Timberg family maintains a website, timbergally.com.

For general *On the Mezzanine* interest, see Louvish, Chandler, and Mitchell; and Mikael Uhlin, marx-brothers.org/marxology. "Do away with their former characters": *Variety*, January 14, 1921. For evidence that Groucho was called Mr. Hammer in *N'Everything*, take a look at the Chicago Palace Music Hall theatre program for June 28, 1920, viewable at digital.chipublib.org. The accepted "birth of the greasepaint moustache" is in many sources, including *Groucho and Me* and Arthur Marx, *Son of Groucho*. The two 1921 publicity photos are printed in Mitchell's *Marx Brothers Encyclopedia*; larger versions can be found online. The "candid backstage photo" is in the personal collection of Frank Ferrante. Paul Wesolowski determined its date and location. It shows a happy, greasepainted Groucho holding his infant son, Arthur, born in July of that year. Robert Moulton confirms that the *Mezzanine* publicity photos were taken on December 16, 1921. Adam Gopnik's comment about Groucho's makeup is from "Talking Man," *The New Yorker*, April 17, 2000.

The *Mezzanine* review quoted at length is from the *New York Clipper*, March 9, 1921. I'm especially indebted to Robert Moulton for calling this item to my attention, and for insights regarding Herman Timberg's syncopated jazz patter. Benny Leonard: See Louvish; Chandler; *Variety*, February 11 and April 8, 1921; and *New York Evening Telegram*, July 8, 1921. Hattie Darling is quoted in Chandler. "It is the effrontery": *New York Dramatic Mirror*, July 30, 1921. "An entire musical comedy show": *Billboard*, October 29, 1921. "Rough stuff": *San Francisco Chronicle*, February 6, 1922. *Billboard*'s snarky passage is from June 4, 1921. *Variety*'s "more thoughtful" assessment is from June 2, 1922. "More pretentiously": *New York Sun*, March 15, 1921. "An outstanding smack of smartness": *Variety*, March 18, 1921. *Humor Risk*: See Adamson, Arce, Louvish, and Uhlin. Buying the act from Timberg: *Variety*, January 27, 1922.

British tour: *Variety*, May 12, June 9, June 23, June 30, July 7, and August 11, 1922. Details of the shipboard vaudeville bill are from a "Programme of Entertainment" from the event, photographed and shared on Facebook by Frank Ferrante on October 23, 2015. Some details of the London opening, including Groucho's ad lib about language, from Crichton and Mitchell. The London *Stage* and *Telegram* reviews are quoted in *Variety*, August 11, 1922. Groucho's letter appeared in *Variety* on the same date. The Russian dancers' names are from a newspaper ad reprinted in *The Marx Bros. Scrapbook*. The manager's apology is from Crichton. Impressions of E.F. Albee are from Trav S.D., *No Applause—Just Throw Money*, and Crichton. Albee banning jokes: *Variety*, September 15, 1922. For more on the British tour and the falling-out with Albee, see Louvish.

II. TAKE IT FROM ME

Impressions of Will B. Johnstone are from Margaret Farrell, "*I'll Say She Is*: The 'Laugh-a-Minute Revue' that Made the Marx Brothers," *Studies in Musical Theatre*, vol. 7, no. 1 (2013); Adamson; Groucho in *The Marx Bros. Scrapbook*; and Margaret Farrell in personal conversation. Mikael Uhlin has conducted much invaluable research, including interviews with Will B. Johnstone, Jr., and my descriptions of Johnstone owe a lot to his work. Some basic biographical details are from obituaries in the *Brooklyn Eagle* and *Kansas City Star*, February 7, 1944. Henry Charles Payne quote from *Chicago Inter Ocean*, March 15, 1903. "Makes faces while drawing" and "most impish grin" are from O.O. McIntyre, "New York Day by Day" column, May 10, 1931 and June 12, 1933. Johnstone's train companion was S.J. Perelman, when the two journeyed west to write *Monkey Business* for the Marx Brothers. Perelman's account is in his essay "The Winsome Foursome," published in *Show* (November 1961) and *Esquire* (September 1981) before landing in the posthumous Perelman anthology *The Last Laugh*. History buff and athlete: Uhlin. "Fond of the drink": Margaret Farrell, *I'll Say She Is* talkback at Marxfest, May 25, 2014, available on YouTube. Johnstone's contributions to *A Day at the Races*: Adamson. B.J. Lewis is quoted from his column, "Incident-ly," *Knickerbocker News*, February 11, 1944. Football diagrams: Uhlin. The Johnstone-Beckman romance is from Uhlin, and from Margaret Farrell in personal conversation; the parrot anecdote is from Will B. Johnstone, Jr. by way of Uhlin.

Betsy: *New York Clipper*, October 14; *New York Sun*, December 12; and *New York Evening Telegram*, December 12, 1911. Also, Gerald Bordman, *American Musical Theatre: A Chronicle*. *Miss Princess*: *Variety*, November 15 and *Brooklyn Eagle*, December 24, 1912; and *New York Dramatic Mirror*, January 1, 1913. *The Red Canary*: *Reading Times*, September 25, and *Variety*, October 31, 1913.

Lina Abarbanell, star of *Miss Princess*, *The Red Canary*, and ten other Broadway shows, would also enter musical theatre history in another fashion. Her daughter, Eva Goldbeck, would marry the composer-lyricist Marc Blitzstein. Blitzstein's protégé, Leonard Bernstein, would include Lina Abarbanell's name in a scat lyric for his opera *Trouble in Tahiti*. (If you don't believe me, see Eric A. Gordon, *Mark the Music: The Life and Work of Marc Blitzstein*.)

Fiddlers Three: *Lima Times Democrat*, November 11, and *Hamilton Daily News*,

November 24, 1919. Description of *Sunshine* is from *Cumberland Evening Times*, December 16, 1919. More on *Sunshine*: *Trenton Evening Times*, April 9 and 12, 1919. Alexander Johnstone's partnership with Bert Williams: *Variety*, June 18, 1920. There is a detailed account of Alexander's *Sympathetic Twin* troubles in the *New York Clipper*, June 9, 1920. His obituary appears in the *New York Times*, June 9, 1956.

For background research on Joseph M. Gaites, and insight into his character and his role in our story, I am relying heavily on Mr. Rodney Stewart Hillel Tryster. "The M stands for Minimum" is from *Harpo Speaks*. The origin story of Joseph M. Gaites, as well as his physical description, appears in a long profile from the *Duluth Herald*, and other papers, September 17, 1910. "The honor of being robbed by Gaites": *Morning Telegraph*, January 24, 1900. Groucho on road shows: *New York World*, 1927, Smithsonian's Groucho Marx Collection. Gaites as grocer: *Variety*, May 25, 1912. George Jean Nathan's thoughts about Gaites: *The Smart Set*, May 1913.

Descriptions of *Take it From Me* (all 1919 unless otherwise noted): *Syracuse Journal*, January 21; *Billboard*, February 5; *Brooklyn Eagle*, April 1; *Philadelphia Inquirer*, February 29, 1920 and March 2, 1920. The lyric for "I Like to Linger in the Lingerie" is quoted from the published sheet music. Cartoonists' Night: *Brooklyn Eagle*, April 16. The importance of a success for both Gaites and Johnstone is noted in *The Telegram*, April 20. American Cartoonists convention: *New York Evening World*, May 22. There is a detailed account of the show's financial success in the *New York Clipper*, July 14, 1920. Gaites keeping the show on the road too long: *Variety*, March 15, 1923. Additional impressions of *Take it From Me* are from Margaret Farrell, who also described Will's meticulous bookkeeping. Johnstone to write for the Shuberts: *New York Clipper*, April 9, 1919.

Love for Sale: Gaites signs Kitty Gordon: *New York Clipper*, September 10, 1919. Margaret Farrell, referring to Will B. Johnstone's diaries, states that the gimme-a-thrill plotline common to *Love for Sale, Gimme a Thrill*, and *I'll Say She Is* was Johnstone's creation. (As suggested in the main text, I had surmised that it was Gaites' idea, because it's not nearly as complex or imaginative as Johnstone's concepts for *Take it From Me* and *Up in the Clouds*.) Jack Wilson and his similarity to Cantor, as well as the tale of the mislaid baggage, is from the *Toronto Evening Telegram*, November 4, 1919. "Wall Street Blues" and "Give Me a Thrill" included in the score: *The Music Trades*, September 27, 1919. "Unique characters": *Harrisburg Telegraph*, October 6, 1919. Kitty Gordon's nine gowns, and their cost: *Syracuse Herald*, October 16, 1919. There are some lovely photographs of Ms. Gordon in some of these gowns in *Theatre Magazine*, October 1919. "A rather disasterous [sic] tour": *New York Clipper*, December 10, 1919.

Up in the Clouds: "More of a plot..." is from the *New York Dramatic Mirror*,

June 4, 1921. Details of the plot are from the same article, as well as *Billboard*, July 16, 1921; *New York Evening Telegram*, January 1, 1922; *Variety*, May 13, 1921 and January 6, 1922; and *Chicago Tribune*, July 3, 1921. Incidentally, the name Jean is an important one in the Johnstone cosmos. Will and Helen named their daughter Jean; and there were subsequent Jeans in the family; Jean is Margaret Farrell's middle name. Tom Johnstone's music for the song "Jean," from *Up in the Clouds*, was used for the song "Hail Napoleon" in my adaptation of *I'll Say She Is*. "Condensed" *Love for Sale* with James Watts: *Variety*, July 21, 1922.

Shubert Advanced Vaudeville: See Trav S.D., *No Applause—Just Throw Money*. Also, "Vaudeville Tangle Keeps Performers Hunting Jobs," *Billboard*, December 16, 1922; and "Unit Notes," *Variety*, September 22, 1922. There is much to glean about Shubert vaudeville from other sources cited here regarding both *The Twentieth Century Revue* and *Gimme a Thrill*. Impressions of the Shubert brothers from Foster Hirsch, *The Boys from Syracuse: The Shuberts' Theatrical Empire*, and John Kenrick, *Musical Theatre: A History*. *Hollywood Follies: Variety*, September 22 and October 6, 1922. Charles Moy: *Variety*, February 22, 1923. Sam Toy and rice story: *Variety*, March 29, 1923. "Not such a much": *Billboard*, December 9, 1922. Sketch with Harpo and Chico as mechanics: *Variety*, October 13, 1922. "The Marx boys may greatly profit…": Sime Silverman, *Variety*, December 8, 1922. "Shubert Unit Losers for This Season": *Variety*, February 22, 1923. *Twentieth Century Revue* stopped by the law: *Indianapolis News*, March 5; and *Variety*, March 8, 1923. Thanks to Robert Moulton for help sorting out the timing of the Indianapolis incident.

Gaites in Fall River: *Variety*, October 6, 1922. Gaites quotes, and description of *Gimme a Thrill*, from *Variety*, September 29, 1922. This is also the source for "He apparently started off to do a real job…" *Gimme a Thrill* is further described in a review in *Variety*, October 13, 1922; this description confirms that the plot of *Love for Sale* and *Gimme a Thrill* was essentially retained for *I'll Say She Is*. It notes the character of Beauty, the eight nursery rhyme suitors, Wall Street, the Chinatown "hop joint," and the Apache dance, as well as the presence of "I'm Saving You for a Rainy Day." The Gardiner Trio "walking away with" *Take it From Me*: *Philadelphia Inquirer*, March 2, 1920. *Everybody* liked Max and Moritz.

III. YOU MUST COME OVER

The discussion of musical revues derives from years of study and observation, informed by Gerald Bordman, *American Musical Revue*; Robert Baral, *Revue: The Great Broadway Period*; John Kenrick, *Musical Theatre: A History*; Mary C. Henderson and Alexis Greene, *The Story of 42nd Street*; and Stephen Sondheim, *Finishing the Hat*.

The "Chicago critic" quote about *Up in the Clouds* is from the *Tribune*, July 3, 1921.

Quotations from Will B. Johnstone's diaries are courtesy of Margaret Farrell. Many are included in her *Studies in Musical Theatre* article about the history of *I'll Say She Is* (see earlier note). This article is an important source for the circumstances under which the Johnstones met the Marxes. Impressions of Ned Wayburn are from Louvish; Wayburn's own 1925 book *The Art of Stage Dancing* (which is available for free at Project Gutenberg, so enjoy yourself); and Trav S.D., *No Applause*. Friendship between Groucho and Will is from Johnstone's diaries, as relayed to me by Margaret Farrell. All quotes from Will B. Johnstone, Jr. are by way of Mikael Uhlin, Marxology.

Early title *You Must Come Over*: *Variety*, May 3, 1923. For what it's worth, Kyle Crichton, in *The Marx Brothers*, also attributes the title to Gaites. Johnstone originating the thrill plotline is from Johnstone via Farrell. The review quoted here ("It would seem that with such a vehicle as this...") is from an undated, unlabeled Boston newspaper clipping (circa September 4, 1923) in the Smithsonian's Groucho Marx Collection. Harpo's "cut the cards" gag: That this is what the typescript refers to is confirmed by an April 8, 1924 Baltimore review, in Groucho's scrapbooks at the Smithsonian, which mentions a "courtroom skit in which cards were cut with an ax." Connection between the courtroom scene and *Irish Justice*: *Cumberland Evening Times*, March 10; and *Variety*, May 28, 1924. According to Margaret Farrell, Johnstone was also working on an idea he called "the newspaper show," a theatrical project that went unrealized. Details are few, but it sounds like *As Thousands Cheer* (discussed in this chapter); also like the Federal Theatre Project's "Living Newspapers" of the late thirties. Ms. Farrell suggests that *Try and Get It* (which Johnstone pitched to the Marxes in Wayburn's office) and "the newspaper show" are one and the same.

Announcing Harding's death from the stage is in Steve Stoliar, *Raised Eyebrows*, and others. Groucho told the story on *The Dick Cavett Show*, December 16, 1971, from whence I swiped the "I got a lot of laughs" quote. I think it's unlikely that Groucho was irreverent when announcing the death of the President of the United States. (There is more discussion of the nature of the typescript throughout Act Two of this book, particularly the second chapter.) "Less than one year ago we were doing *Home Again* in London": Robert S. Bader notes in correspondence that by this time, *Home Again* was a "vastly different" show than it had been in 1914.

Birth of the Napoleon scene: The *Chauve-Souris* version originates in Crichton. Information about the Society of Illustrators show, and Johnstone's involvement, from the *Morning Telegraph*, May 10, 1923. Margaret Farrell confirms that Johnstone was writing about the Illustrators show in his diary concurrently with *I'll Say She Is*. The 1973 interview in which Groucho discusses writing the Napoleon scene is in

The Marx Bros. Scrapbook. The "later version" of the Napoleon scene can be found in *The Groucho Phile.* The original document from which it was transcribed is in the Groucho Marx Collection. (I have examined this script, and it contains no departure from the *Phile* text, nor anything to verify or contradict my hypothesis that it's an early-thirties road script.) Groucho's answer to "Do you write your own stuff?" is from a 1924 article by Colgate Baker, also in the Groucho Marx Collection.

A final word on dating the typescript: At the May 31, 1923 tryout in Allentown, "Johnstone rushed backstage to add a line that mentioned the title of the show" (information from Johnstone's diaries via Margaret Farrell, *Studies in Musical Theatre*). Presumably, this refers to the exchange at the end of the Theatrical Agency scene, in which the Agent asks, "Isn't she a beauty?" and everyone else replies, "I'LL SAY SHE IS!" But this line is present in the typescript, which suggests either that the typescript originated a few weeks later than I estimate in the main text (i.e., after rehearsals had concluded), or that an extra page with the new line was interpolated. I'm guessing the latter.

IV. I CAN'T GET STARTED

Competing versions of how the Marxes got involved with *I'll Say She Is* are from *Groucho and Me*, *The Groucho Phile*, and *Harpo Speaks*, referenced as Groucho's and Harpo's memoirs in the main text. A "later, less folksy telling" is in *The Marx Bros. Scrapbook.* Chico meeting Tom Johnstone in front of the Palace is from Kyle Crichton, *The Marx Brothers.* It's likely that Crichton's version of the story is a) exactly what the boys told him and b) false.

For James P. Beury's background, especially the Conness-Till period, I am relying on revelations unearthed, and dots connected, by Rodney Stewart Hillel Tryster. Edward Robins as a "Belasco leading man": *Moving Picture World*, February 13, 1915. For an excellent detailed history of Conness-Till, see Kevin Plummer, "Historicist: Early Cinema, Made in Canada," torontoist.com (May 16, 2015). Details of the prizefight footage caper, and Beury's "a fortune was waiting," from Peter Morris, *Embattled Shadows: A History of Canadian Cinema, 1895-1939.* Details of the studio fire derive from Kevin Plummer's article as well as *Variety*, June 4, 1915. Robins and Beury present *Annabel Lee*: *New York Dramatic Mirror*, June 30, 1917. Beury's acquisition of the Walnut Street Theatre comes from the *Philadelphia Inquirer*, March 13 (including the dollar amounts); *New York Clipper*, March 17; and *Variety*, December 3, 1920. Details of the renovated theatre are from "The Call Boy's Chat" column, *Philadelphia Inquirer*, October 24 and 31, 1920. The same column, on December 12, offers us Beury "on the job daily with his architect"; Beury having at some point "appeared behind the footlights himself" and "directed and managed a stock company in Toronto"; *and* the line about Beury's cane being made from the original roof supports. Booking deal with the Shuberts: *Variety*, May 19, 1920. *The Green Goddess: Dramatic Mirror*, January 1, 1921. In 1925, Beury produced Tom Johnstone's *When You Smile* (*Buffalo Courier*, September 15, 1925).

Rehearsals begin: *Philadelphia Inquirer*, May 13, 1923. Vaughn Godfrey as director or co-director of *Up in the Clouds*: *Variety*, January 6, 1922. Muriel Hudson quote: *Philadelphia Inquirer*, May 21, 1923. Background on the Melvin Sisters is from an unidentified clipping, circa May 30, 1924, Groucho Marx Collection. "Banking on their judgment of this city": *Philadelphia Inquirer*, June 3, 1923. "The Call Boy's Chat," *Philadelphia Inquirer*, May 27, 1923. So many of the *Inquirer* items in this section are from "The Call Boy's Chat," from here on I'm not going to specify so unless it's important for some reason. Also, for the rest of this section, I'm just going to say *Inquirer*, without the *Philadelphia*. What do you think, I just sit around writing endnotes all day?

Details of the Allentown opening are from Will B. Johnstone's diaries, courtesy of Margaret Farrell. Review of the Philadelphia opening: *Variety*, June 7, 1923. "Reminiscences of *Up in the Clouds*": Chicago clipping, October 15, 1923, Groucho Marx Collection. Only show in town: *New York Clipper*, June 13 and 27; *Variety*, June 21, 1923. "Coolest spot in town" and "typhoon fans": *Inquirer*, July 1, 1923. "Word of mouth": *Variety*, June 27, 1923. Peggy McClure: *Inquirer*, July 29, and *Variety*, August 2, 1923. Florence Hedges: *Inquirer*, June 10 and July 22, 1923, and April 27, 1924. Cecile D'Andrea: *Inquirer*, June 3 and July 8, 1923; and *Yonkers Statesman*, January 17, 1925. Mildred Joy: *Inquirer*, August 19, 1923. The boys sing Minnie's praises, and Minnie Marx quote: *Inquirer*, June 17, 1923. Groucho's book on comedy: *Inquirer*, July 1, 1923. The Studebaker story, in its mythic form, is from Groucho Marx, *Groucho and Me*, and elsewhere. The possibly *true* story (and the wonderful "I can't get started" line) is from the *Inquirer*, August 26, 1923. The point about Groucho's costumes was elaborated upon by Paul Wesolowski in personal conversation.

Who's Who curtain: *Inquirer*, June 10 and 17, 1923. Tony Biddle is quoted in an *I'll Say She Is* ad, *Inquirer*, June 9, 1923. Flattering Philly: *Inquirer*, May 27, June 3 and 24, and July 15, 1923. Conflicting reports about just when *I'll Say She Is* would transfer to Broadway can be found in *Variety*, August 30, 1923 and April 23 and 30, 1924; *Kansas City Star*, December 19, 1923; *Philadelphia Inquirer*, March 23 and May 11, 1924; *Brooklyn Daily Star*, May 12, 1924; and other fine publications. "We created *I'll Say She Is* for Philadelphia consumption": *Inquirer*, July 8, 1923.

"Alive to the times": *Inquirer,* September 2, 1923. The "Call Boy's Chat" column was still trumpeting the show's success, as evidence of Philadelphia's civic greatness, on October 28 and December 30, 1923, and March 23 and June 15, 1924. Gaites and Beury's closing announcement: *Inquirer,* August 26, 1923.

The circumstances under which *Thumbs Down* usurped *I'll Say She Is* at the Walnut are suggested in *Variety,* August 9 and 30, and September 13, 1923. Robert Moulton, guessing at Beury's reasoning, says: "If you have a financial interest in two shows, and one could tour and make money, and the other is a dud but you have a theatre that now gets traffic no matter what, then maybe you would put the one on the road and bring the other into the theatre you own."

Frank Ferrante noted Groucho's affection for the Walnut in personal correspondence. Ferrante adds: "A patron at one of my [1993] Walnut performances showed me a color photo of Groucho entering the lobby of the Walnut from that [1974] visit." Also: "An elderly gent approached me after a performance there of *Groucho: A Life in Revue* and said to me, 'I saw Harpo Marx drop knives on that very spot seventy years ago.'" Groucho's line about "the most important thing…" is from Chandler, *Hello I Must Be Going.*

Boston: "Nose dive" from *Variety,* September 20, 1923. Slow business and tough competition: *Variety,* September 6, 13, and 27, 1923. That the main competition came from the *Follies,* featuring Gallagher and Shean, was confirmed by Robert S. Bader in conversation. Groucho's "Bunker Hill" remark is from Crichton. Chico/Patricola trouble: *Variety,* September 20, 1923. Yankee Girls episode: *Buffalo Courier,* February 3, 1924. Boston review and cast listing: *Boston Globe,* September 4, 1923.

V. ISN'T SHE A BEAUTY?

For research and insights regarding Lotta Miles / Florence Reutti, especially on her family and early years, I am indebted to Professor Pau Medrano Bigas of the University of Barcelona (who is a delightful correspondent and the author of a scholarly thesis about the use of advertising by pioneer tire companies), Robert Moulton, and Rodney Stewart Hillel Tryster.

The 1973 Groucho quote is from *The Marx Bros. Scrapbook.* Early biographical details of Florence Reutti: *Buffalo Evening News,* January 30, 1924, and *Buffalo Courier,* February 3, 1924. Joseph F. Reutti's obituary is in the *Buffalo Evening News,* February 16, 1921. Florence's early work with Henrietta in Buffalo: *Buffalo Courier,* August 7, 1908 and February 28, 1909. The life and first marriage of Henrietta Reutti is a whole rich soap opera unto itself. It's not relevant enough to the Marxes or *I'll Say She Is* to include in these pages, but if you're curious, *New York Herald*, November 22, 1912; *New York Press*, November 23, 1912; *Variety*, November 27, 1912; *Buffalo Courier*, March 7 and 13 and May 16, 1913; *The Saratogan*, May 15, 1913 and December 18, 1914; *New York Evening Telegram*, October 3, 1915; and *Troy Times*, May 22, 1918 ought to get you started. Jean Newcombe as original Lotta Miles: *Syracuse Post Standard*, October 3, 1919. (This is the article that places both Newcombe and Reutti in *Fifty-Fifty, Ltd.*.) I should note that Professor Pau Medrano Bigas doubts that Newcombe was really the original Lotta Miles.

"Notable Women of History": *Photoplay*, July 1916. *Florence Rose Fashions*: *Motography*, July 22, 1916; and *New York Dramatic Mirror*, October 28 and November 18, 1916. "The Most Photographed Beauty in America," and Dr. Genthe quote: *Fort Wayne Journal-Gazette*, July 14, 1918. Discovered by B.S. Moss: *New York Clipper*, January 8, 1919. Changed name to Florence Court: *New York Clipper*, August 20, 1918. Robert Moulton confirms the date of Florence's marriage to Raymond Court. More thoughts on *Fifty-Fifty, Ltd.*: *New York Clipper*, July 16 and 23; and *Washington Times*, August 10, 1919. See also *Theatre Magazine*, December 1919. *Linger Longer Letty*: *San Francisco Chronicle*, August 26, 1922; *Variety*, September 1, 1922.

Tangerine: "Lotta Miles" was in the show, according to *Variety*, December 16, 1921. Of special interest is the fact that *Tangerine* played for a year at the Casino Theatre. There is no Lotta Miles, Florence Reutti, or Florence Court listed in the record, but she may have been a replacement. (*Tangerine* opened at the Casino on August 9, 1921.) It seems unlikely that *I'll Say She Is* was Miss Miles' *second* engagement at the Casino if nobody mentioned it at the time, but it's possible. I haven't found any 1924 references to *I'll Say She Is* being her Broadway debut, either. Lotta Miles in Ziegfeld's *Frolic*: *Variety*, January 6; *Rochester Democrat and Chronicle*, February 12; and *Chicago Tribune*, March 20, 1922. Separation from Raymond Court: *San Francisco Chronicle*, August 26; and *Variety*, September 1 and September 22, 1922. The September 22 article has most of the details, and the quote from Justice Marsh.

Cast in *I'll Say She Is*: *Variety*, September 13, 1923. "Rich clear soprano voice": *New York Clipper*, January 8, 1919. The long quote from Miss Miles is drawn from the *Hamilton Evening Journal*, January 18, 1924. "Poise and acting ability": Undated Detroit review, circa October 9, 1923, in the Smithsonian's Groucho Marx Collection. Stage appearances with the Marxes in 1931: *Hamilton Journal News*, October 28; and *Buffalo Courier-Express*, December 4, 5, and 9. *Waterfront Lady* is available for free at archive.org. If you spot her, let me know. In 2014, film scholar and author Michael J. Hayde told me that a 1921 silent film produced by the Kelly Springfield Tire Company, *Blowout Bill's Busted Romance*, had turned up at the

Library of Congress, and I got all excited—but then Professor Pau Medrano Bigas assured me that the actress billed therein as Lotta Miles is not Florence Reutti but another Lotta Miles altogether. Information about the Kelly comedy shorts can be found in *Printers' Ink*, November 25, 1920; and *Ostego Farmer*, February 17, 1921; and also, apparently, at the Library of Congress. Obituary: *Hamilton Journal News*, July 13, 1937.

VI. GUNNING FOR HIGH NOTES

Variety's rather poor sentence is from October 25, 1923. Charles Collins is quoted from *Chicago Tribune*, October 16, 1923. O.L. Hall is quoted from an unidentified clipping in the Groucho Marx Collection, circa October 15, 1923. Andole brawl: *Variety*, November 15; *Chicago Tribune*, November 10; and *Milwaukee Journal*, November 9, 1923. Dispute with *Abie's Irish Rose*: *Variety*, November 1 through December 6, 1923; also George C. Warren's syndicated column, "Behind the Back Row," December 4, 1923. Groucho's insomnia: *Buffalo Courier*, December 9, 1923. Antics in Chicago with Hecht and MacArthur from *Harpo Speaks*. The Charlie Chaplin quote was used extensively in ads for the show, from this point forward. That Chaplin actually saw the show, and that he saw it during its pre-Broadway run in Chicago, was confirmed by Robert S. Bader in conversation. An advertisement in the October 18, 1923 *Chicago Tribune* specifies that Chaplin attended the October 14 performance.

Metcalfe and Sullivan, and Groucho's goddamn good quote, from *The Marx Bros. Scrapbook*. Metcalfe in *The Street Cinderella: Billboard*, September 23, 1918. Goodman Ace is quoted from the *Kansas City Star*, December 27, 1923. Additional details on Groucho and Goody are from Hector Arce, *Groucho*. The tale of stagehands' struggle is from an unidentified Kansas City clipping in the Groucho Marx Collection, circa January 1, 1924. The Hamilton and Buffalo reviews, dwelling on the charms of Miss Miles, are in the *Hamilton Daily News* and *Hamilton Evening Journal*, January 24, 1924; *Buffalo Evening News*, February 2, 1924; and *Buffalo Courier* and *Buffalo Morning Express*, February 5, 1924. The Syracuse review quoted is from the *Syracuse Journal*, February 22, 1924. Beury in Panama: *Philadelphia Inquirer*, March 23, 1924. Harpo's ultimatum: *Harpo Speaks*. Gaites negotiating with bands: *Variety*, April 23, 1924. The *Inquirer*'s rapturous words: April 29, 1924. Gaites' departure, and becoming an agent: *Variety*, April 30, 1924; and April 15 and July 29, 1925.

Refitted by Herbert Ward: *Variety*, May 14, 1924. Ward was apparently already working on the show, as he's the credited art director on published sheet music covers for both *I'll Say She Is* (printed prior to the Broadway run) and *Gimme a Thrill*. Ward is listed as art director in the *I'll Say She Is* Broadway program, too, but whether the scenery was refitted for Broadway is worth some doubt. Robert Moulton cites *The Stage*, in its June 5 New York review: "The scenery shows deplorable signs of wear and tear on the road." However, in his diary entry for May 19, 1924, Will B. Johnstone notes that "the new costumes showed to advantage," so we can verify *some* attempt to gussy up for Broadway.

"Look, Chico, we're not good enough": *Groucho and Me*. In his 1959 autobiography, Groucho says very little about *I'll Say She Is*, his account consisting mainly of the tall tale of romance between producer "Broody" and inept chorus girl "Ginny." He doesn't mention the Johnstones, but casually insults the music, the production, and the entire non-Marx cast, as "amateur night in Dixie." He calls the score of *I'll Say She Is* "the most undistinguished one that ever bruised the eardrums of a Broadway audience."

Innocent Eyes: The correct opening dates of both shows are in the May 14, 1924 *New York Evening Post*; see also *Brooklyn Daily Star* and *New York Sun*, May 17, 1924. Reviews of *Innocent Eyes*: *Post* and *Sun*, May 21, 1924. I know that when I was researching the *I'll Say She Is* tour I came across some negative reviews of *Innocent Eyes* on the road, and thought to myself, *Look at that*, Innocent Eyes *got negative reviews on the road*, but goddamnit, I don't seem to have saved or noted them, and in this one instance you're just going to have to take my word for it. *Innocent Eyes* got negative reviews on the road. I promise. For more on the *Innocent Eyes* situation, see Arce, *Groucho*. The Casino's no cut rates, and non-Shubert production: *Variety*, June 25, 1924.

The list of 1924 shows is derived from theatre pages of the *New York Times*, *Post*, *Herald-Tribune*, and *Sun*; the *Playbill* website; and the Internet Broadway Database. "No worse than a bad cold" is one of the many thumbnail smears on *Abie's Irish Rose* perpetrated by Robert Benchley. Robert Moulton adds that *Mr. Battling Buttler* was alternatively known as *Battling Buttler*, which is the title of the film Buster Keaton made from it; and that *The Potters* became a W.C. Fields film. As long as we're adding things, Owen Doyle's *The Nervous Wreck* also formed the basis of Danny Kaye's feature debut, *Up in Arms*, and I'm thirsty.

The history of the Casino Theatre and its notable productions owes something to Gerald Bordman, *op cit*, and John Kenrick, *op cit*. (What were the odds that both of those guys wrote books with the same title?) "Magnificent decrepitudes": *New York Evening Post* review of *Cocoanuts*, December 7, 1925. "Poverty-stricken revue": *Groucho and Me*. Kane's Warehouse: *Marx Bros. Scrapbook*. Groucho makes the same point in more detail, without naming Kane's, in *Groucho and Me*. It's not clear whether this tale applies to the pre-Broadway tour, the Broadway production, or both. Will B. Johnstone's list of borrowed scenery is from his diary, May 29, 1923, courtesy of Margaret Farrell.

If, like me, you feel acutely the absence of the Casino Theatre from our planet, you can find some sliver of consolation by visiting other buildings designed by Francis Kimball. None has the Moorish grandeur of the Casino, but suggestions of the its majesty are revealed by close attention to the Chamberlain-Burr-Day House on Nook Farm in Hartford, Connecticut (a neighbor to the Mark Twain and Harriet Beecher Stowe houses); as well as the Corbin Building (13 John Street, Manhattan), the Church for All Nations (417 West 57th Street, Manhattan), the Montauk Club (25 Eighth Avenue, Brooklyn), and the Emmanuel Baptist Church (279 Lafayette Avenue, Brooklyn).

VII. MAY 19, 1924

All publications cited in this chapter are from 1924 unless otherwise indicated.

Groucho in Broun's syndicated column: *Buffalo Courier* (etc.), May 19. Woollcott's "acrobats" line is in *Harpo Speaks*.

The 8:42 curtain time was recorded by John Anderson in his review, *New York Evening Post*, May 20. Oddly, Will B. Johnstone recorded in his diary that the show began at 8:20. But the officially advertised show time was 8:30 (see the theatre page of any New York paper that week), and I must conclude that it's more likely Johnstone made a casual error in his diary, and the show began twelve minutes late, than that the show began ten minutes early.

Variety on "Do It" from the Philadelphia review, June 7, 1923. The 1931 film of the Theatrical Agency scene is widely available in public domain compilations and on YouTube. It's transcribed in Chandler, *Hello I Must Be Going*. Ben Taggart is the ship's captain in *Monkey Business* and a cop in *Horse Feathers*.

The humorous description of the Apache dance is from "Four Marx Bros. Queer Hit: Rough Revue," Ashton Stevens, circa October 15, 1923 (Groucho Marx Collection). Beury and Wanamaker arrested for obscenity: *Variety*, June 6, 1923. "Go ahead, shoot": *Variety*, May 28. The "most vivid surviving description" is from an unidentified Boston clipping in the Groucho Marx Collection, circa September 4, 1923. The same clipping includes details about the Wall Street scenery, including that it resembled a spider's web—so the spider and web references in the typescript were intended literally. For Damon Runyon and the culture of Broadway, see Jerome Charyn, *Gangsters and Gold Diggers*.

Variety traces the Tramp Ballet to *Pinwheel* in its review of *I'll Say She Is*, May 28. To appreciate the dark profundity of the mirror scene in *Duck Soup*, see Adamson. For a dissenting view, see Coniam. "Love from Elsie": Franklin P. Adams, "The Conning Tower" column, May 23. Anderson on "The Instigation of Socks," etc.: *Evening Post*, May 24. Harpo's rope gag is described by Kyle Crichton in *The Marx Brothers* and Glenn Mitchell in *The Marx Brothers Encyclopedia* as being accomplished with the use of a double. When we staged the bit in 2014 it was clearly best accomplished not with a double but with a backstage run-around. Bill Marx, in *Son of Harpo Speaks*, recalls Harpo and Chico reviving the rope gag for later appearances, without a double. A tip of the hat to Matthew Coniam for this clarification, and another to Mikael Uhlin for tracing the hypnotism theme to *On the Mezzanine*. The Marxes' hypnosis joke ("Trying to induce the Broadway producers…") is from a 1924 article by Colgate Baker, in Groucho's *I'll Say She Is* scrapbooks, Groucho Marx Collection.

Napoleon scene: "Glimpses of the Moon" was dedicated to Bebe Daniels, who had starred in the silent film *The Glimpses of the Moon*, based on the Edith Wharton novel. The sheet music, published in 1923, had Bebe Daniels' picture on the cover, and contained an advertisement for the film; the song was clearly interpolated into, rather than conceived for, *I'll Say She Is* (or its predecessors). That the "sell the couch" ending was used on tour and on Broadway is confirmed in Ashton Stevens' Chicago review ("Four Marx Bros. Queer Hit: Rough Revue," circa October 15, 1923), and an undated Broadway review, both in the Groucho Marx Collection. Another interesting detail about the Ralph Barton cover for *Judge* is that Harpo is identified as "H. Marx," and Groucho as "J. Marx"—throw this on the mountain of evidence that Arthur's stage name was widely known before his brothers'. The unrealized 1928 Napoleon movie project is from Coniam, who cites the February 25, 1928 *New York Evening Post*.

I stand by my description of the 1931 Theatrical Agency short as "the only part of *I'll Say She Is* for which we have an original cast performance on record" (besides "some incidental gags and Harpo's knife-dropping routine"). But Mikael Uhlin would like me to add that there is, in a sense, another. In 1970, the Rankin/Bass studio released an animated television special entitled *Mad Mad Mad Comedians*. The show featured cartoon versions of various comedians, including the Marx Brothers, in a five-minute version of the Napoleon scene. Groucho, then 80, performed his own vocal role, with Paul Frees voicing Chico and Zeppo. Despite the value of having Groucho's line readings on record, he sounds sleepy, and the scene just isn't very funny in this form. There's intrusive musical scoring, and a terrible laugh track that chuckles at almost every line, even lines that aren't supposed to be funny. The script is so severely edited that much of the best material is missing, and the point of the scene is lost. But if Mikael Uhlin would like me to add something, I add it.

Similarities between *Gimme a Thrill* and *I'll Say She Is* were noted by the *Philadelphia Inquirer*, June 5, 1923; *Variety*, June 7, 1923; *Boston Globe*, September 4, 1923; and *Variety* again, May 28. An unidentified Chicago clipping from October 15, 1923 (Groucho Marx Collection) also makes the connection.

VIII. "A MASTERPIECE OF KNOCK 'EM DOWN AND DRAG 'EM OUT HUMOR"

All publications cited in this chapter are from 1924 unless otherwise indicated.

The burlesque argument: "Frank burlesque," *Variety*, April 16. "Extravaganza, if you wish": *Variety*, May 28. "Regular burlesque stuff": Arthur Pollock, *Brooklyn Daily Eagle*, May 20. "As ever turned a wheel": *Syracuse Journal*, February 22. (Burlesque circuits were known as *wheels*, and burlesque shows which played those circuits were called *wheel shows*.) "Girlesque tutti frutti": *Buffalo Courier*, February 5. Chorus girl Mary Carney is quoted from the *Herald Tribune*, August 10. Groucho's chorus girl lingo is from an unidentified clipping, circa 1925, in his scrapbooks at the Smithsonian. *Times* and *Sun* reviews of *Cocoanuts*: December 9, 1925. *Cocoanuts* itself is described as a burlesque show in *Variety*, November 4, 1925, and *Philadelphia Inquirer*, November 24, 1925. The characterization of Groucho as somewhat "Victorian" in morals is from Steve Stoliar, *Raised Eyebrows*. For more on the twin evolutions of vaudeville and burlesque, see Trav S.D., *No Applause—Just Throw Money*. For more on the neo-burlesque movement, see the neo-burlesque movement. Sime Silverman on Groucho's cleanness is from his review of *Cocoanuts*, *Variety*, December 16, 1925. Harpo's adventures working in a Freeport brothel are memorably preserved in *Harpo Speaks*, and discussed again in this book, Act Two, Chapter VIII. Thanks to Robert Moulton and Robert Bader for adding their thoughts on the burlesque argument, and to Trav S.D. and Melody Jane for knowledge and wisdom on the subject.

Minnie breaking her ankle on opening night is in *every* source. Go look at the books on your shelf, on any subject. It's in at least twelve of them. If you're still not satisfied, see *Variety*, May 28; *New York Times*, June 1; and *Zanesville Times-Signal*, June 8, and see how you like it.

Broadway reviews: Robert Benchley, *Life*, May; Arthur Pollock, *Brooklyn Daily Eagle*, May 20; John Anderson, *New York Evening Post*, May 20; John Corbin, *New York Times*, May 20; Burns Mantle, *New York Daily News*, May 20; Gene Fowler, *New York Daily Mirror*, May 20; *New York Times*, June 1; Alexander Woollcott, *New*

York Sun, May 20 and May 24, and *Vanity Fair*, December 1924; *Variety*, May 21; *New York Evening Post*, May 24; "Ibee," *Variety*, May 28; *Christian Science Monitor*, May 26; *Harrisburg Telegraph*, May 26; Burns Mantle, *Buffalo Morning Express*, May 31; Brett Page, *Charleston Gazette*, June 1; Dixie Hines, *Huntington Press*, June 1; George Jean Nathan, *American Mercury*, July; Robert Garland, *Variety*, June 11; David Carb, *The Bookman*, August; Alison Smith, *Picture Play*, August; Fay King, *New York Daily Mirror*, October 20. Gilbert Seldes is quoted from a review of *The Cocoanuts* in *The New Republic*, January 20, 1926.

Regarding Kaufman's supposed fatherhood of Groucho's character, Groucho himself added to the confusion when he told Kaufman biographer Howard Teichmann (*George S. Kaufman: An Intimate Portrait*), "Kaufman molded me. Kaufman gave me the walk and the talk." Teichmann acknowledged that Groucho's statement was "generous," and Groucho walked (and talked) it back in *The Groucho Phile*.

Matthew Coniam's thoughts about Chico are from *The Annotated Marx Brothers*. Gilbert Seldes is quoted again from the January 20, 1926 *New Republic*. The *Post* review of *Animal Crackers* is quoted by Louvish. Life as Broadway stars comes partially from *Groucho and Me*, *Harpo Speaks*, and Crichton. Minnie's ginger ale business: *Variety*, November 26. The *Herald Trib* quote about Minnie is from August 3. Harpo's Town Hall recital: *New York Sun*, June 4. The recital probably never took place; I haven't found any other reference to it, and Robert S. Bader doubts it very much. Heywood Broun still hadn't seen the show at this point according to his June 24 column. On November 6, he reported that he'd finally seen it, and made that remark about Harpo and pathos. Harpo as "the brains of the band," *Evening Post*, December 15, and then everywhere.

Margaret Farrell notes that in Will B. Johnstone's diary, entries dealing with the Napoleon scene are marked with a star—indicating, perhaps, that he was building an argument to demonstrate his authorship of it. The Napoleon scene was, in fact, plagiarized widely after the success of *I'll Say She Is*, and concern for his property is what motivated Johnstone to send his typescript to the Library of Congress. In 1926, an official version of the Napoleon scene appeared in vaudeville, billed as "The Famous Comedy Scene From *I'll Say She Is*—Napoleon's Waterloo." Will and Tom were the credited authors, but the Marx name was not invoked; the lead roles were played by Phil Doyle, Harry McDonough Jr., Bobby Dare, and Dorothy Howe. I wish I knew more. *Yonkers Statesman*, March 13, 1926.

The Marxes and the Theatre Guild: *Post*, December 13; *Evening World*, December 31; *New York Women's Wear*, December 31; *Times*, January 4, 1925 (with a very nice photo of the boys in Napoleon getup with a smiling Lynn Fontanne); and *Philadelphia Inquirer*, January 4, 1925. Pickford and Fairbanks: Unidentified clipping, Groucho Marx Collection. Anne Nichols' note to the Brothers is preserved in Groucho's *I'll Say She Is* scrapbooks, Groucho Marx Collection. (The note is also signed by William De Lignemare, designer of *Abie's Irish Rose*, sometime producer, and author of *My Impressions of Roumania*; he and Nichols were intermittently engaged.) Nellie Revell story: *Post*, July 17. "Box party": *Herald Tribune*, July 17. Nellie Revell's review: Syndicated column of October 7, *Syracuse Journal* and such. Roller skates: *Post*, October 23; *Sun*, October 24. "They went down Broadway": Unidentified clipping, headlined "Police Summon Marx for Unwise Parks," Groucho Marx Collection. A photograph of the boys rolling down Broadway on skates appears in the 2011 expanded edition of Robert S. Bader's *Groucho Marx and Other Short Stories and Tall Tales*. "Thrill contest": *New York Sun*, June 4. Eddie Cantor and beards: *Variety*, July 23. *Greatest Show in the World*: *New York Sun*, July 11, and *New York Commercial*, July 12. "This stage isn't as deep as it looks": *Post*, June 12. Chico's remarks about comedy: *Post*, June 28; and *Sun*, June 30. Westbrook Pegler and wonderful nonsense: Paul Sann, *The Lawless Decade*. John Decker is quoted from an undated *Evening World* clipping in the Groucho Marx Collection, circa July 1924. Percy Hammond's "amateur antics" line: *Chicago Tribune*, December 23, 1914.

The controversy about whether Groucho and Kaufman look alike (a tough break for both of them) is reconstructed from numerous clippings of Hammond's *Herald Tribune* columns, some of which are reprinted in *The Groucho Phile*, and many more of which are in the Smithsonian's Groucho Marx Collection. The unidentified journalist who suggests Groucho is aping Frank Tuttle is quoted from a clipping in the Groucho Marx Collection. The "press agent" line is from Samuel Hopkins Adams, *Woollcott: His Life and His World*. F.P.A.'s "Marxman" line is from his column, "The Conning Tower," undated, Groucho Marx Collection. Woollcott's "nightmare": *Sun*, September 20. Woollcott on Julius Marx and Lotta Miles: *Sun*, October 23. Confusion over Lotta Miles' name: *Sun*, September 29 and October 3. Lotta Miles dressing room interview: Unidentified clipping, Groucho Marx Collection. Lotta Miles' divorce: *Brooklyn Eagle*, November 7; and *Variety*, November 12. Lotta Miles' sister's wedding: *Variety*, January 7, 1925. And have you heard, "Carlotta Miles Doesn't Diet to Keep Her Figure," *Boston Globe*, March 8, 1925.

WHN radio appearance: *Bridgeport Telegram*, July 8. Groucho's bungalows: *Post*, July 15 and July 17; *New York American*, July 15, and *New York Illustrated News*, July 15. Building a theatre: *Variety*, January 21, 1925. The theatre was going to be in Chicago. Democratic Convention, Klanbake, and William Gibbs McAdoo: Two unidentified clippings, Groucho Marx Collection; and George Jean Nathan, "Art for the Democrats," *American Mercury*, July. More background on McAdoo and the 1924 convention from Wikipedia. (You've got to expect that once in a while.) Harpo and Heifetz: *New York Herald Tribune*, November 23. Cavett's "insult in quotes" line is from the 1991 HBO documentary *The One, The Only...Groucho*. "People do not care...": Colgate Baker, "The Wonderful Four Marx Brothers and Their Show," circa June, Groucho Marx Collection. "You can't stabilize these Marxes": "Four Easy Marx at the Casino," unidentified clipping, circa May 20, Groucho Marx Collection. "Delightful companions": *Theatre Magazine*, August. "Faith in *I'll Say She Is*": "*I'll Say She Is* Strong on Comedy," unidentified, May 20, Groucho Marx Collection. Groucho on comedy: "Ability to Hold Audience is Good Comedy, Says Marx," unidentified, Groucho Marx Collection. Groucho on vaudeville: Colgate Baker, *op cit*. "Beautiful ambiguities": *Evening Post*, undated "Two on the Aisle" column, Groucho Marx Collection. Harpo on *The Green Hat* and reading habits: *New York Review*, December 6. "Sitting alone in his study": Unidentified clipping, Groucho Marx Collection. Cartoon: *Judge*, February 1, 1926. Woollcott quoting Groucho's complaints: *New York Sun*, December 5. Chico as the handsome one: *Evening World*, circa December 1924, Groucho Marx Collection. More on Harpo and "brains": *Evening Telegram*, July 17; *Evening World*, circa May 30 (Groucho Marx Collection). "Literary hidalgos" is from an undated Percy Hammond column, Groucho Marx Collection. Chico on Groucho and Harpo needing the limelight is from Maxine Marx, *Growing Up with Chico*. Zeppo and Chico and nightlife: Unidentified clipping, Groucho Marx Collection. Zeppo in traffic court: *Evening World*, July 25. Chico in traffic court: "One-Fourth of the Marx Brothers Visits Three Jails for Auto Mixup," unspecified clipping circa November 1924, Groucho Marx Collection; and *New York Graphic*, December 2. Cartoonists in the audience, and the Marxes as cartoonists: *New York Bulletin*, October 2. Harry Hershfield's *Abie the Agent* is also referenced in *Animal Crackers*, when Chico mistakes Roscoe W. Chandler for the strip's star character, Abe Kabibble; for more on this scene and the confusion it has wrought, see Coniam's *Annotated*. Gold watch for Beury: *Post*, September 24, and *New York Morning Telegraph*, September 24. Sealskin dressing gowns: Unidentified clipping, Groucho Marx Collection, circa October 1924. Beury's midnight supper: Unidentified clipping, December 12, Groucho Marx Collection. Bachelder on the cast's perfect attendance: Unidentified clipping, Groucho Marx Collection. Chico missing his entrance: *Post*, September 23. Harpo on "the unpardonable sin of stagedom": *Kansas City Star*, October 19.

"The clowning antics...": *New York Daily News*, February 6, 1925. Boston reviews quoted are *Boston Daily Globe*, February 10, 1925; and *Harvard Crimson*,

February 13, 1925. Boston success is noted in *Variety*, February 18 and March 4, 1925. Coolidge inaugural is from the *Globe*, March 4, 1925. *Too Many Kisses*: *New York Sun*, February 28 and March 4, 1925; *Variety*, March 4, 1925; *Oakland Tribune*, April 20, 1925. *A Kiss in the Dark: New York Sun*, April 4, 1925. Woollcott on Boston, *Sun*, March 18, 1925. Chicago disappointment: *Variety*, April 20 and May 13, 1925. Woollcott's backstage drama: *Sun*, April 24, 1925.

Groucho's *New Yorker* piece titled "Boston Talk" appears in the April 4, 1925 issue. The Marxes' association with *The New Yorker* extended to an advertisement the magazine placed in the playbill for *The Cocoanuts* at the Lyric in 1925. Under a splendid art deco caricature of the Brothers by *New Yorker* artist Victor Bobritsky, the ad reads: "*Groucho says*—'I have never read a magazine more entertaining than *The New Yorker*.' *Chico says*—'There is nothing I enjoy more than a copy of *The New Yorker*—unless it's two copies.' *Zeppo says*—'To me *The New Yorker* is a source of interesting information which I don't get anywhere else.' *Harpo says*—'Whenever I do speak I want it to be a good word for *The New Yorker*.'" In the September 28, 1929 issue, there was a tender obituary for Minnie Schoenberg Marx, written by Woollcott.

Detroit: *I'll Say She Is* "will be held as long as business warrants," *Variety*, June 3, 1925. The story of Chico's disappearance and reappearance is assembled from the following accounts, all 1925: *New York Sun*, June 8 and 9; *Joplin Globe*, June 9; *New York Times*, June 9; and *Variety*, June 10 and 24. Thanks to Bob Gassel for the *Detroit Free Press* account, from the June 10 edition.

Kaufman's line about the Barbary apes is ubiquitous, but let's cite Howard Teichmann, *George S. Kaufman: An Intimate Portrait*. Woollcott's subtle swipe is from his syndicated column, "Second Thoughts on First Nights," dated December 13, 1925. *Variety*'s Kaufman and Berlin fantasy is in its review of *Cocoanuts*, December 16, 1925 (though I've tightened up the dialogue just a little). The *Times* review of *Cocoanuts*, quoted here, is December 13, 1925.

Act Two

I. *JE SUIS MARXISTE, TANDANCE GROUCHO*

Why a Duck is a 1972 book, edited by Richard J. Anobile, which combines stills and dialogue from the Marxes' films. This was a pre-home video way of experiencing a movie at home, at will. Anobile followed it up with *Hooray for Captain Spaulding* (applying the same technique to *Animal Crackers*, which had been in legal limbo when *Why a Duck* was published), and was later responsible for similar volumes on Laurel and Hardy, W.C. Fields, and Buster Keaton, as well as "video novels" of *Star Trek; Play It Again, Sam; Mork and Mindy; The Maltese Falcon*, etc. Anobile's *Marx Bros. Scrapbook*, something else entirely, is as indispensable as it is controversial.

Mel Brooks' "healthiest of all the comics" remark is from Kenneth Tynan, "Frolics and Detours of a Short Hebrew Man," *The New Yorker*, October 30, 1978.

II. DO IT

The Woollcott speech quoted is drawn partly from his opening-night review of *I'll Say She Is*. "This is Woollcott speaking" was his standard radio introduction.

It's unclear to what extent Will B. Johnstone is responsible for the plots of *Monkey Business* and *Horse Feathers*, but it's worth noting that these two films, more than any other Marx project besides *I'll Say She Is*, treat Zeppo as an almost-equal member of the team—or at any rate, they use him more effectively and more generously than *Cocoanuts, Animal Crackers*, or *Duck Soup*. That there was a proto-Margaret Dumont character in *Mr. Green's Reception* was confirmed by Robert S. Bader in conversation. Groucho's line about "a big woman in the act" is in *The Marx Bros. Scrapbook*.

III. ZVBXRPL

Mikael Uhlin notes that another member of the Johnstone family, with whom he'd corresponded, spelled Will's nickname "Grampit." I use "Grandpit" following Meg's example. Since we're in the neighborhood, Harpo's book calls Sam Marx "Frenchie," while Groucho has it "Frenchy." I prefer Harpo's spelling and use it for no better reason than that.

IV. THIS BROADWAY SONG

For analysis of the supposed Quackenbush/Hackenbush controversy, and other strange tales of real and imagined grievances about names in Marx Brothers movies, get thee to Coniam. Criticisms of the Johnstones' music: *Variety*, May 28, 1924; *Variety*, June 7, 1923; *Brooklyn Eagle*, May 20, 1924; *Toronto Evening Telegram*, February 12, 1924; *Syracuse Journal*, February 22, 1924. That lyrics of the kind Johnstone wrote were inherently generic and disposable is supported by Burns Mantle's description, in his *New York Daily News* review of May 20, 1924, of "Tom Johnstone's songs, fitted to Will Johnstone's 'I Love Yous.'" Information about competing versions of "How Dry I Am," Irving Berlin's "The Near Future," and the song's origins, is from Wikipedia (get with it) and James J. Fuld, *The Book of World-famous Music: Classical, Popular, and Folk.* Irving Berlin on Kaufman's hatred of music is from Jeffrey Magee, *Irving Berlin's American Musical Theater.* The story of Kaufman insisting that Berlin cut "Always" from *The Cocoanuts*, which can be found in any book ever published in the world, is "one of the great fables," according to Bader, who adds that Berlin wrote to Groucho in 1959 to correct the false account. Nevertheless, Groucho continued to sing "Always" and tell the story, into the seventies.

V. CINDERELLA BACKWARD

Hollywood types reading this chapter will be thrilled to learn that I've adapted *Merrily We Roll Along* for the screen. Write to me.

"How late do you stay open?" is from *Duck Soup.*

Kevin Fitzpatrick is so prolific, it's hard to keep up. Since his introduction in this chapter, he's written and published *Under the Table: A Dorothy Parker Cocktail Guide*, *The Algonquin Round Table New York* (to which I contributed an illustration, and in which he kindly refers to me as "the Marx Brothers' representative on this planet"), and *The Governors Island Explorer's Guide*; and edited and published *Dorothy Parker: Complete Broadway (1918-1923).*

VI. UP IN THE CLOUDS

On his Will B. Johnstone page on the Marxology website, Mikael Uhlin notes that Will B. Johnstone, Jr. vividly remembered the song "Up in the Clouds," just as Meg Farrell does.

Dick Cavett "felt the earth move" when Woody Allen told him he had "endless" ideas for films; see Robert B. Weide's *Woody Allen: A Documentary.* Arthur Marx's "father and son" line is from a photograph of an inscription, posted by Frank Ferrante on Facebook. Woody Allen's line about Picasso and Stravinsky is on the back cover of the 1972 LP *An Evening with Groucho.*

VII. SELECTIONS FROM THE MARXFEST DIARIES

The diaries quoted in this chapter were originally published, in somewhat different form, on marxfest.com.

"Waxing wroth" is from *Horse Feathers.* "Left-handed moths" are from *Animal Crackers.* I won't explain *every* reference in this section. I shouldn't have to tell you that "the party of the first part" is from *A Night at the Opera*. I *should* tell you that "additional credit in the *Academy Bulletin*" is from Adamson. Harpo at Henderson's: Pissing himself, Harpo, *Harpo Speaks*; shitting himself, Groucho, *The Marx Bros. Scrapbook*. Moskowitz: *Horse Feathers*. "Peasie Weasie": *Harpo Speaks*, Louvish, Chandler, and others. Groucho and Dinah Shore's charming rendition can be seen in *The Marx Brothers TV Collection*. The Schang gag: *Harpo Speaks*. Groucho discusses the Leroy Trio, with varying degrees of candor and whimsy, in *Groucho and Me*, *The Marx Bros. Scrapbook*, and *The Groucho Phile*. He also tells the story in concert on the 1973 LP *An Evening with Groucho*. "I Wonder What's the Matter With the Mail": *Marx Bros. Scrapbook*. "There's a Place Called Omaha, Nebraska" is a song by Groucho and Harry Ruby. It appears in *The Groucho Phile*, and on the 1952 Decca LP *Hooray for Captain Spalding and Other Songs by Harry Ruby and Bert Kalmar Sung by Groucho Marx*.

VIII. THAT FROG

"Because you share a love so big…" is from *The Muppets Take Manhattan* (1984), music and lyrics by Jeff Moss.

The list of shows whose scenery supposedly wound up in *I'll Say She Is* is from *Groucho and Me*. "Groucho Himself" is Adamson. "Then out o' the hat, it's that big first night" is from "Another Op'nin', Another Show," Cole Porter, *Kiss Me Kate*.

To the story of Robert Moulton and Paul Wesolowski helping Seth Shelden with his Harpo horn, Moulton adds a detail: Before meeting up with Seth the day after the show, they were searching for the grave of Manfred Marx. Moulton remembers a discussion of the importance of Harpo's horn, during which Seth said, "Well of course it's important—it's his voice."

The 2014 *I'll Say She Is* reviews quoted are: Martin Denton, nytheaternow.com, August 12; Bruce Chadwick, History News Network, August 11; *Time Out New York*, August 11; Adam McGovern, "A Night at the Avant-Garde," *Fanchild*, August 24; John Brennan, "Revival of the Marx Brothers' *I'll Say She Is* a Rousing Success," *The Examiner*, August 24; Jose Solis, stagebuddy.com, August 22; and J.K. Clarke, theaterpizzazz.com, August 19. For more, visit illsaysheis.com.

Harpo after the final performance is, of course, from *Harpo Speaks*. In his "Conning Tower" column of June 28, 1924 (more than seven months prior to the Broadway closing), F.P.A. says he went "uptown, and met with A. Marx the harpist, and I hid a deal of silverware up my sleeve." Perhaps Adams did this on two occasions, or perhaps Harpo is conflating two events. Harpo's close friendship with Woollcott lasted until Woollcott's death in 1943. Harpo's first child was named William Woollcott Marx, after his godfather Aleck. There is a charming letter from Woollcott to Harpo, dated May 19, 1934 and published in *The Marx Bros. Scrapbook*, in which he notes the tenth anniversary of *I'll Say She Is*, and of their friendship. Woollcott closes, "I love you dearly, and think the chances are that I will continue to do so until one of us dies. After you, Alphonse."

INDEX

ABOUT THE AUTHOR

Noah Diamond is a writer and performer, best known for *I'll Say She Is*, the Lost Marx Brothers Musical, for which he adapted Will B. Johnstone's book and lyrics. He has played the role of Groucho in various incarnations of the show. Other Groucho performances include productions of *Animal Crackers*, *Groucho on the Air*, *Music of the Marx Brothers* at 54 Below, and *Wish You Were Here: Groucho Marx* at the Jewish Museum. He has served on the Marxfest Committee, organizing New York City's Marx Brothers festival, and as Marx Brothers Historian to the 93rd Street Beautification Association, for whom he created the short film *The Brothers*.

With his partner Amanda Sisk, he co-produced and co-wrote the books, music, and lyrics for the Nero Fiddled musicals, a series of political satires seen in New York from 2003 to 2008. The pair also co-produced Noah's solo multimedia show, *400 Years in Manhattan*, as well as *Groucho on the Air* and numerous special events.

His previous books are *400 Years in Manhattan*, based on his stage show of the same title; and *Love Marches On*, a saga of Broadway in comic strips, set in the years 1925 and 1975.

He lives in Manhattan with Amanda, Eleanor Roosevelt, Bagley, and Kanika. He maintains a website at noahdiamond.com, and never refers to himself in the third person.